TIME TO GO SOUTH

A modern Odyssey from France to Greece

Ann and David Berry

Copyright © 2016 Ann Berry, David Berry

All Rights Reserved. No part of this publication may be reproduced, stored in a retrieval system, or transmitted in any form or by any means: electronic, mechanical, photocopy, recording or otherwise, without the express permission of the authors

Ann Berry and David Berry assert their joint right to be identified as the authors of this work.

Contents

PRELUDE 5

CHAPTER 1 10

CHAPTER 2 26

CHAPTER 3 38

CHAPTER 4 53

CHAPTER 5 69

CHAPTER 6 83

CHAPTER 7 96

CHAPTER 8 109

CHAPTER 9 121

CHAPTER 10 135

CHAPTER 11 149

CHAPTER 12 166

CHAPTER 13 180

CHAPTER 14 193

CHAPTER 15 207

CHAPTER 16 220

CHAPTER 17 233

CHAPTER 18 247

CHAPTER 19 261

CHAPTER 20 275

SOME SAILOR'S TERMS 279

END NOTE..280

Prelude

Port Napoleon, France, 1873 miles to Gouvia. Six weeks to launch.

The boat hoist launched *Aderyn Glas* quietly into the water while a small crowd of friends watched and passed whispers around. Ann and I held our breath as the water lapped up her sides but she settled well enough. After a while I pressed the button to start the engine and an alarm began screaming. We looked at each other and started to worry.

You have to be tough to live in Port Napoleon. The sun burns and bleaches everything and the hot hairdryer *Mistral* desiccates anything left and makes whirligigs of dust before crashing and whistling through your rigging. When the rain comes it comes in like a tropical storm and the dry dust underfoot becomes a slurry that paints everything khaki. The mosquitoes are big as birds, silent as ghosts and bloody as vampires and fatten the brass-band frogs that haunt, invisible, the marsh at the roadside. The insects hide in the showers, under toilet seats and feed in the restaurant under the tables, lancing through puny clothing and injecting anti-coagulant to make your wound bleed and itch for days. The frogs deprive you of sleep with their deep throated tuba voices and the smells are the burnt smells of the dusty Camargue. You have to be tough to live in Port Napoleon.

'I've found us somewhere to live in Port Napoleon,' Ann had said looking up from her laptop, 'while we tear the boat apart. That way we won't have to worry about tidying up each night after work.' And so the year began in a blue box.

Aderyn Glas is our transport and our home. We like to think of her as Welsh but she is English, from Plymouth, designed by Moody and built by Marine Projects in 1992. And it was in Plymouth that we kissed goodbye to our family and slipped into a cold grey morning in April. We crossed the Channel and spent a happy summer meandering through the French canals, festooned with masts and booms and rigging and a plant pot on a string. We reached Port Napoleon, at the mouth of the Rhone, as the nights drew in and we felt the first cool clutch of autumn. We abandoned her there to rest for the winter while we headed in the car for Spain.

We had chosen her name with care. When we bought her she was called *'Cara'* after someone's wife, girlfriend or daughter, but we wanted a name that reflected the sense of freedom she brought us. We had to choose carefully, it had to be a name that other nationalities could pronounce and should not be objectionable in any language. To pronounce "*Aderyn Glas*" run the English words: "a daring glass" together and you have it in one.

But Welsh names can be tricky. The Welsh have a wonderful word "*cwtch*" which means a cuddle but if you say it in America it means something totally different so be careful. There's the famous story that travels around the Welsh pubs of an English couple who moved to Wales and were keen to name their newborn son with a Welsh name so they chose *Allanfa Dan*, I suppose because it had a strong English ring like Alan Dan. But translated from Welsh *Allanfa Dan* means fire exit. Think of the time he will have in school.

Aderyn Glas sat patiently on her twin keels for six weeks while we ripped her apart and modified and scrubbed and built and fixed and painted and polished and added solar panels and replaced a radar and patched up a radio. For the first week we lived in the converted container – the blue box – that Port Nap grandiosely calls a bungalow before we moved on board and worked and lived and ate twelve feet up in the air in the middle of a boatyard surrounded by seven hundred other boats.

Finally we launched her into the shallow water and tied her to a pontoon. Then there were more things to do which we couldn't have done ashore and new things to fix like the oil pressure alarm that had scared us all when we turned over the engine and fitting the alternator controller and fixing the stern anchor into its bucket and hoisting the dinghy onto the davits and washing off the ochre

Camargue dust and pumping up the fenders and making new ropes for them and mooring lines and don't forget the stern anchor warp.

And we fought the mosquitoes, my god, how we fought those mosquitoes! We had blue lamps and ultrasonic things and sprays for the body and sprays for the air and lotions and anti-histamine and things you plug into the mains *that must not be used in a confined space*, and nets and nets and nets and three fly swats and after a week our lungs were shot from the stuff we were breathing and the mosquitoes still pierced our clothes and left bright red itchy patches and bleeding blisters as trophies.

'We need a *Mistral*.' said Ann and as soon as one came we wished that Scotty could beam us up. The hot hairdryer wind blowing at twenty knots or more for days on end is enough to drive you over the edge. Look out of the window and the skies are clear and blue, but listen for a moment and the roaring and clanking and shrieking tells you all you need to know about the weather forecast. *Mistral*. They say they last one day or three days or multiples thereof but life changes when a *Mistral* blows and time becomes subjective.

And while all this was going on we met some great people, Owen, Peter, Olaf and Jenny and their dog, the gentle Jason, who were all so kind and generous with their time and advice.

She's a tad under ten metres this Moody Eclipse, our home, and that tad is important when the marina fees increase on the dot of ten metres. The fact that we overhang each end by a huge amount doesn't bother the typical *Capitaine* who only reads the registration papers and we save a lot of money that way. She's a wonderful cruiser for two people with a large saloon, heads and shower, and two cabins. We sleep in the forepeak which is the biggest and coolest cabin – the other being alongside the engine tends to get hot – and although the bunk is pointed there is room enough to be comfortable so long as you are first into bed and grab the space that your feet need. We have two steering positions, one out in the cockpit, where you might expect to find a wheel, and one opposite the settee in the saloon from where she can be driven like a motor cruiser. Step down from the saloon and you find the galley which is well fitted out and behind you as you cook is the fridge which can be run from battery or mains. When we sit in the saloon we can see out on all sides, except astern, through an array of glass, and despite the greenhouse effect this is far better than sitting in the bowels of a cruiser and not seeing what's going on around us. She's a lovely boat, but she does have a problem: she lists like a drunk.

This is not a casual 'I think perhaps if I look askance my boat may have a small list,' this is a full blown, 'I think my boat is sinking but only on one side and look at that mast it's like a windblown tree,' kind of list. She stands out in a marina. In an anchorage people worry about her: is that boat sinking? It is so marked that a prairie grows above the boot-top paint line on the port side. But, all-in-all, she's lovely.

As May became old we sat in the sun and we planned. Then we tore up the plans and tried again. At first the plan was to go to Spain but we found we couldn't do that because we'd already been resident in Spain for three months and they have this absurd law which allows them to chain a resident's boat to the quayside until he pays a tax. So we decided to travel to Sardinia on a scouting trip for the next season when we would go the whole way to Greece. Then we decided that if we were that far it would be silly to come back and that we may as well go to Greece this season. And we forgot that the boat was full of all sorts of bits and pieces and equipment and kit that we had intended to take ashore in Spain or France and put in our car and drive home. We planned in detail and we planned strategically. We planned where to go to ensure we could get food in the best supermarkets but we couldn't decide whether to go around Italy or hop to Corsica and Sardinia then drag across to Sicily. It looked too far. We looked at Tunisia and then I wanted to go to Malta. And Rome which is in the opposite direction. Then Ann wanted to fly home from Elba to be at granddaughter's christening. We planned and we planned and we planned. And in the end we planned to go to Marseille, thirty miles away.

Then came a day. It was a day like none before. A day when we knew that to stay longer was simply to prevaricate. Sure there were still things to fix but we were taking an engineer with us: me, and I think we knew that if we didn't leave now we would never start the odyssey. We looked into the barrel of six months and two thousand miles, pulled up our gangplank, cast off our lines, waved the first of many goodbyes.

And left.

Chapter 1

Day 1, Marseille, France, 1836 miles to Gouvia.

The man stood on the water on the port side of our boat. He was at least two hundred metres from the shore. He was dressed like a fisherman and I could clearly see a look of expectation on his face. Behind him two more men watched us motor slowly passed from where they sat relaxing at a table, their lunchtime sandwiches and wine nearby. The water came to mid calf and mid table leg and our wash would lift it another six inches. A row of tall sea fishing rods formed an honour guard for us. It was only a few feet away. The bulky fisherman tucked his long rod under his arm and made frantic pushing motions with his hands.

'I think we're too close to the edge of the channel,' Ann said nervously.

I looked at Rachel who didn't agree but I turned the wheel anyway and sidled to the right a little.

It was so good to be on the move again. We were overwhelmed by a sense of escape, of freedom, we felt that we could now simply go anywhere we wanted to. Go south and we would eventually get to Africa, to Algeria. Go west and Spain would capture us, east was Italy. We could escape the Mediterranean altogether and slip through the Straits of Gibraltar into the Atlantic, or we could cruise exotically the coast of Egypt. Or maybe through the Dardanelles to the Black Sea and the mysterious Danube. We could visit Malta or follow the trail Homer mapped out for Odysseus.

Ann checked something in the dictionary, a small frown made a crease in her forehead and a wisp of blonde hair straggled over her sunglasses. '"*Odyssey – a series of wanderings, a long adventurous journey*" - that's us,' she grinned, the frown disappeared and the whole world was ours for the taking.

So strong was the feeling of freedom that even the momentous decision to travel two thousand miles at about six miles per hour and to live nowhere else but in a space ten metres by three for six months; and to live in each other's company twenty-four hours of every day of that six months, passed over us and didn't even merit a comment. The air was fresh and smelled clean after the dust we'd become used to and *Aderyn Glas* motored along happily. Ann was happy busying herself with the charts and the plotter in between taking spells in the cockpit. And I was happy feeling the boat beneath me, obeying the helm, purring along.

At the mouth of the channel from Port Nap we'd turned right, away from the industry and the anchored tankers, and headed out towards the sea. The water wasn't yet pure Mediterranean blue but we were still in an estuary. The breeze was ahead of us so we unfurled the sails and tacked to the left. The huge genoa, our headsail, is the powerhouse and hauls us along like the wing of a jumbo jet. The mainsail, despite its name, only adds about half a knot to our speed and is far more complicated to set. So much so that we often sail on with only the genoa deployed.

With the motor off the speed dropped away but in the sudden quiet life was even more beautiful. We'd not heard the sounds of a boat under sail for over a year. The small wavelets lapped at the hull and occasionally a rope creaked. Behind it all the background swish of the hull cutting through the sea. We lay back in the cockpit and allowed the sounds to lull our senses and the sun to warm our faces, and the breeze to stroke our hair. We relaxed. Unwound.

But behind, to the north, a pack of hounds had our scent. The line of sails spread across the horizon from Martiques and weaved energetically towards us, tacking from side to side. Ann watched them grow with narrowed eyes. 'They're racing and we're cruising. Don't get all competitive,' she said emphatically.

'Run!' I said, 'haul up the mainbrace and split the spinnaker. We'll be around the next headland before they can board us.'

But she didn't see the humour. 'Don't compete, you'll only look silly. Remember that dinghy racing course when you found yourself in the lead and panicked and missed the mark and everyone overtook you. We're in a plastic bathtub laden down with everything you can think of with not enough sail area and a list like the last moments of the *Graf Spee*.'

'Shhhh... not so much of the "plastic".' I could remember the relief when I found I wasn't in the lead any more.

The first yacht to arrive was twice our size, had more canvas than *Cutty Sark* and heeled like an F14 in a nine-g turn. She passed close astern with a swish of water and shouts from her excited crew. There were at least a dozen broad men on deck and they all seemed to know what they were doing. 'Well oiled,' said Ann ambiguously.

The second yacht was a tad smaller but no less determined. She came quickly from the other side and also aimed at our stern. I touched the wheel to flee from her path and she passed us by with shouts and a wave from a cheerful *Capitaine,* his race going well, his ship slapping and groaning.

The fleet passed us by despite the little tweaks I made to the sails when Ann wasn't looking. All of them. The big and the small the short and the tall all dodging and weaving. They all passed us by. Until only a tatty little twenty-something overgrown dinghy was left, way behind the rest, crewed by a man and a girl *cwtched* up in the cockpit. He had one eye on the course and the other on his girl and one hand on the tiller. He sailed passed us as if we were a lighthouse.

'Are we sinking?' I grumbled, wondering why we were going so slowly.

'Just incompetent.' Ann always knows the right words.

The feeling, like the fleet, soon passed.

We headed southeast then east trying to keep sailing but giving up in the end as the wind died. We practised our worry technique. We worried that the entire racing fleet were heading for Marseille and so there wouldn't be any space left when we arrived. We are highly motivated and polished worriers.

Phillip and Mary had been our friends and guides through a fair number of canal miles last year and they'd told us, in no uncertain terms, to go to Marseille. When Phillip retired they spent eight years sailing around the areas we were heading for and what they didn't know we wouldn't need to. Mary thought the approach to Marseille was breathtaking and Phillip said you could buy anything you needed in Marseille.

Mary was right. The view at the entrance is sandstone coloured and spectacular. On the left the ancient Fort Saint-Jean curves around the entrance with the cathedral behind it, and on the right the Pharo and the citadel towers above the natural inlet to the harbour. The basilica of Notre Dame, with its glistening golden statue of the Virgin and Child, looks down from the hill above the city. The Vieux Port is a basin in the heart of the city and was once its only harbour. Now it's a marina for hundreds of boats like us. Only most of them are bigger. Ahead of us were frightening phalanxes of masts.

The welcome quay, the *quai d'accueil,* was on the right and as we hung about wondering what to do next the *Capitaine* turned up in his super rigid inflatable boat and after a brief quiz pointed at the most difficult to enter berth I'd seen for a long time.

Astute Ann knows when to leave. 'It's like the canals.' she said and walked forward grinning before I could offer her the helm. She was right though, dead water and no breeze, like you never get in Britain with its currents and quixotic winds. Would I ever get used to it?

'Canals or not, Ani sir, it's tight in there.' I always seem to call her *Ani* when I'm nervous.

We touched the quayside gently and Ann stepped off. We had crossed our first bit of Mediterranean. We had taken our first bite of elephant. Four hours sailing, two hours motor, thirty-seven miles, 31C in the shade.

Next day we walked around Marseille old port in tee-shirt and shorts and watched the watchers watching the boats. Both came in all shapes, sizes and colours. Marseille is one of the most ferociously independent and cosmopolitan cities in France and it was a bit of a culture shock for us after the peace of the canals and the desert of

Port Napoleon. A bloody fish stall where *madame* cut newly dead fish with dexterity and a sharp knife, and stuffed the liver back under the ribs, rubbed shoulders with stalls of glass jewellery, scented soaps, sunglasses made in China, and super-cooled ice-cream all hiding under coloured umbrellas. We drank water and beer and coffee and water again to try to stay hydrated but it was oven-hot in the caldera of apartment buildings that ringed three sides of the port. There is a chandlery just off the quay and we found that Phillip was wrong, they didn't stock a Sardinia chart nor a Sardinian flag.

Ferries came and went regurgitating chattering, dripping people or swallowing more into their bellies. Passengers were tourists or locals, backpacking students and happy holidayers and kids and bikes, all easily identified and all trying to hide from the heat. The ferries were noisy and smelled of diesel fumes. They kicked up a wash and gave no concessions to the long lines of moored cruisers. Their smells added to the heat. We found a supermarket and hovered in its air-conditioned cavern until our sweat-wet clothes became cold and our faces lost their beetroot colour.

Little open topped busses wound around the town and in the afternoon when everyone sensible ran for shade we sat on the top deck of one that wound through the backstreets and up the hill to the basilica, then down again and along passed beaches sparsely populated with sunbathers, swimmers and paddling children. When the bus passed the promenade we could see the Frioul archipelago a few miles across the sea, it was our next destination. The bus wound through the backstreets and into shopping areas teeming with people, noisy and bustling, hot and smelling of tarmac. It passed a stadium, toured the *Centre Ville* then turned near the cathedral and terminated with intent near an ice-cream shop. We felt scorched and realised that from that moment onwards we would have to do something more to protect our skins.

We were going to have to do something to keep *Aderyn Glas* cool too. When we got back she was an oven.

The medium-rise apartment buildings and sheer mass of masonry that surrounds the old port act like heat stores and radiators and pump heat into the port continuously. The result is that the quayside area all around the basin reaches temperatures higher than those outside the city. And, some days, not a breath of wind takes the heat away.

So we hoisted out all our sunshades: the boom tent and the bridging piece that joins the cockpit bimini to the spray hood and we arranged a prop to ensure an airflow between the two. From above she would look more like a tent now than a boat, covered in grey canvas, but she would stay cooler. Then we hosed her down and hosed ourselves down in a carefully controlled accident. We turned on all our fans, including the big mains powered office fan brought all the way from Britain, and opened all the hatches. But it was still hot.

At the end of a long hot day what we needed most was a shower. Ann hopped in through the door of the ladies and met a man coming out of a cubicle with his wife. She checked: it was the ladies. *'C'est normale.'* It's normal, it's France. Courageously, she threw her towel over the cubicle door and turned on the shower and discovered something else about French marinas. High pressure water shot from everywhere, the showerhead, the pipe joints and the tap. It soaked everything around, the cubicle, the shower room, the towel and Ann's clothes.

'But at least' she said, 'it was cooling.'

We stayed for another couple of days, *bimbling* around and feeling the excitement of a visit to a city on our own boat which still seemed a little exotic to us. In the evening we sat in the cockpit with a salad and a wine bottle in the centre of this dusty hot marina and marvelled at how wonderful this life was.

'Let's stay,' Ann smiled, laying back and relaxing.

'Time to go.'

On 23rd of May we left, springing out of our tight little berth and missing our neighbours by a creditable three inches or so. Since *Aderyn Glas* never goes where she's asked in reverse I was pleased to miss everyone by any margin at all. We crossed the harbour, fuelled and departed taking all the photos we'd been too anxious and too busy to take on the way in, cutting across the traffic, much to Ann's annoyance.

'Stop messing around, let's go!'

'Yes Ani sir.' There is no doubt who is captain but unfortunately Ann always manages to outrank me. 'Off to Frioul.'

Day 3, Frioul, France, 1830 miles to Gouvia.

Not far from Marseille are a number of dusty, scrubby, rocky islands: the Frioul archipelago. They are the complete antithesis of Marseille. Ile d'If was where Alexander Dumas had the man in the iron mask incarcerated (so we were told) and the twin island of Frioul was a quarantine island where ships heading for Marseille would be held until their crews presumably either died or did not. Frioul had a port and was our destination. It is actually a pair of small islands joined by a causeway, a pair of grey-white ridges poking out of the sea each a mile long and one tenth of that wide. The archipelago is the target of hundreds of visitors who catch the ferries from Marseille each summer day. It is a nature reserve and visitors come to walk and wonder or simply to escape the heat of the city on the beaches.

For us, ironically, it was an anxious crossing of six miles of sea because the 23rd of May was a holiday and we worried about whether we would find a berth. We are consummate worriers. But the forecast was changing and we needed to leave Marseille and move onwards away from the Bouche du Rhone and the dread *Mistral*. How naïve we were! The *Mistral* would continue to upset our plans for weeks yet.

We played at sailing. The wind was wrong but at that time I had a dislike of voyaging solely on engine. Halfway to the island I flushed the holding tank, which is what our toilet drains into, intending to pump it to the brim with seawater then dump it overboard. Unfortunately I got it wrong and pumped the contents through the vent and down the side deck. So I spent a happy hour with disinfectants and mops and finally a seawater flush while Ann steered, also happily, with sails barely filling and an occasional waft of chlorine on the dying breeze.

Owen, from Port Nap, had briefed us about arriving at Frioul: 'You pick up a buoy with your stern-line,' he said. 'then motor towards the quayside. If you're lucky there will be a *Capitaine* to help you with your bow-lines but more often not. But remember this,' he spoke with emphasis, 'however long your stern rope is it will not be long enough and you'll stop short of the quay. Just like I did. Just like everyone does.'

'But now I know.' I thanked him. He looked at me with a pitying smile.

The approach to Port Frioul is passed the prison island of Ile d'If and the south end of the breakwater. The nineteenth century causeway that joins the two islands forms a sheltered bay and that is where the port is. The marina fills two sides of the port with concrete quaysides and you are welcome to moor in the normal Mediterranean way, sticking either your bow or stern into the quay and hauling on a line at the other end of the boat. In Frioul the line is fed through a buoy. Later we would find lines already laid in marinas, the so called "lazy lines".

We approached from the north and I had a momentary shock as I looked towards the shore and found a ship between us and the harbour where there was no room for a ship to be. When my brain sorted out what I was seeing I realised the ship was concrete, a building in the form of a ship, cream and white and complete with concrete anchors cast on the concrete bow.

We had a twenty-five metre rope we'd brought to take ashore in all those anchorages we'd read about where you need a twenty-five metre rope to take ashore. So we unhanked it and tied one end to a stern cleat, ready for action. There was no answer to our radio calls so we headed for the obvious *Capitainerie* and I nudged the bow into the quay so Ann could leap off and find someone to point us in the right direction. It was lunchtime and hot and not a breath of wind in the shelter of the harbour. We knew about hot lunchtimes from our canal travels and didn't expect *les Ports de Plaisance* to be any different to the canal locks. Eventually the *Capitaine* arrived from the direction of the nearest bar and told us affably we could moor anywhere so we elected to stay near the office and the showers thank you.

I coaxed *Aderyn Glas* away from the quayside and motored around in a big circle, this time aiming at the buoy that was to take our twenty-five metre stern-line. Surely we wouldn't need more? And of course, we did what everyone else did in Frioul, stopped embarrassingly short of the quay. So we tied on an extra length, watched the *Capitaine* smirk a little and trickled on to the quayside. *We don't care, we're safe*, I thought, and pulled the mooring line so tight the buoy disappeared under the surface.

But in the afternoon the wind increased and blew right into the bay and onto our stern. After a while the water in the harbour picked up and the boat slopped back and forth. Other boats arrived looking windswept and wet and moored around us. Frioul was a popular destination that holiday weekend.

I had pulled that stern-line as tight as I could but as little wavelets formed in the harbour the anchor began to crunch against the quayside bollard and we had to use the winch to pull the stern-line even tighter and haul us off the quay. The wind became so strong that we tied ourselves to our neighbours and bridled the stern to the buoy, a rope to each side to hold us square. On one side of us was a Frenchman and on the other a Belgian and we all cheerfully mucked in to make our boats secure.

Yachts arrived in a steady stream until there was no space left on the quays. Then more yachts appeared. Each was met by the *Capitaine* who now roared around the harbour in his rubber duck RIB and directed skippers to a suitable berth by waving his arms and shouting and whistling. Latecomers were found places amongst those already berthed, and when there was no more space the *Capitaine* continued to accept yachts and found space where there was none. No-one was turned away despite arrivals continuing on well into the evening. We eyed the tiny shower block and single toilet beside the *Capitainerie*.

'Unisex showers,' Ann voiced my thoughts. And so it was to be.

Next day the wind had eased and the overcrowded harbour slowly emptied. The *Capitaine* had jammed his short bulky body into a plastic chair outside his office and smoked while he watched boats leave.

'Beaucoup d'argent?' I asked and he grinned.

We went walking, already half in love with the first island we'd visited.

'Frioul is an archipelago and these are two islands,' Ann had been reading the French magazine *Cabotages,* something that had impressed me greatly until I realised it was printed in English as well as in French. 'the islands are Pomegues and Ratonneau, and the causeway wasn't built until 1822. They were,' she added, 'dead scared of getting the yellow fever that had decimated Barcelona in 1822.'

I felt my eyes glaze a little.

'Hospital Caroline, named after one of your ancestors the Duchess du Berry, was opened in 1828.'

'My mother always swore I had French blood in my veins.'

'Remember that French waitress's reaction when she found out you were a Berry?'

'Didn't get me a free drink though,' I said truthfully.

'Humph!' She went on, 'The thing is the ships would anchor in the bay for the required amount of time and any sick people would be carted up to the hospital, literally maybe, where they stayed until the ships were eventually cleared to go into Marseille. But the lovely irony is that the hospital was closed in 1941 because of a typhus epidemic. Try finding logic in that! The hospital only catered for about fifty patients anyway and there was 100,000 square feet of it.'

I did the sums, on *Aderyn Glas* we had somewhere less than two hundred and fifty square feet for the two of us, and oddly shaped at that.

'Maybe we should hoist a quarantine flag and get more room.' I mused.

'It's listed now,' she read and looked around, 'it's on top of that hill with a view of Marseille. Must have been hard on the patients seeing the city and knowing they wouldn't reach it.'

It seemed to be the place to go so we set off to find it.

We passed the concrete ship with the concrete anchor which is the home of the Coast Guard, and found a rocky cove full of beautiful turquoise water and noisy kids. We'd watched them all arrive on the morning ferry and march off and wondered where they were going and now we'd found them. There was a space on a rock and we clambered onto it, already hot and kicking ourselves for not bringing water to drink or swimming kit. I plunged hot feet into the cool water and expected them to sizzle. Around us were low cliffs and birds soared and wheeled, the sea was clear and clean, the sky was wall-to-wall blue and I decided to stay forever.

'Time to go,' said Ann with impeccable timing as I nodded off.

So we bought a small bottle of water from the kiosk on the beach and climbed the bare stony hill, dripping, to the hospital with the view. But the buildings were surrounded by a fence to protect us from the building works, and the building works from us, so we could only get a glimpse of Art Deco architecture and that didn't really mean too much.

The sun beat down so Ann took her shirt off and put it over her head and we walked down the dusty, desert path to a castle that overlooked the sea to the west. There was a *calanque* – a cove – so full of anchored cruisers and smaller boats that you could step across them from one side of the *calanque* to the other.

The sea looked lovely. Ultramarine in the depths and turquoise in the shallows, flat and calm like a sea should be, inviting and benevolent, clean and playful on the shore. We paddled again in another turquoise cove then made our way back home.

In the afternoon the wind picked up enough to make us take the boom tent down. The sky stayed blue. Ann gave me a look that said *Mistral* and we tossed a coin into the sea to appease Poseidon, just in case.

Jean came for a drink. He was the Belgian guy from the thirty-foot Bavaria next door and was sailing single handed to Lefkas 'but don't tell my insurer's I'm doing single handed night passages.' Did everyone sail single handed to the Greek Ionian islands?

He was fit and skinny and about forty, shorter than my six feet, smoked cigarettes and unimaginatively drank Belgian beer. Luckily we had some of his favourite brew. We sat in the shade of our cockpit bimini and talked about the usual things: where we'd been and what we'd seen, where we were going, the good and the bad ports. He knew there was a *Mistral* due, which is what we'd thought, so we decided there and then to wait in Frioul until it was over. If we had to be delayed by wind then Frioul was a good place to have wind in.

The *Capitaine* didn't think so. We went next day to pay him for more nights and he became quite agitated. There is a *Mistral* coming, he told us, as if that explained everything and would instantly change our plan.

We were puzzled. A *Mistral* is always a northerly or north-westerly and from that we were sheltered, being on the east side of the Island with the village street of restaurants and tourist shops to the north. We said as much to the *Capitaine* but he got excited and insisted that we move from our berth to the corner of the dock. He showed us exactly where on his aerial photo.

'*Côte à côte. Comprenez?*' He held his hands palm to palm. Alongside. Okay with us, we agreed, we'll move this evening.

This only increased his agitation and he insisted: '*Maintenant! Maintenant!*' As if he could hear or taste the first whispers of wind already. '*Maintenant!* Go! *Allez!*'

So we caught a little of his panic and dashed off to move the hundred metres or so to the corner.

Outside the office we almost collided with Jean. Breathlessly we told him the story and with fearful glances to the north the three of us began untying the two boats ready for a dash to the corner. We pulled ourselves backwards from the quayside, hauling on the ropes passed through the eye of the buoy until we were well clear. Jean did the same and almost collided with us as *Aderyn Glas* swung around. I swore. Couldn't he have waited for a minute? I banged her into forward gear and aimed at the corner. Jean had put himself in such a position that we couldn't move away from the quayside and we almost scraped our hull as we travelled towards the supposed shelter of the magic corner. Any second we expected an avalanche of wind to blast us sideways across the bay and demolish us on the rocks opposite.

We tied up alongside. Then moved again when the *Capitaine* arrived and waved his arms about because we were not tight enough into the corner. Jean had tucked in behind us but was told to move to the other quay so that we were bow to bow at right angles. By now we were expecting a hurricane and tied ourselves to the quayside with every line we could muster. Jean tied a line right across the corner of the quays so we did the same in the opposite direction. Our French neighbours came along later and tied up behind us with a smile.

Then we took down all our sunshades and lashed on anything that could blow away.

And waited.

And waited. Expectant.

No *Mistral*.

Next day, for something to do, I walked around the boat opened hatches and lockers and generally checked everything. In the aft bilge of the saloon a small puddle of water had formed, a couple of cupfuls. I puzzled over it for a while then rang my daughter, a chemist.

'How do I tell if water is seawater or fresh?' I asked Amanda after the usual pleasantries.

'Taste it?' She replied a little quizzically, 'I thought that was obvious.'

'You've not seen this stuff, it's swilling about in the bottom of my bilge. I drink it and die horribly. I was expecting some clever alchemy, potions and motions, boiling up of dead pigs bladders and mixing in a ground up eye of toad. They have those here, you know, in the supermarkets.'

'Well, you could do that if you want, although I have to warn you pigs bladders smell a bit in the heat. Or you could take a sample and let it evaporate in the sun until you either do, or don't, have a nice film of salt.' Her tone told me she'd expected me to think of that.

'I should have thought of that.' I said, 'It must be the heat. Raining there is it?'

So I did what she'd said and, lo and behold, we were sinking.

'My God,' Ann the blasphemer, 'We're sinking.'

'At this rate, and assuming we don't bale anything out, we'll sink just this side of China.' I was, though, a little more worried than I let on. 'I expect it'll mend itself.' Things often did, I'd found, leave them alone and they'll get better. Like worms.

Still no *Mistral*.

So we hopped on a ferry to Marseille for supplies. There was nothing to buy in the village where even the morning bread had to be ordered in advance. Jean had told us there were no supermarkets in Cassis either, so if that was to be our next port we really needed to fill the fridge.

By the time we got back the temperature had gone from very hot to meltdown and it was airless, no wind from any direction. The mosquitoes were clocking up scores despite all my creams and sprays and lamps and gadgets and nets and a wind would help keep them at bay. Any wind! But there was no *Mistral* again that night, only the sweltering heat. We began to believe it must have missed us somehow and that it would be okay to move onwards. Then, in the morning, a little whisper sprang up but from the south, straight into the bay.

'*L'apres midi*,' the *Capitaine* walked passed and drew the wind in the air with his cigarette. '*Bien sure*.' The French couple next door smiled at us again.

The whisper became a breeze and swung around to the south east. We waited. All evening and into the night. Eventually we went to bed. Overnight the temperature dropped.

Another day dawned. No *Mistral*. The sky was grey overcast and it spat a few drops of rain. *Mistrals* don't rain. *Mistrals* blow under clear blue skies. The wind was from the north though.

'*L'apres midi,*' the *Capitaine* was off to get his morning baguette and the French couple giggled.

Late in the morning two customs men turned up to check our papers. They only wanted the registration papers, that said we were a tad under ten metres, and our passports and turned down our offer of a drink. They talked a little rugby to put us off guard and why were *l'équipe francaise* rubbish this year but wait till the next Six Nations, then, sternly: *did we have anything to declare*? Like what I wondered? Were we smuggling brass band frogs from Port Napoleon to Frioul? They wandered off saying something about the *Mistral* arriving that afternoon and grinning but they left in their launch well before it was due.

In the afternoon the *Mistral* turned on like someone had thrown a switch. We were up on the bare cliffs near the southern end of the island and had to bow our heads and shoulders into the wind as we started back towards our home. Dust lifted off the paths and attacked our eyes and noses and ground between our teeth. The seas to the west of the island were already spinning spume from shredded wave tops and where the wind was funnelled up the *calanques* and the other small valleys it was strong enough to shove us bodily around.

The crowded anchorages of the holiday weekend were now deserted and boiling cauldrons. The gulls couldn't fly, blown and twisted in the air, they struggled to travel a metre forward then, tired, they turned for a rest and immediately lost ten. The noise grew from a whisper to a roar. The wind kept on accelerating. On each side of the path the scrubby bushes whipped violently. We reached the causeway and looked down into the harbour. The wind was hurtling from the corner of the quayside where *Aderyn Glas* was moored and out over the harbour so ferociously that it kicked up waves only a dozen metres from the quay. But she was safe, our home, sheltered where the *Capitaine* said she would be safe.

We smiled at the French couple in their cockpit and they smiled back.

That evening the wind shrieked through our rigging and the bimini rattled until we took it down, scared of it blowing away. We took the fly nets off and locked down the hatches. At 1:30 in the morning the noise was so great we had no choice but to lie awake and listen. I dragged myself out of bed, had a look around and took down the fly net from the door, no mosquito could fly in this. At 4:30 it was blowing even harder and the boat was moving and snatching at the warps. I crawled out on deck and checked all the ropes. The solar panel support was vibrating and I tensioned the guy ropes to stop it, worried that my expensive panels would be damaged.

At daylight the wind still howled and all the boats kicked against their warps.

'Would you want to meet one of these at sea?' Ann asked unnecessarily.

It was good that we couldn't see into the future or we would have stopped right then.

Next day life returned to normal though outside the harbour it looked rough. In the afternoon four German boats arrived looking very beaten up. We talked to Jean and our French neighbours who had both decided to leave the following day. Jean had an appointment in Nice with his niece, which was nice, at the end of June, and the French couple were going to Siota. We had chosen Cassis or, if we didn't like the look of it, the *calanque* in front of it called Port Miou.

People left and I felt the usual sense of sadness at having to say goodbye to new friends and beautiful places.

'We could stay a little longer,' said Ann.

'Time to go.' I said.

The bilge was wet again.

Chapter 2

Day 9, Port Miou, France, 1816 miles to Gouvia.

We motored south towards the lighthouse and the dragon's teeth archipelago of Ile Riou and even though it was calm Ann wouldn't let me cut between the islands and the mainland. The dramatic coastal cliffs were four hundred feet of sheer, vertical, white rock, speckled with black and eroded by rain and they grew out of a sea so blue you could scoop a handful of its blueness. We passed around Cap Croisette and headed east with Rachel the robot driving and Cassis our destination. The cliffs were cathedral columns, the *calanques* cleaved with an axe struck deep to make their sides sheer. Tripper boats gasped in awe and were lost little dots in the photographs. Gulls squabbled and screamed above the noise of the engine. It was hot again.

Ann stretched on the foredeck to soak up sun and get away from the engine noise.

We went to Cassis, the small town that was reminiscent of Honfleur in Normandy, not because we had to but because Olaf the big Norwegian guy had said it was attractive and because the forecast warned of a force seven. Brave yachtsmen like us run for shelter when the windspeed is force six.

'Force seven!' Ann complained, annoyed, 'We've only just got over a *Mistral* and now we're getting a force seven.'

I felt like saying 'I don't make the wind.' But I knew her answer would descend to a personal level and the state of my bowels so I stayed silent.

Ann had banished the faithful, patient, Rachel and was killing dozens of swimmers by going up the wrong side of the yellow beach marker buoys. 'Oops!' She said, 'Now we'll get chased by Great White sharks after all that blood but I was distracted by all those naked men. Surely the judge will let me off.' Naked men decorated the ledges along the mile to the harbour, some were shy, some had nothing to be shy about, some could dip a foot into the water from where they lay, at least a foot, even cold as it was.

'Do you want the binoculars?' Ann asked, 'There may be one or two women.' But there weren't.

Cassis was a horrible little place that day, jam packed full of motley craft randomly crammed into a small harbour through which day-tripper boats ploughed every so often at twice the legal speed. It was so tight that to turn our little yacht we had to motor through the whole serried array until we reached the far quayside then had to dodge an incoming tripper boat that wanted the water we were on and *get your little plastic bathtub out of the way or I'll bash you thanks.*

So we left and that was a mistake. We should have clung to the unwelcoming place with fingernails in the pontoon, or nailed our hands to the quayside. We should have pleaded and paid twice and feigned illness, or engine trouble, or bad bowels, but in ignorance we left.

Back at the *calanque* at Port Miou we were met by a *Capitaine* in a battered red plastic dinghy. He was a grizzled fifty, wore shorts and a tee-shirt and had a cigarette in the corner of his mouth. He helped us tie our bow to a buoy then took our twenty-five metre line over the stern to a ring on the wall behind us, standing carelessly in his boat. Then he brought the end back and stopped short with a smirk on his face and holding the end of the rope aloft. More rope.

"*Calanque*" is the French word for a cove or fiord and the one at Port Miou is a mile long with a dog-leg entrance that sealed off the sea and a yacht club that lined the banks all the way to the shallow end. On the western side cliffs towered a hundred feet towards the sky above a German World War II naval installation but on the eastern side the skyline is more rounded and much lower. An arm of rock that in a few thousand years will be eroded away turning the *calanque* into a beach and a reef and a cliff. The moorings for visitors are between the entrance and the yacht club on the eastern side around the dog-leg bend and *Aderyn Glas* was strung like a hammock between a buoy and the iron ring in the cliff wall.

We dropped our inflatable dinghy over the stern and heaved the outboard onto it. Amazingly the motor started after the third pull, evidence that doing absolutely nothing to an engine is better than all this preventive maintenance you read about in the books.

'Draining the carburettor last year and putting fresh petrol in the tank this year might have had something to do with it.' Ann had taken the RYA diesel course so knew all about petrol engines!

I checked the bilges for water. In the aft bilge where we'd seen the water accumulate before there was a puddle. We bailed out about a quarter of a bowl of seawater, more than last time. This little leak was getting worrisome.

But it was hard to worry right now. It was calm and peaceful. People strolled along the cliff path in the sunshine and looked down at those lucky sailors touring the coast in their boats and sitting in their cockpits with drinks and food, surrounded by *such beautiful* lapis lazuli water. Their lives serene, part of nature, moving with the rhythm of the sea.

A little later we went in the dinghy to a plastic landing stage that belonged to the club. The outboard motor shattered any feeling of serenity. It clattered and buzzed, spat water and gasped oily smoke. Spray spattered us from the bow and we arrived with wet bums. There is no way to climb elegantly from a bobbing dinghy to a bouncy-castle floating pontoon so we crawled on hands and knees. To balance on one of these pontoons you would have to be a trampolinist.

Up on the top of the rounded cliff on the Cassis side we found a view, an ice-cream parlour and more naked men, though thankfully the last two were not in the same place. So we had one each.

'Force seven,' Ann said when we climbed back on board, 'we've never been on any yacht in a force seven. I'm glad we're going to be sheltered in here.'

A little later a different *Capitaine* turned up and judged we were too close to the damaged and dilapidated hulk that was our neighbour and tied our stern-line to a different ring on the cliff. Then he wanted an extra line to pass through our mooring buoy in case the first one broke. Throughout the evening boats were arriving and the *Capitaine* met them and moored them between the buoys and the cliff.

'Plenty of space here,' I said relaxing in the cockpit with a glass of *blanc* in my hand watching the people on the path watching us, 'look how the *Capitaine* spreads everyone out. It's very good of him.'

The water was peaceful, the gash of sky between the cliffs was clear, and if there was a wind we were too well sheltered to notice. It was a little bit of heaven.

It was hell. We woke in the early hours to the sound of the wind and by the time we climbed out of bed at eight o'clock the boat was rolling around like a pig. Strung between the buoy and the cliff she was sideways on to the seas that reflected around the dog-leg and stormed down into the *calanque*. By the time I'd eaten breakfast, balanced in the cockpit, I knew I had to get off the boat or spend all day throwing up. As she rolled we grabbed at handholds and braced ourselves as if we were at sea in a storm. We locked down the cupboards and put away anything that could fly. I noticed the old familiar feelings. I was getting seasick! Seasick on a mooring. It was hard to believe but it was unmistakable.

On the next berth a boat full of affable seventy-year old Frenchmen were busy casting off. At first I thought they must be heading out into the storm, didn't they know how bad it would be? But then they turned and motored passed us further into the *calanque* looking for a quieter berth. We watched with interest as the *Capitaine* arrived and showed them a berth near the bouncy-castle that wasn't much better than the one they'd left. We decided that if the French were not going to be offered a better berth then the Welsh certainly wouldn't be, so we abandoned ship.

We took the dinghy to the *Capitainerie* and climbed the cliff to the cape to look at the sea. At the top trees bent in a rhythmic dance as the wind curled around them and there was dust and spray in the air. Below and beyond the *calanque* the seas were blown into shreds of white and the waves amplified where they funnelled into the entrance. The bay was empty of boats. We sat on a ledge and looked at the fury.

Down in the *calanque* a mad Canadian cast off his mooring and turned his yacht towards the sea. When she hit the incoming combers she shuddered to a standstill, her bow buried deep under foaming, turbulent water, her mast and rigging shaking from the blow. Slowly she shook herself free and started to move forward again only to crash into the next wave. Over and over this happened, her bows rising until we could see half the length of her bilge from the top of the cliff, then she crashed down and buried herself under the next solid roller. The crew, mainly teenage and young adults, clung and huddled together in the cockpit. Jammed against the rails. Strapped to the boat. No-one made a sound. No-one screamed. Slowly, incrementally, she gained on the waves and slowly she battered her way out of the entrance and across the bay to the sea. She headed away from both Cassis and Miou. Away from any sort of shelter.

A day-tripper boat arrived from Cassis packed with tourists who had paid to see the *calanques* and here you are *monsieur-dame your first* calanque *and please be sick over the side not on my foot*. The boat was a ship, fifty metres long and probably displaced hundreds of tonnes and it was thrown around as much as the yacht had been. The passengers screamed as the bows were buried and screamed again as the bows reared up to the sky and water was flung the length of the ship drenching them all. And screamed once more in free-fall as the bows crashed down to fling the white sea wide on each side. And went on screaming in fear not fun until the boat was well inside the *calanque*. Then they did it all again as they left.

'Force seven,' I said, 'poor bastards.'

From where we were we could see *Aderyn Glas* being thrown around, rolling violently and snatching at her lines, but there was nothing we could do. She was safe enough, the lines were strong, but it was an anxious time. This was our home.

We knew now why the *Capitaine* had spread the boats out so much, if we had been closer to our neighbour we would have locked masts together.

We hiked around the cliffs and found a blow-hole and amused ourselves shooting pine cones four feet into the air. After a while we found ourselves in a sheltered, tree-lined cove of inviting cool blue water. It was amazing that this deep little *calanque* was so completely sheltered that we couldn't feel a breath of wind. The little beach was crowded and the water's edge was filled with adults and children having noisy fun. In the surrounding trees people had slung hammocks and were lazing in them, arms and legs carelessly thrown over the sides and heads and torsos arranged in the shade. We had cleverly left our swimming kit on board again so we had to be content with paddling and looking longingly at the deeper water. The scent of barbecue filled the air and made us hungry so we scrambled back onto a rock and ate the sandwiches Ann had brought. It was tremendously hot and the normal thing to do would be to return to the boat and dive deep into the blue with a mask and snorkel and chase the fish and search for mermaids. But we knew the wind would be as strong as when we left, and *Aderyn Glas* just as untenable.

In the end exhaustion made us return. We'd left the small cove and hiked the cliffs and found the delightful little hidden beaches and swimming pools that brought the tourists to the area. And we'd tried to walk to Cassis but it was too far so we had an ice-cream and a drink. But ultimately we had to return.

I took a pill especially brought for the purpose of quelling my tendency to throw up. The wind was as strong as it had been that morning but the direction had changed enough to reduce the swell coming around the dog-leg into the mooring. *Aderyn Glas* still rolled, but not as much. We sat in the cockpit in the early evening, damp from the spray we'd collected during our dinghy trip but no longer so uncomfortable and, in my case at least, no longer feeling the horrible eye rolling, giddy, toxic imbalance of incipient seasickness.

A purple Mohican haircut climbed over the stern followed by a broad grin on a painted face and a young muscular body written all over in body paint with a truncheon bulge in the front of tight, pink swimming trunks. On the cliffs behind a chorus of hoots and whistles from a crowd of tipsy blokes and us half-rising from our seats near the wine bottle and what the hell is going on please and why didn't we buy the pepper spray?

But a grin like his couldn't be malevolent and, while he sat a little unsteadily on our cockpit coaming, we couldn't help but grin back.

Among cheers and jeers from his mates on the shore he told us he was getting married and had to get drunk and do some dares and he was well on with the first and we were one of the dares. We talked in bits of English and bits of French and he was drunkenly in love with his baby and Ann got the wrong end of the stick and asked him whether his baby was a girl or boy and that confused everyone for a moment or two.

His mission was to get a kiss from the Welshwoman and to get the Welshman to drink from his bottle of *Pastis*. I could see Ann struggle with the idea of kissing this water nymph with the big grin for about a millisecond. Cheers rang out, loud enough to start an avalanche in the Alps.

Then he produced from down the bulging front of his trunks a bottle of milky liquid for me to drink from. I'll drink *pastis* at any time and from any place, but from *that* place? Despite the coolness of the sea, the *pastis* was a little warm. Cheers and whistles and echoes from the cliffs, shouts and grins and waving hands.

Ann, worried that this drunken bridegroom might not make it back to the beach, donated a swimming float to his growing collection of trophies. Finally we thought about a photo but as he posed, balanced on the edge of the transom, the boat moved and he fell off into the sea.

'What a nice young man,' said Ann primly waving to his mates on the cliff path, 'maybe you should carry pastis around with you.'

'I don't have the room,' I said, 'not with the beer keg and your wine carafe.'

Later the swell decayed and we went to bed early, tired and tipsy, my seasick pill pulling my eyelids down. There's nothing like a good night's rest to perk you up. At 5:30 in the morning the fridge alarm went off.

There are essentials on a boat. Things you cannot survive without. The list of essentials is somewhat personal and depends where in the world you sail. Ann lists radar, EPIRB, flares and the life raft amongst hers. She's a pessimist. My list has the engine, mosquito killers, scented nappy sacks and, of course, the fridge. I'm a hedonist.

Without the fridge the wine gets warm and you have to forage for food every day which becomes a major limitation. So when the alarm started screaming in the early hours I thought the end had come.

Ann has developed a defence mechanism: if anything goes wrong at night she immediately goes into a deeper sleep. She could thus be eaten by crocodiles, abducted by aliens or carried off by Errol Flynn who would slide down the sail knife in hand with his other arm around Ann's waist, and she would know nothing about it. So it was up to me to crawl out and stop the noise. I grumbled, mumbled and spluttered indignant curses, as befits a man woken from his rest, while Ann lay pretty and peaceful, her face smooth and calm and blameless. Someone had switched the fridge off. For a moment I had an impulse to wake innocent Ann and point out that since it hadn't been me it must have been her, but I couldn't find the courage. Another second and I realised that where the switch was located it was liable to be kicked by anyone sitting on the settee so it could have been me. In any case it was me who put it there so I'd lost the argument before it began.

Then I was overwhelmed with relief: I had not woken her.

Next day started calm. The water was flat and a deeper blue than the blue sky. We'd survived a second beating, one by Aeolus and one by Poseidon. I tossed a coin into the water and watched it sink to the bottom.

'Time to go,' said Ann over breakfast.

'Time to go,' I agreed and gave Rachel some waypoints to remember.

The forecast was for a usable force three though with the threat of a thunderstorm in the afternoon. Thunderstorms at sea scare me, we carry this great tall lightening conductor thirteen metres above our deck which waves at the passing clouds. *Here I am*, it says, *strike here*.

We headed for Sanary-sur-Mer, a small port halfway to Toulon and, more importantly, this side of the infamous Cap Sicié which the sailors on this coast refer to with some twisted pride as their own Cape Horn. With a possible thunderstorm ahead we were happier not to try passing the cape until the next day.

So we sailed a lot then motored a bit along the coast, more or less southeast passed green hills rising to six hundred feet but sloping gently, not like the cliffs to the west. We launched ourselves across the four mile bay from La Ciotat to Bandol in calm seas with a light wind and reached Sanary in late afternoon. We called them on the VHF radio and the box squawked some kind of reply which, of course, neither of us understood. So we headed in and tied up on the welcome quay. Ann went off to find the man behind the radio while I chatted briefly to a British yacht that was, he said, taking the last available berth and isn't it tough around here this time of year? I looked around at the empty marina spaces and thought he must be joking. Ann came back with a long face and told me the marina was fully booked. The *Capitaine* had been very apologetic but there was a racing fleet on its way in and that was that. This was only the fourth place we'd visited and our eleventh day and already we had been refused. For a couple already paranoid about not being able to find room in these marinas it was a death blow. In the high season we wouldn't find anywhere and what would we do then?

Panic clutched at us.

We had no option but to go backwards to Bandol. It was the last day of May.

It's only three miles from Sanary to Bandol but it's a long three miles and took a tremendous amount of energetic grumbling and worrying on my part before we got there.

Day 11, Bandol, France, 1798 miles to Gouvia.

And they had space.

It's a big horrible place really, spread out all over the bay with pontoons growing from the quayside and a great long hike from the visitor's berth around to the showers and the *Capitainerie*, but they had space so I loved them.

The berths at Bandol are fitted with lazy lines which are totally misnamed because you have to be fit, young and healthy to handle them and I'm none of these so I make up for my shortfalls by swearing a lot and using the sheet winch, which is cheating. Normally these things are ropes already attached to heavy ground tackle by the marina owners. They call them "mother and daughter" where the mother is a heavy rope for tying to the cleats and the daughter a lighter line that attaches the mother to the pontoon. As a boat arrives one of the crew picks up the daughter line, either by fishing for it with a boathook or from the hand of a convenient *Capitaine*, and walks along the boat with it to whichever end, bow or stern, sticks out into the harbour. He then pulls hard to get the mother line off the bottom and over a cleat. A wise man uses his crew for this job, but if the crew refuses he wears thick gloves because the ropes are always covered with the muck from the bottom of the harbour and often have sharp little shells and even fishhooks stuck in the roving. I always forget the gloves until I'm balanced, straining, on the stern then it's too late and all I can hope is that the mud comes from a place so depleted of oxygen that there are no organisms to get in the slashes that the shells are going to make in my hands.

The knack is to balance the lines at each end of the boat until it is the right distance from the quay with all the ropes at the right tension to hold the boat against whatever forces are expected: wash and wind usually.

In Bandol the ropes had been replaced with chains. Did this mean they expected trouble? I wrapped one around a stern cleat but later tied a rope snubber to the chain and pulled it tight with the winch. The snubber would act like a shock absorber. All this left me hot and sweaty and the shower was half a mile away and when we reached it, it was closed until tomorrow at four o'clock thank you and don't complain.

We checked the bilge and emptied a whole litre of water from it. A whole litre! This problem was going from worrisome to significant on the scale of things. I still couldn't work out where the leak was so we had a glass of *blanc* and watched the sunset. It had been a day to worry.

We stayed in Bandol for two nights until the forecast was perfect for us to round Cap Sicié. To be honest it didn't have much to attract us, the showers were so far away we seriously considered that rowing there in the dinghy might have taken less energy than walking, and the town itself was a typical seaside holiday town. There was nothing wrong with it, but you can see the same facades, bars, shops and ice-cream sellers virtually anywhere on the coast of any country in Europe.

Moored next to us was a UK boat whose owners had sold up and bought some *gites* in France. We had the usual chat about the places we'd been and the things we'd seen, which on our side wasn't much at that stage, and where to go and how to get there. Sardinia, they recommended, but stamped their combined feet and insisted we buy an up-to-date pilot book for it. 'And don't go in August,' they said.

Overnight the seasons moved and we didn't feel a thing. From the last day of May to the first day of June. From Bandol spring to Bandol summer, from eighteen euros a night to thirty-eight euros a night. The high season had arrived.

The first day of June was a fete and we found a café and watched the world celebrate for a while, drinking in the aromas of coffee and beers and the sounds of a French holiday. Then we went shopping. Jean, our neighbour in Frioul, had arrived and we exchanged a few words but he seemed in a hurry to get somewhere, so we said goodbye to him and never saw him again, another *goodbye*. We went and chatted to another English couple of about our age, Samantha and Harry who had brought their motor cruiser all through the French canals and were now turning around and going back again. They had simply fancied a dip in the ocean before setting off for home and had reached Bandol. We told them they really must visit Frioul on their way home, but they were in a hurry so we wished them goodbye too.

'Retirement is good,' said Ann.

'And sailing is full of *goodbyes*,' I added in a rare sad moment.

'Toulon?'

'Toulon,' I sighed, and next day we said goodbye to Bandol. And left.

Chapter 3

Day 13, Toulon, France, 1779 miles to Gouvia.

We were sinking. The end of the odyssey was being spelled out by the rhythmic drip, drip of seawater that leaked through our sterngland. I lay on my belly and sweated in the stifling confines of the dirty bilge where the propeller shaft went through the gland and out to the sea and watched the steady drip, drip, of seawater. The gland leaked and there was nothing I could do. The odyssey was finished, we had to go back.

We had arrived in Toulon after a long hot day of too little wind and too much engine and tied up in the friendly but overcrowded marina in the heart of the city where the staff spoke English and helped with the mooring. Behind us two huge yellow ferries of the Corsica and Sardinia line swallowed cars and trucks and simmered black smoke and noise into the atmosphere. In front, where the quayside ran along the edge of the town, the ever-present day-tripper boats came to swallow people. Toulon is a naval town and the busy helicopters, the stealthy submarine and the sleeping aircraft carrier had taken me back to those days when I had to work for money instead of being rewarded for being old. Like Marseille it had no cooling breezes but plenty of high rise concrete to concentrate the heat. It's a chaotic town, the new amongst the old, the fast roads punctuated with life preserving pedestrian crossings, *but watch your step* monsieur, *these* chauffeurs *kill and don't notice*. It's a town where there are more ice-cream shops than bars on the quayside and hot dust coats you like batter.

We had risen early to try to work before the heat became too bad. The night before I had emptied three litres of seawater from the bilge and that was after only eighteen miles of motoring. *Three litres!* So in the early morning we had tried to follow the trail of water back to its source and had emptied the cavernous cockpit locker of all the essential junk we carried: fenders, fuel cans, bike saddles, chain, oars, hammocks, brushes, pumps, flares, grab-bags, engine oil and so on. The trivia that might become important one day. Then

I had mined under the floorboards, hot and dirty, cramped and aching and less than pleased at having to do it at all and why can't we hire an engineer? A proper one? And even less pleased when there wasn't the trace of a dribble or a drip of water to be found.

So then I had crawled head first into a space too small for me and it hurt like hell and my head filled with blood because I was suspended upside down wondering if I could ever get back out of this piddling little locker where the water collected. And I had found not one, but two holes that drained into it and had stuffed a wire through them one and thus found there was a path from the sterngland to the bilge and thus found the drip, drip, that was going to sink us. *Hooray!*

And instantly I knew we didn't have the right tools and the gland looked rusty as hell. And I *knew* if I started playing with it and forced it too hard the whole gland would fall apart in front of me and we would sink before we could even get to a crane.

We checked the lines and started the motor. Ann put the boat into stern gear and pulled against the mooring lines, while I watched the gland. As soon as the propeller shaft started rotating the drip became a spray of water that flew in an arc all around the compartment. This really was serious.

We sat on either side of the saloon and looked at each other with suitably serious, long, glum faces. Ann waited for me to give her an option she could go with. We're very democratic, we have a vote each and Ann has the decider. Unless we're actually sinking.

I laid it out for her: 'Anyone sensible would abort this project now and go back to Port Nap, and that's what we should do. In two days we could be out of the water and a mechanic could fix our gland.' I did the engineer's classic wipe of a dirty forearm across a sweat-laden brow and tried to look sad, but even as I said the words I could tell that going backwards didn't enter into Ann's head. Ever.

'Or we could try and fix it here. The worry is that I could make it worse.' I thought that was very probable. I've attacked lots of corroded steel bolts over the years and none of them ever unscrewed, they all disintegrated in a mass of rust and I thought this one would go the same way. I also didn't have a spanner of the right size which meant I would have to cobble something together which was even more likely to destroy the screw. If I failed then either the gland would be a mangled mess that would need major work in a boatyard and our odyssey would be over for the year, or I would break the gland stem and the sea would flood in and we would sink quickly. Straight to the bottom and stay there. And probably no insurance payout for being so stupid.

I sighed. I knew what the plan was already, before I even made the suggestion: 'Or I suppose we could continue and keep an eye on it.' I found myself mumbling the words, hoping subconsciously that she wouldn't hear them.

'Yes!' She agreed instantly, 'We'll buy all the tools you could possibly need to fix it before we leave the city and see how we go.' Ann was happy again, though she had more faith in my abilities than I had. I wondered how she could ignore something so potentially catastrophic. Terminal optimism perhaps.

But I convinced myself that so long as we didn't try a long sea crossing, such as across to Corsica, before the problem was resolved it was safe to agree. And she was so happy.

I went to look at it again. Lay and watched it drip. The propeller shaft runs through a tube that is bonded to the hull called the gland stem. The gap between them is stuffed with a cord packing filled with grease and that's what stops the sea coming in. It's all very old technology invented long before Nelson – although they didn't have too many propellers back then.

To compress the packing and stop the drip you have to tighten the nut a little. The problem for me was that the gland nut was in an impossible position and covered in rust. Rust meant weakness and rust meant the nut had welded itself to the stem. And I needed a really big spanner to fit the really big nut and a really short spanner to fit in the space and the spindly, *corroded* gland stem didn't look as if it was going to stand the stress without snapping and stress was what I was feeling most and maybe I would snap too. *Pull* on the spanner, *snap* off the gland stem, *whoosh* goes the water, *glug* goes the boat.

Drip, drip.

We decided to do whatever we could to reduce the flow then buy whatever tools we could find that would stand a chance of solving the problem. The first, obvious, thing to do was pack ever more grease into the gland. Greasing the gland is something that has to be done every time the engine is started anyway because the cord rubbing on the rotating shaft needs grease to seal it. There's a little pump to force the grease into the gland. The seal wear meant the gap that the grease had to fill was now so big that grease was not filling it completely and reliably. So I forced in more grease and by slowly rotating the shaft by hand as I did so I could stop the drip. At least we wouldn't sink until the engine ran.

Ann put a drip tray under the gland to catch any drips that snuck through when our backs were turned and we went shopping. We bought more grease because we were going to need a lot. We learned that the French for grease is *graisse*.

We found a cyber-cafe and asked the internet. *Leave it alone*, the internet said with a collective voice, *if it's not pouring in you will only make it worse*. But no-one defined what *"pouring in"* was.

We also found a *bricolage* and they had a Stillson wrench, the thing pipefitters use to tighten up large nuts. So we bought one.

We tried to relax a bit: unwind, de-stress, it's hot and sunny and we're not actually sinking right now. We walked the short distance to the shops across the manic road that ran behind the quay and found a modern shopping centre and an old town. We spent money, which is always good therapy, buying a French SIM card to reduce the phone bills a bit. We tried to buy a French dongle to give us 3G access to the internet but we didn't have a French address so *tant pis monsieur*. This meant we had to go on using Ann's contract mobile to download weather forecasts whenever we couldn't get wi-fi and this cost a fortune.

We found a large supermarket and bought provisions and citronella candles *contre les moustiques,* which were the only things we'd not yet tried, and sagged for a while in its air conditioned interior. It seemed that as fast as we were getting acclimatised and tanned the air temperature was climbing one step ahead of us. We'd found Marseille hot, *it's a city*, we'd thought. Now we found the city of Toulon hotter. And dustier and drier. And noisier. Was it *citier*?

We spent all evening debating our decision to carry on. It occupied us over dinner and into the night. Next morning the drip tray was dry. I went back the *bricolage* and bought another Stillson, the last they had. The gland had a locknut and I reasoned that I would need two big spanners. We left Toulon in the late morning and headed east, towards the Porquerolles, the next islands along the coast. Away from Port Napoleon and certain salvation. I watched the gland as Ann started the boat moving. It sprayed water everywhere. I shut the hatch quickly and smiled at her.

'Les Porquerolles,' I said, '*on-y va.*'

'*Allons-y,*' she insisted, 'no wonder they never understand you.'

The weather was hot under a blue sky and there was a little wind at the harbour mouth so we hauled out the sails. If we could sail some of the way we could save the stern gland some wear and reduce the amount of water that would trickle in. As we cleared the harbour and turned east we caught a rising wind that was somewhere near the forecast force four already. We crossed the bay and the sea state increased until, as we cleared the shelter of Cap Sicié, the full force hit us from behind, from the west. The four was a six. Ann passed up lifejackets and strops without a word, it was going to blow! We took in a big chunk of the main and the genoa and powered along. The growing seas started to roll *Aderyn Glas* and we started getting a little wet. I hauled the mainsail fore and aft to stabilise her and let the wind get to the genoa better. By this time we were doing the maximum hull speed of about seven knots with a following wind, a scrap of mainsail and a furled genoa. Spray was lifting off the crests and blowing passed us and the noise was increasing. The seas were coming at an angle from astern so I had to sail up and down the waves or let them wash me towards the uninviting shore. It became hard work. We stopped the normal routine of half hour watches when Ann decided this was too much for her to handle. She was right.

The shore was miles away to our left. A long way ahead was a cape we would have to round to reach the islands, the tip of the Giens peninsula. We were bouncing about feeling far from safe. The Porquerolles were still a couple of hours ahead of us and I began to worry that by the time we got there this wind would have grown into a gale. We had no options, there was nowhere on the mainland that offered us any shelter and we certainly couldn't turn and go crashing back into the following seas. We were running before the wind. It's the quietist point of sail. It's so quiet sailors carry out "running repairs" when sailing like this. I didn't miss the irony.

It kept on building, the seas, the wind. The wind was a warm blast and carried on it the scent and taste of the salt spray stripped from the wave tops. The noise was overpowering. The rigging gave out a discordant howl as the wind vibrated the various lengths of the wire stays, and the seas had the frightening, sucking, slurping, noises of shingle moving on a beach.

It became a fight to keep the boat straight.

Wave after wave rose up from behind and I spent most of my time looking over the stern. As each one approached the noise increased. It would start to lift us, stern first, the bow pointing downhill. I would turn the wheel and send *Aderyn Glas* surfing down the leeward side of the wave and she would accelerate, but as she did so the wave slid under her anyway because it was travelling faster than she could. On the crest we would look down into a pit and she would decelerate, point her nose towards the sky and would slip backwards into the following trough. Each time I would straighten her up, turning into the roll if need be, and snatch a few seconds to correct the course before the whole thing started again.

After hours of this we could see the entrance to the Porquerolles archipelago and it was too small! The way in is between the main island and the end of the Giens peninsula and the gap was simply too small for me to get the boat through. Panic clutched at me. What the hell could we do? To sail right around the islands was impossible to even think about, it would add hours and we were already exhausted. We could see boats of all sizes cowered in the shelter behind the peninsula. I steered roughly east until the waves ran at right angles to our course, straight through the gap. I was too tired to do anything more imaginative than turn *Aderyn Glas* so that the waves were directly astern.

Turn the wheel and hope.

Turn the wheel and deal with the consequences.

Ann stood and gripped the cockpit handholds and stared behind us watching the combers arrive.

The shallows picked up the sea to an even greater height and the wind stripped the crests into driven spray that flew creaming passed us from the stern to the bow while the wave growled beneath us. Then we were surfing so dramatically down each wave front that it was impossible to go anywhere but in the wave's direction. But that's why I had waited before tuning in. The waves were right behind us. We surfed through the gap.

The marina was over to the right and we nudged our way towards it. Every time we teetered on the top of a wave, or found a second or so in the trough, I turned the wheel towards the marina only to have to turn away again a moment later as the next wave arrived. Incrementally we crabbed towards safety. After a while we were able to steal more and more metres in the direction we wanted rather than the one the sea had planned for us. Incrementally we narrowed the gap and incrementally the seas and the wind reduced. Enough, eventually, for us to head for the marina entrance and, with a struggle, put the sails away, start the engine and get ready for entering a berth.

We were not safe yet. At sea it may be rough but the chances of hitting something are small. This is not true in a harbour. Ann balanced wet and salt encrusted on our side decks and threw out all the fenders we had. I guessed I must look the same, wet and white with salt crystals.

The marina is built in a bay on the north of the island and protected by a breakwater like a comforting arm wrapped around the fingers of pontoons. Inside the water would be calm but there was nothing much to stop the wind which would blow us sideways. We entered the marina fast with the throttle fully open and swerved inside, heeling wildly, until we faced into the weather.

Then we stopped as abruptly as if we had brakes. We looked around. Ahead, to the west, was a low shoreline covered in trees, behind us were the landing places for the ferries and the marina itself – the offices and the crowded pontoons. Behind the marina and sweeping around to the south was the village, mostly shops, yacht services and apartments. South of us was a shallow harbour with some moored boats but in this wind we wanted a pontoon berth.

The wind was only a little less strong than it had been outside and it was blowing onto the sides of most of the berthed boats meaning it would be a tricky bit of boat handing to persuade *Aderyn Glas*, with all her freeboard, into a space.

I took us towards the fuelling berth because it was parallel to the wind which would make it easier to drop Ann off. She could then go and talk to the *Capitaine* and get us a berth. But I didn't reckon on a fool of a kid pump attendant, who clearly knew nothing about boats and how hard it was to handle one in conditions like this, point blank refused to let us stop even for the few seconds it would take for Ann to get ashore. I should have ignored him, or shot him, but trying to steer and have a shouted argument in French was too much. And I didn't have a gun.

So I took us towards an unpopulated jetty and put the bow into it. It was about forty-five degrees to the wind and Ann just had time to leap off and tie a line before *Aderyn Glas* slewed around. I waved to Ann and she ran off while I tried to keep the boat from doing too much damage to herself. It was difficult, and noises came from the bow that I didn't like much where the side of the boat was crunching against the planking. I struggled to hold her off. All around me were sailors sitting on their bums or talking on the quayside and not one of them offered a hand. In the end a young guy with a rucksack and walking gear came and helped. He knew nothing of boats but could see I was having trouble. With his help I was able to sort her out a bit then he waved and wandered off. Whoever he was I was really grateful to him.

Ann returned and pointed at what was essentially the outer harbour wall. She looked relaxed and happy. Only Ann can look relaxed and happy in a situation like this. She has such faith in us.

Anywhere you like on the breakwater, she'd been told.

It wasn't a particularly reassuring sight. It was full of boats with only a few slots left that we could aim for. And it was going to be a completely cross-wind landing, get it wrong and we would be blown sideways onto a whole string of moored boats.

To move from where we were to that side of the marina meant we had to turn completely around. The only way we could do that was to head the boat into the wind. If the wind blows sideways onto her hull *Aderyn Glas* always turns her bow away from the wind and once she starts to turn nothing can stop her. Turning in a wind is exactly like balancing a broom on your fingers, if it starts to topple you have to be quick to catch it and our boat is the same. If we were caught out and the bow was pushed around there was no way to get it back and we would quickly be blown onto the boats on the next pontoon. I looked at the yachts moored there, they all looked very expensive.

The most difficult bit would be getting away from the jetty without this happening. As soon as we let go of the rope the bow would want to go downwind. As the Irishman said, if we wanted to get *there* the last place to start from was *here*.

As if we weren't worried enough already the crunching noise of boats colliding made us look around startled. A large yacht had arrived and had managed to get blown sideways onto a line of moored boats a short distance from where we were headed.

There was the noise of costly things breaking and a lot of shouting. A girl from the *Capitainerie* ran full pelt down the pontoon, leapt into a parked RIB and roared across the water to help untangle the mess. A forty-something foot long boat with a strong wind blowing against it is hard to move and it took three RIBs, a lot of people on the moored boats pushing and a tremendous amount of shouting, most of it lost in the wind, before the yacht came free. I understand now why captains of large yachts all have permanent red faces, it's nothing to do with sunshine, it's embarrassment.

It was our turn. We had a briefing session. When things are difficult we always talk them through. I would go full astern until there was enough flow over the rudder to give me a chance of steering the stern around. Only then would Ann let go of the rope. If I could get the stern to turn to port there was a good chance of getting the bow up into the wind before it blew us too far around.

Somehow it worked. At some point I thought *to hell with it* and went for it. I could feel *Aderyn Glas* coming around and as soon as her bow started turning into the wind I went full ahead and steered the stern in the opposite direction. *Broom balancing.* She was unstable: as soon as she moved away from the wind she had to be corrected or she would move even further from the wind.

Now we had to cross the short distance to our chosen berth. We had selected it with great care. A slot between two boats that were covered in fenders and had crews on them to help. We knew those guys would help, they were probably as scared as we were.

I crabbed across the distance, the bow turned into the wind and at the last moment turned her straight and drove into the gap with the motor full astern to stop us. It felt like all those lovely cross-wind glider landings: *hold it level, kick the rudder pedal, full airbrake, back on the stick, wait, wait...*

Welcome to the Porquerolles. I threw a whole euro into the water for Poseidon and grinned at the guy next door.

Day 15, Porquerolles, France, 1765 miles to Gouvia.

We grinned at each other, too. We were wet and coated in salt and hot and sweaty but filled with adrenalin and *safe.*

We washed our fine *Aderyn Glas* to get the salt off and washed ourselves with the hose to get the salt off us too.

It was late afternoon and we didn't feel like much more than a drink, a bite to eat, and a relaxing evening doing nothing at all and worrying even less. The wind was still bowing the violin strings of the rigging but we hardly noticed it now, it was almost pleasant. The Ensign looked more shredded, as did the Welsh Dragon. Only the new French courtesy flag looked fresh.

Ann went to check the bilge. Even without using the motor much enough water had leaked in to worry her, so she poured anti-worry medicine into our biggest wine glasses and we put the problem out of our minds until morning. We weren't going to sink overnight.

The boat on our port side was Dutch. Hans was the captain of *Dream* – tall, slim, maybe forty with a ready smile and good English – and charming Katarina his wife and they invited us over for a drink. They were going where we were going, Greece, Corfu, Gouvia and ultimately Preveza for the winter.

He had decided to travel across to Italy via Elba while we had finally decided on Corsica, Sardinia and Sicily. We'd heard that the marinas on the Italian mainland charged enormous amounts to rent a patch of water and a bollard to tie up to, and thought that the islands would be cheaper. Hans gave us a look that meant *I am too polite to argue with someone I have just met but you must be joking, mate!*

Later we lay in bed and listened as the wind sang and felt the gentle, rhythmic roll of our home under us. We thought this was a little bit of heaven and had no idea then that this was nothing compared to what would follow and that both heaven and hell awaited us.

Next day was beautiful, the sky was deep blue again and the wind had dropped. The light was the light of the Impressionists, of Cezanne and Braque, so hard you could cut it, silvery-white and glittering as the sun it flowed across a landscape of low hills and woods, fields and squat cliffs, and the small, neat village.

Happy day-trippers poured from the morning ferries out of Toulon and other places on the mainland and flooded into the village to hire mountain bikes by the dozen, or hurried or strolled off towards the nearby beaches. Mothers, fathers, children, aunties, uncles, cousins, walkers, cyclists, naturists and naturalists, swimmers and explorers, the noisy and those in search of solitude, the old and young, wealthy and poor all tumbled off the ferries and headed to the village. The cafés did a brisk trade in breakfast coffees and croissants, and those who didn't have breakfast croissants had breakfast ice-cream. We sat and watched with a secret, satisfied smile, this was our life not our holiday.

We had to move berth, the breakwater was booked for the next few days by a regatta who we knew would stream in through the entrance in a boisterous, shouting cavalcade as evening arrived, racing stories and tokens of manhood shouted from the decks all fuelled by testosterone, adrenaline and gassy beer. So we moved back across the water towards the centre of the marina. It should have suited us to be closer to the village and the shower block but we were still tired and resented the extra work.

We'd already scouted around a little and knew there was a slipway and a hoist in case the gland really gave trouble, but I still had no intention of trying to fix it. *Drip*, it went in the dark bilge bowels, *drip, drip*.

We *bimbled*. This, you understand, is a Navy word and means what it sounds like. To *bimble*: a bit of pottering, a bit of tootling, of walking along mind in neutral a bit of, well, nothing very much. The kind of thing you do on a day like this when there are no pressures but lots of new things to see and do.

We bimbled our way to the *Plage d'Argent* along sandy lanes, deeply shades by trees, because there are no paved roads on the Porquerolles. Everyone travels on foot or on a mountain bike.

But the Silver Beach disappointed us. True, the sand was silvery but, although the water was crystal clear and shallow, the beach itself was strewn with the fallen leaves of the palm trees that fringed it and the sand was like concrete. Maybe this is how it's supposed to be in a nature reserve. The beach curved in a natural bay bounded by rocks and about five hundred metres across. Out passed the line of yellow beach markers a gaggle of yachts lay anchored and tilting in the slight swell. Ann stretched out on a towel and I went for a swim at last.

In the water lived a hideous creature like nothing I'd ever seen. I snorkelled above it in three feet of water and I was scared it might attack me. A brown, ugly thing about a foot long it looked like the stump of a long dead sailor's limb lying on the sandy bottom.

After a minute or so of staring at each other the stump started swimming away and changed colour and I realised I was watching a cuttlefish. When I moved, it stopped. When I stopped, it moved. It pointed it's ugly stubby tentacles at me but headed in jerks towards the weeds and rocks at the edge of the bay. I followed, horrified, curious. My phobia of wild things in the sea revved along in top gear. From time to time it would give me a pretty display of bright colours and I wondered what it was signalling. *Don't eat me* probably, or *do you want a good time ducky*, or: *you touch me and I'll get my brother the giant squid to sort you out, bimbler!* In the end it reached cover and I lost it in the weeds, and though I came back soon afterward with Ann, we couldn't find it again.

The cuttlefish wasn't my only surprise of the day though. As we had a beer in the bar on the beach and looked out over the turquoise water and through the anchored yachts towards the distant mainland an aircraft carrier motored massively passed, complete with its attendant destroyers. Yesterday, in all that wind and sea, I'd thought the gap between the island and the mainland was too small for *Aderyn Glas*. Now here was a full blown aircraft carrier popping through the gap like it was an ocean wide. Just bimbling back to Toulon.

I watched it slowly turn to line up for the channel and was glad I wasn't a yacht coming the other way. Ann gave me a look I couldn't interpret but there wasn't a smile in it. Puzzlement maybe.

'*The* place to go,' our new Scottish neighbour told us as he borrowed an extension cable, 'is the next island, the Parc National de Port Cros where they have these underwater panels to tell snorkelers about the habitats. But woe betide you if you anchor in their precious Poseidon grass.' He looked suitably stern. Like a skinny, tough schoolteacher.

'We'll take the ferry,' I suggested next morning as we waved him off, 'see you later.' But the ferries didn't run until July.

So we went cycling instead.

I thought the little folding clowns' bikes we'd carried all the way from Britain would be able to cope with the dusty main tracks that were hammered hard by the passage of countless feet and bike tyres each day so, full of optimism, we set off along the coast to the next beach, Notre Dame. On the way we were going to cross the island to investigate the deserted beaches on the south side.

I should have known from the start it was a mistake and I should have gone back to bed or sat still until the urge to explore had passed. By the time we'd cycled the hundred metres or so from the boat to the chandlery Ann's front tyre was flat and I realised we didn't have a pump so I had to go back for it. The weather was hot and pumping up the tyre didn't cool me down. Nor did the quizzical, and sometimes downright rude, looks we were given by the other cyclists. They were all riding things that looked as indestructible as the Forth rail bridge, but we had six gears and so what if the wheels were a bit on the small side?

The sky was blue from end to end and the air was a furnace. The only breeze came from pedalling the bikes and once we were out of the village, the only noises were the ones we made and the background of birdsong. The scent was of wildflowers, the view was of low rolling hillsides and occasional trees and I could have stayed right there for the rest of my life.

But instead, we struggled up and down the dirt tracks in the heat with both our tempers getting shorter until finally I crunched a small stone with my gear change and wrecked it. Now I had one gear. I swore at the bike and kicked it and rested it in the shade of a tree but neither threats nor kindness healed it.

Ann stopped and rested out of earshot. Her brain transmitted the message *we should have hired proper bikes,* but she said nothing. Nothing I could hear anyway.

After I'd cooled down I resorted to some levering with the cycle spanner and managed to repair it enough to continue in a grinding, graunching way until we found a really necessary cool little bay, deserted except for a jet skier and his girlfriend who obviously thought they were going to have this lovely secluded beach all to themselves and who are these English fools on kiddies bikes? *Tant pis!*

We went for a paddle and Ann got tar on her shoes. Tar is death on a boat. It gets everywhere and nothing removes it. Ever!

So we headed back with me in a foul temper, missed the beach we were aiming for altogether and ended up back at Plage d'Argent where the water was colder than before and there were no cuttlefish.

Eventually we pushed the bikes most of the way back home and sealed them in their bags forever. Never to remove them again.

For therapy I went and bought an anemometer in the chandlery and immediately felt better. I love to spend money on toys. The wind speed gauge that should have been attached to the top of the mast had, with infinite irony, blown away in a Port Napoleon *Mistral* during the winter. Now, with my new toy, I would be able to tell when the wind was strong enough to justify my terror.

The night was hot and filled with the zinging of mosquitoes and the chirp of cicadas. Next morning was perfect. The problem with such an endless series of hot calm days in such a beautiful place is that you lose the will to move. If this is paradise how can the next place be better? So let's stay here. The spirit of the Porquerolles was seducing us, soaking into us, calling us with Siren songs, persuading us to stay.

'Let's stay forever,' I said. Ann agreed. It took a real effort to actually decide that – tomorrow – we would head for Saint Tropez.

On the 8th June we left. It was a totally uneventful passage across calm seas and we took turns sunbathing on the foredeck while the stereo played sixty's pop songs or classical pieces and Rachel steered and navigated. There was no life and few boats and we arrived off Saint Tropez five hours later with the stereo blasting out "Land of Hope and Glory".

Chapter 4

Day 19, Ste Maxime, France, 1726 miles to Gouvia.

Saint Tropez. 'Sounds wonderful, doesn't it?', Ann smiled, 'visions of Brigitte Bardot and Roger Vadim strolling the narrow streets or drinking arcane cocktails in small, special backstreet bars that only the *cognoscenti* would know, while they discussed "And God Created Woman".'

I joined in the dream: 'Or Bardot sunbathing on secluded, sheltered, beaches dotted around the tiny, rustic village with its little harbour where local, dilapidated, lateen rigged fishing boats bobbed in the sheltered water. Or buying the morning catch of fish to grill in the corner of some soon-to-be-famous, penniless artist's attic while he slept after a night of drinking and arguing and debating and drinking and fighting and drinking.'

Pop! That was my dream bursting.

Aderyn Glas had arrived off the marina and we'd taken one look then crossed the bay and tied up in San Maxime instead. The sheer tonnage and bright sparkle of the superyachts moored in the harbour and its approaches meant that Saint Trop' was not for the likes of us and its neighbour was close.

We were moored near the jetty that the ferries used to take the day trippers across the bay and expected, a little miserably, to be rolled around a lot from their wakes but it proved to be quiet enough. There was fuel and the usual free electricity and water, a chandlery and a shower block presided over by an impressive *madame concierge* that she only opened at times when we didn't need it.

It was a hot and poky concreted place with hardly a supermarket, too many holiday makers and too many mosquitoes. It was expensive too, we were getting into the high rent corner of the Riviera. 'You know,' said Ann with emphasis: '*The* Riviera!'

We bailed two litres of water out of the bilge after five hours of motoring.

We took the ferry next day across to Sainte Tropez – how could we not? – and went to look for Brigitte. The marina was, as we expected from our fly-by, full of the most breathtaking vessels including one huge superyacht with a British flag and a stainless steel anchor (no, I'm serious, a huge stainless steel anchor on a ship). Its liveried crew were polishing away at the stainless steel stanchions of the guardrail and I wondered if they would polish the anchor later. The wavelets played fascinating patterns of light onto the highly polished, deep blue of her immaculate hull.

Sainte Tropez is a small village with a harbour and narrow streets that wind up the hill to a fort. The three, four or five story buildings that ring the harbour, now the marina, are all uniformly pastel coloured apartment buildings and most have either a tourist shop or a restaurant on the ground floor. The uniformed side streets are the same, though here and there is a tree in a pot or washing hung rebelliously from a window.

We wandered around trying to find the magic with everyone else who was trying to find the magic. The noises were the noises made anywhere in the world where a cosmopolitan crowd of tourists wandered through narrow streets looking for something to look at, a chatter of foreign tongues and excited kids, growling adults and crying babies. The smells were of tobacco and breakfast food. We peered into expensive art gallery windows and saw tourists peering at conveyor belt art. We squinted at interminable menus printed in many languages in an endless series of restaurants whose waiters chattered in many languages and tried to seduce us with their few English words. And we climbed the hill to the fort and looked out over the town, passed peacocks and cannon. But we couldn't find a hint of the magic. Eventually we shrugged and hobbled back over the precision laid cobbles to the quayside to eat our sandwiches next to the lateen rigged local fishing boats and the queue to the women's toilet.

The fishing boats, at least, seemed to be genuinely old but every one of them now belonged to the *Saint Tropez Lateen Club* and were perfectly painted and preserved examples that had probably never had their decks soiled by a fish scale. Except on one where a seagull tore apart a fish carcase while we watched. I would bet, too, that their sails were made of the finest modern plastic sailcloth. Sainte Tropez played to my overdeveloped cynicism gene.

The town's marina was lined with the large and magnificent vessels of the rich and famous. The huge multi-decked floating palaces crowded in amongst the ocean racing powerboats that were mostly floating engines and the RIB tenders of the even larger ships that were too big to get through the harbour entrance and so had to anchor outside. Deep blue hulls, cream, grey, and white hulls, highly polished, flickered light at us. The variety of flags added colour: red or blue British, orange and green Italian, the French *Tricolore* of course, and many from tax-haven Georgetown. Some yachts carried powerboats, jetskies and RIBs craned onto their sterndecks or hauled into garages in their sterns like the holds of ferries.

We meandered to the other side of the harbour in time to line up with the other tourists to gawk at some beautiful, graceful, young girl who flowed down the *passerelle* at the stern of her yacht and floated barefoot across the street to where a chauffeur was held a door open for her. A hugging scrap of multi-coloured mini-dress, the crew who stood formally and respectfully at ease, a Chelsea Tractor with black anonymous windows and the discrete security all added to the enigma. Like everyone else we didn't have a clue who she might have been or how she managed to walk barefoot on the hot tarmac without screaming, but it was clear she must have been famous and could afford the best chiropodist.

We found a chandlery near the harbour office and headed for the door to buy something we could use that would also serve as a memento, a polished steel shackle or bolt with "*souvenir of Saint Tropez*" stamped on it. Perhaps we could only afford a stainless fishhook. But we never found out. Being the owner and captain of a yacht doesn't even guarantee you entry to a chandlery in Saint Tropez and we weren't allowed inside. The sign said "Crew Only" in large letters and there was a rope across the door. A posh and expensive rope but still a very effective rope. The assistant behind the counter glanced briefly at us as we tried to unhook it and shook his head dismissively.

'I suppose,' said Ann, 'it would be no use taking my shoes off and floating along the pavement?'

'You'll just burn your feet and expect me to kiss them better. Anyway we probably can't afford a shackle here, and I'll bet everything they sell is made of stainless or gold, did you see that anchor?' I tried to imagine what kind of creature the shopkeeper had in mind when he wrote "Crew Only" – the image of our beautiful celebrity calling in to buy a bolt or a can of grease, or even a stainless steel toilet seat didn't seem to fit.

The late afternoon was cloudy, oppressive and hot. Eventually the heat wore us down and we queued for the return ferry and wondered why we'd bothered.

Saint Tropez is a myth, a place to keep in your dreams, somewhere to spend your life wanting to go; just don't go there. There's nothing there except people waiting to take money from you and herds of tourists determined to keep their euros in their pockets for as long as they can. It's not attractive, the beaches are non-existent, the streets are too clean, the houses are too stereotyped and are all newly painted in whatever colours the local authority have decided on for the season. The harbour is full of expensive machinery and busy with ferries that constantly disgorge ever more hopeful tourists. There is no Brigitte, no Roger, not even an existentialist philosopher to stare at.

On the return home we sat inside the ferry to avoid any more sun.

Life was due to get harder, but we didn't yet know it.

The weather is absolutely the greatest influence on a cruising yacht. Where we go, when we go, how we get there and whether we arrive in good condition or not all depends on the weather between the start and end points of each leg. It's not enough to look out of the window and make decisions based on what you can see and feel. Flat out *Aderyn Glas* can do seven knots and weather systems can do twenty-five. Every day we travel we need to know where the weather systems are, where they are going and what winds are associated with them. The winds whip up the seas and so it's good to know what the wave height will be too. Weather forecasts and their accuracy are, literally, a matter of life and death to us and we'd had a few examples of the forecasts being wrong, both in the *calanque* at Miou and between Toulon and the Porquerolles. Now that we faced our first sea crossing from Sainte Maxime to Calvi on Corsica, we absolutely needed the best forecast we could get. We wanted a risk-free crossing that would bore us stiff with its routine and yet preferably under sail to save the fragile stern gland.

Yes, the plans had changed again. We had discarded the plan that was going to take us along the coast to Monaco and decided instead to head off for the first of our islands. In part this was because we had lost a little time in those places where we'd had to wait for weather windows, and in part because we were keen to get on, to start the voyage proper, rather than bimble around the coast. Also the forecast was good for us: a gentle wind would blow us away from France and towards Corsica over the Ligurian Sea.

We had many ways to get forecasts. Our favourite was an internet site called *passageweather.com* which gave us windspeed and direction, precipitation and wave heights, for the coming week. We also used GRIB files which gave the same data for the same time period with the exception of wave height. For both of these we needed internet access and finding it was always an issue for us. Ultimately we could get a low bandwidth dataset from the Passageweather site using the modem in Ann's mobile but the cost was prohibitive.

After that, in order of preference, came the forecasts provided by marinas, which were usually good and also web based but local in area and normally restricted to a twenty-four hour prediction, and by the local coastguard services via a VHF channel. In France the latter was of no use to us since it required a level of French that was beyond us. Further along the coast and at the north end of Corsica we found Monaco radio that provided an English version, but that was in our future.

Normally there was a variation in forecasts which resulted, presumably, because they required a degree of interpretation of data but we learned to live with that and generally chose the most pessimistic. We also found that there was a huge local modification of the general weather field caused by cliffs, headlands and other features, together with the presence or absence of thermal sea breezes that are far stronger than those we were used to in Britain.

But we checked the weather as best we could, which in Saint Maxime, meant a visit to the *Capitaine* for a twenty-four hour prediction that he downloaded from his favourite website. For us, because we planned to cross to Corsica, he went as far as providing a picture of the whole route for which we were grateful. The guys in the motorboat next to ours looked with some envy at the charts that predicted a steady, calm sail all the way across the Ligurian Sea.

So we left early next morning, early for me being ten o'clock. We filled our tanks then headed out into the bay leaving behind us hillsides densely covered with trees and holiday homes. There was a little breeze so we hauled out the sails to catch it but we made only about two knots. As we cleared the Saint Tropez cape and set course for Corsica the wind began to increase and so did the boat speed. It became instantly clear that the forecast had underestimated both the wind and the sea. The wind was stronger and much noisier than the useful force four maximum we were promised, and was from a direction that created a side-on chop that made *Aderyn Glas* roll horribly. Ann did the first hour and by the time I was halfway through the second the corkscrewing was bad enough to make me feel queasy. Ann, sat in the side of the cockpit, seemed unaffected and I knew there was no point in suggesting we turn back yet. I also knew we could not take another twenty hours of this sort of motion. My new toy told me the windspeed was around twenty-five knots.

'See,' I said, 'if we hadn't bought this nice little anemometer we wouldn't know it was bad here.'

Ten minutes into Ann's watch I could see she was uncomfortable. The moment had come.

'Twenty-odd more hours of this, Ani darling,' I said with a grin that was more a baring of teeth, 'I won't mind if you think we ought to turn back.'

She only hesitated for about a second or so. It was rough enough by then to send the odd spray over us and little white crests flew freely from the tips of the choppy waves. The thought of a twenty hour long fight was enough to make us turn around. We were two and a half hours out of Sainte Maxime but we couldn't get back there because it was pretty much directly upwind, so we turned northeast and headed for the next bay along the coast, to Frejus.

It was a struggle. We trimmed the sails until we had a scrap of main and little more genoa and we flogged close to the wind at about four knots for three hours. We were wet and cold and tired and completely unable to find the entrance to Frejus and when we did we had to approach through hordes of kite surfers and wind surfers who revelled in the unexpected hurricane.

The entrance was a gap in a beach and on either side the rollers growled onto the sands. What made it all so much more dangerous was the wind which was now directly astern. We had no choice but to have faith and try to surf our way into the gap that presented itself, but before that we had to take in the sails and that meant turning completely around to head into the wind to ease the pressure on them. Ann was at the helm and misunderstood what I said to her, we needed a really fast turn as a wave passed below us but instead she put the helm over gently and took us around slowly, thinking that I would need time to handle the sheets. The result was the wind and seas caught *Aderyn Glas* broadside on in the surf zone and we nearly capsized. Seven tonnes of boat began to roll over and be destroyed on the shore. Time stopped. Our home and our odyssey literally teetered on the edge of destruction while the combers roared and the wind pressed against her. Down below there were a series of crashes as various things fell over the floor, the heavy cooker top leapt across the cabin, the books deserted the bookshelves, fruit fell about the floor and a wastebin leapt into the toilet bowl. Anything that was not tied down crashed onto the nearest available floorspace. Ann and I held on, there was not much else we could do. I'd opened the throttle and Ann had the wheel hard over to push the stern around. The sheets were loose and the boom was in the water. Slowly the stern came around and she came back up. I caught the boom and we breathed again. Our lovely, beautiful *Aderyn Glas*.

We took in the sails then had to spin the boat back towards the shore. This time there was no mistake, Ann pushed the stern around with the throttle wide open and the wheel hard across. She aimed at the surf-filled gap and charged. On either side the roar of the surf filled the air. Inside the entrance we discovered we had a sharp turn to the left to make. Ann swerved violently then stopped. All the noise of the surf and the flying spray was behind us. The posh new marina of Frejus was in front of us. And the wind was already pushing us sideways.

Day 21, Frejus, France, 1716 miles to Gouvia.

We radioed the *Capitaine* and he waved us into a berth next to a small motorboat. The wind kept trying to take control and there was no way this was going to be a soft landing so we hung out every fender we could find. I tried to angle the boat against the wind in a move best described as damage limitation and crabbed towards the berth. The *Capitaine* waited to take our lines and hand Ann the stern-line but it was impossible to get the rope tied on before the wind slewed us around the small boat alongside. I hoped for help from its crew but no-one showed up. So we swung around but luckily we didn't do any damage and I was able to get her straightened up by winching hard on the stern-line with the sheet winch.

Exhausted we flopped in the cockpit.

Exhausted we had a couple of snappy moments about the near death experience on the way in. Exhausted, but then elated that we'd made it reasonably safely to the berth, we listened again to the discordant music of the wind in the rigging of the assembled boats and the growl of the surf outside the marina. We were learning all the time, still on the steep part of the learning curve.

'Maybe one day we'll learn that the sea is not for us.' I thought aloud, 'Why do we do it?'

'Because you enjoy it,' said Ann, and she really believed I did.

Frejus is a clean, modern marina complex surrounded by apartments and the odd designer shop, palm trees with uplighters and open spaces to saunter around in an evening. The showers were clean and the water was hot, there was a choice of chandleries with no silly notices on the door. Ann followed a lady with a shopping bag and thus found a supermarket near the beach. Which was where we bumped into Hans from *Dream* whom we'd last seen in the Porquerolles.

The downside of Frejus is that in any kind of blow it all gets very difficult. For a start the entrance is through the surf zone, and as we'd discovered, that could be a real death-trap. After that the arrangement of the pontoons and buildings seem to amplify whatever wind blew from whatever direction. The result can be the kind of trouble we watched next day as a French yacht was blown sideways onto a line of moored boats across from us on the next pontoon. Her captain managed to snag a host of mooring lines and the more he struggled to get free the more he became attached like a fly in a spider's web. The pot-bellied idiot of an owner climbed onto his foredeck clad only in shorts that, for a fat man of about sixty, were frighteningly skimpy. He waved his arms and ordered his neighbours and the staff around as if they all worked for him and he paid them a wage. Ann and I sat and watched bemused from the comfort of our cockpit. In Britain a captain in trouble would accept all the advice he could get and be grateful for it and then would be more likely to slink away, red-faced with the shame of it all.

Not this guy. He stood and shouted and directed and ordered and absolutely no-one listened or did anything he told them to, which was just as well. It took the combined efforts of two of the *Capitainerie* workboats and helping hands from the neighbouring yachts to free him and get him into a safe berth.

So Frejus in a wind is not the place to arrive or to leave, but when we were tied up we felt safe. At least the wind would keep the mosquitoes away. I was doing well lately, the DEET and the other chemicals together with the nets kept my bite count down to around three or four new bites each day. And the Bonjela kept the itching to a minimum.

Hans came for a visit and brought his laptop for me to fix. Somehow he'd managed to delete his GRIB program and so had no weather forecasts. Someone had told him I was good with computers which I deny, but this was easy and I fixed it and we had a look at the weather forecast together. The wind was going to blow like this for a few more days yet so we were all going to have to wait a little longer and learn to love Frejus. Hans told us he was aiming at Macinaggio on the northeast side of Corsica which was much further than Calvi, our preferred landfall. But he had a bigger boat and a couple of visiting friends to help crew it and wanted to get on.

'What harm is a little bad weather anyway?' he said with something resembling bravado.

Later that evening we chatted to a Scottish couple who had retired to France and they warned us about whales. Curtiss happily told me that it was common to see whales basking on the surface between the islands. But these, he claimed, would be dying and if we approached too closely they would suddenly thrash about and sink us. Ann and I exchanged a glance that was sceptical if not actually disbelieving.

So we were stuck for a few days once again waiting in the sun for the wind to moderate.

'Right,' said Ann, as we relaxed in the shade of the cockpit, 'a bit of maintenance is called for.'

'Stern gland?' By now it was clear the leak was not going to stop despite my strategy of pretending there wasn't a problem. 'I'll get the tools out tomorrow then and have a go,' I said, half-heartedly. Ann went below and returned with two Stillson wrenches, a can of WD40 and a hammer. I got the idea.

After I'd finished I wondered what all the fuss had been about. The corrosion that looked so horrible that the gland stem would disintegrate as soon as I put a spanner on it wasn't corrosion at all and simply wiped away with an oily rag. The nuts that were so jammed into place that the application of a spanner would twist the entire stem out of the hull like a tooth from a gum and let the sea come pouring in – I squirted with WD40 and they moved as soon as I tentatively tapped them with the hammer. I didn't even need the second Stillson, I simply tapped gently on the gland nut and the locknut and they moved easily to their new positions just a quarter turn from where they'd started. No more than a quarter turn – I knew enough not to overtighten the gland or it would overheat.

The leak stopped as soon as I moved the nut.

I watched, not breathing. No drips formed at the end of the stem. I felt elated. After ten minutes there were still no drips. After another ten I turned the shaft in my hands and there still wasn't a drip. We looked at each other, took a deep breath, thought for a moment, hesitated for another and prevaricated for a third. We didn't speak. Then we started the motor and turned the shaft with the engine. No spray, no drips. I almost began to believe we'd fixed it so we put a drip tray under the stem and determined not to look again until next day, which meant we only checked it every half hour or so until we went to bed. And not one fraction of one drip did we catch.

'It might be okay now,' I said pretending confidence. I couldn't believe it was that simple. Next day the tray was still dry.

'It'll overheat,' I said, pessimistically. We left the tools in easy reach as our minds leapt without hesitation from the fear of water pouring in to one of the shaft seizing solid in the overheated gland, halfway between France and Corsica, while a storm raged around us.

After two nights in Frejus and newly filled up with fuel and water, we left the French mainland and headed for Calvi on the north-western tip of Corsica, a distance of a hundred nautical miles so twenty hours at five knots. We were filled with excitement and apprehension. Excited at the thought of finally leaving the mainland behind and apprehensive because last time we'd tried this we had to turn back.

'Captain Cook,' said Ann, 'starting out into unknown oceans, leaving behind the continent he grew up on.'

'Vasco da Gama, I added, 'Amerigo thingy.'

'Vespucci.'

'Didn't he invent the motorbike?'

'I think that was Honda,' she said. We were getting silly, both of us knew Harley Davidson invented the motorbike and Vespucci was scooters.

For good luck we'd bought a Corsican courtesy flag known as the *Testa de Moru*, the silhouette of a Moor's head on a white background, and we threw a quantity of small change into the sea to pacify Poseidon. This time the forecast was for a calm sea and little wind.

At first we sailed but the breeze wasn't really trying too hard, which was fine by us after the winds we'd had last time we'd set off, so after a couple of hours with the speed down to about two knots we turned the motor on. It was sunny and calm and Rachel was happy steering so we let her. Our Autohelm is called Rachel, named after Sean Young's portrayal of Rachel Rosen the beautiful android from my favourite film of the time, Ridley Scott's *Blade Runner*. The GPS, the chartplotter on the computer and the car satnav systems are also called Rachel – I have no imagination and sometimes it's confusing but we usually know which Rachel we're talking about. So Rachel is our permanent third crewmember and without her we would have to constantly steer and navigate, day and night, in all weathers, so her wellbeing is very important to us.

We stood watch one hour on and one off, although in fact we tended to stay on deck when we were off watch too since there was little else to do to keep us moving. I know the theory is that when you are off watch you should really go and do something different, even if it's catching up with reading or watching a video and we've done both. But this leg was different: it was the first time we'd gone deep into the Mediterranean and neither of us wanted to miss anything. We drank soup and ate sandwiches.

As always we'd calculated our arrival based on an average of five knots then did six or more because we motored rather than sailed. However, an early arrival at Calvi would mean an arrival in the dark so we slowed down to our planned speed. We cruised across the flat water and looked for life. It was all very pleasant so long as you didn't dwell on being alone on the sea fifty miles from the nearest land.

About 12:30 I saw a blue-grey shark about two metres long which, startled by the boat, swam rapidly away in a shallow dive. Late in the afternoon we began to realise that we were motoring through a sea covered with bubbles. After a while it began to dawn on us that the bubbles were not bubbles at all since however much we stared we never saw one pop, but we had no idea what they were. We became fascinated by their sheer numbers. As far as we could see and in all directions they covered the surface rising on the gentle swell and riding down our bow wave. They didn't seem to move under their own power and we began to wonder if they could be jellyfish – something I hate even more than mosquitoes. But the bubbles ranged from about one to two centimetres long which was smaller than any jellyfish I'd ever seen.

There was only one way to settle it we had to catch one. So we stopped and threw a bucket overboard and came up with two. They were small jellyfish with a fringe of electric blue around the base of a shining bubble or sail structure. The bright blue ring held lots of small waving tentacles and I would bet that these were stinging cells.

'Beautiful,' said Ann, who is a Biologist, and busied herself with a camera.

'Disgusting,' I said, as an engineer who had been stung by a jellyfish as a kid and lived in fear of Box and Irukandji being transported mysteriously from Australia just to sting me to death.

We returned the stingers to the sea where they hung upside-down, the sail now being a rudder and the bright blue frill facing the sun.

'I hope you're satisfied,' Ann pouted at me, 'those two will die now.'

'A few billion minus two then, that's good.'

All the rest of that day we ploughed on through fields of jellyfish. Ann searched the books and determined they were *Viella Viella* also known as "by the wind sailors".

'If we could only eat them the world's famines would be eliminated at a stroke.' I thought aloud.

A little later we saw a couple of dolphins in the distance but they didn't want to play with us. There was no sign of Duncan's whales.

Now and then I checked the gland which was neither leaking nor overheating.

Once an hour Ann wrote down our position in the log.

Occasionally we ate something.

Mostly we sat in the shade and drank water by the litre.

Sometimes we played a music CD.

Sometimes we played with the radar but saw nothing.

The radar is not called Rachel, it's called "radar".

When dusk arrived we lowered the table and made it into a berth opposite the inside helm position, and turned on the navigation lights. It was still warm enough to wear shorts and helm from the cockpit.

We have an unbreakable rule for travelling at night: whoever is on watch in the cockpit must wear a lifejacket, be attached to the boat with a strop and carry a torch and the satellite locator beacon, the PLB. The reason for all this redundant safety is that whoever is off-watch is usually asleep and in an hour *Aderyn Glas* could have travelled six miles from the point where the watchkeeper could have fallen overboard. A six mile radius gives an area of about a hundred square miles and even if the sleeping crew were to wake up after an hour (and without a shake and a shout who would?) the chance of backtracking perfectly and finding the missing crew in the dark is small. It wouldn't happen. So we are cautious. We never deviate from this rule.

Darkness brought with it a greater sense of isolation. There was nothing on the radar which meant nothing for sixteen miles in any direction, but we knew that the nearest land was getting on for fifty miles away. As well as man-overboard I worried about heart attacks and broken limbs, about strokes and being attacked by sharks – how could we get help for any of these?

'And lightening strikes!' I said. Ann patiently pointed out there wasn't a cloud in the sky and no hint of a front. 'Duncan's whales then, or giant cuttlefish previously unknown to science!' But all I could see and hear were the blossoming stars, the drone of the motor and the sounds of the hull cutting through the still water.

We slowed down a little more, nervous of hitting things like whales, containers, lobster pots and giant cuttlefish.

It was a moonless night. My first ever moonless, cloudless night at sea. There was a dim glow from the radar and a little light leakage from the navigation lights, but look straight up and there was an almost eerie blackness – and the Milky Way. I'd never seen the Milky Way before and now it curved over my head in an irregular arch like someone had dusted a black velvet sky with icing sugar. One hundred, thousand million stars in our galaxy – the Milky Way – and one hundred, thousand million galaxies. The scale of it all was incomprehensible and took my breath away.

Ann had turned in so I was alone with the vastness and magnificence of it all. The motor purred, the hull swished and the stars were silent witnesses. The sky was spanned by the Milky Way, yes, but there were also the thousands of individual points of light that made up the constellations and the wandering planets. I could only name a few: Orion, the Plough, Cassiopeia. It was all so calm I hauled a cockpit seat cushion from below and lay on my back and drank in the beauty of it. Shooting stars crossed the sky every few minutes and splashed a brief trail of bright light; then were spent. I wondered vaguely how many meteorites there were, on average, every night.

Every fifteen minutes I roused myself to do a scan by eyeball and radar, but there were no other ships out there. After two hours I woke Ann and turned in.

Two hours later Ann woke me and told me excitedly about the red glow on the horizon in front of us. At first she'd thought it had to be a fire, a ship on fire, and she'd turned us towards it to help, but she'd heard nothing on the radio and saw nothing on the radar. She'd watched and the glow grew larger and changed to orange. She was, she told me, quite frightened. In a while she'd realised she'd seen moonrise at sea. I envied her, it must have been some spectacle. My next watch was less exciting: the moonlight had killed the stars.

As we neared Corsica we picked up the lights of yachts heading our way, and when the grey predawn turned to full daylight we began to make out the cliffs to the west of Calvi shrouded in a dawn mist. At Calvi we looked into the marina but decided to ignore its overcrowded pontoons and turned back to pick up a buoy in the bay instead. We felt very pleased with ourselves and celebrated with breakfast and a nap. The idea began to grow that we might actually pull this off. This was exotic Corsica. We'd gone foreign!

Chapter 5

Calvi, Corsica, 1694 miles to Gouvia. Day 24

I went swimming in my shorty wetsuit. Getting into it was an exhausting struggle, I'd not worn it for about two years and it had shrunk tremendously in that time, honest! Eventually, with Ann and I both tugging and straining and me sweating so much I was soaked before I hit the water, my arms and legs were encased and relatively immobile. The bits that made me a man were being slowly crushed and my arms stuck out horizontally at rest, and sprang back to this position whenever I relaxed them. Ann tried zipping the zipper and found I had a choice to make. Zip it up and give up breathing, or leave it unzipped and breathe but suffer a paralysingly cold belly. I went with the latter.

I lowered the ladder over the stern and jumped in, preferring a quick shock to slow, trickling torture. It was cold and I gasped for a bit until the wetsuit was full. Anyone who tells you the Med' is warm hasn't swum in it in the Spring. The water was green and beautiful. *Aderyn Glas* was clean and stable with a small fringe of weed where her list dipped the boot-top on the port side. Small fish played around the keels and shafts of sunlight rippled down to the sandy bottom seven metres below me. It was my first swim for a long time, and my first in the Mediterranean on this odyssey. Ann hummed the *Jaws* prelude.

I tried a little crawl, after all I had been a competitive masters swimmer when I was forty, and in the same age group as Mark Spitz. There the comparison ends, I didn't share his view that swimmers can be competitive into old age. Not that I was old.

'Old swimmers never die, they just crawl away,' said Ann like she'd invented the joke. So I tried again. My arms, however, would not come out of the water, a fact clearly attributed to the all constricting, elastic embrace of the shrunken wetsuit. I was reduced to an amateurish paddling motion much like doggy-paddle. I was pleased I had the snorkel, turning my head to breathe would have been impossible.

I was there to clean the echo sounder transducer which had been causing occasional problems with the depth readout. I guessed it was getting coated with marine life since it was one of the parts of the hull that could not be anti-fouled. I also wanted to clean the barnacles off the log spinner, the little paddlewheel that sits under the hull and sends signals to the meter that tells us how fast we're going through the water. Every so often a crustacean finds its way into the mechanism and stops the wheel rotating preventing us getting any speed information. This is annoying rather than catastrophic since the real navigational information is provided by Rachel the GPS and Rachel the laptop chart plotter program.

The buoyant wetsuit made it almost impossible to stay under the hull and trying to dive was such an effort that, after a very short time, I was gasping and exhausted: my heart racing and thumping. I would dive, fighting to get under the hull then scrape away for a few seconds with my fingernails before I had to return to the surface to gasp enough air to stop the ache in my lungs. After a while I had to concede defeat: scraping off the growth wasn't hard but the solid, buoyant wetsuit made it impossible to finish the job. I felt I was dying. In my hour of triumph over the sterngland I felt I was dying just to get the instruments working and that was stupid. I convinced myself I'd done enough, though, and the rest would keep until the water was warm enough to discard the suit. I checked the mooring buoy we were tied to, lying on the surface and breathing deeply until the aches stopped, then climbed back out, belly and head frozen, arms in a straightjacket death lock and blood depleted of oxygen.

Ann and I struggled again to lever the thing back off me and I eventually draped it over the stern rail where it hung for a day looking despondent, crucified, arms out and hood down, until it dried and was put in deep store forever.

'But I'll need it when I go diving again,' I'd objected, but my logic went unheeded. It's still in deep store today and Ann will regret her burying it so deep when I go diving again.

The citadel was the first part of Corsica we saw as we approached from the French mainland. The majestic walled citadel standing proud on top of the rocky headland was a magnificent sight and the open tranquil bay beyond welcomed us after a wearying twenty hour passage.

The bay is very large and shaped like a comma so that the citadel and town were actually to the north of us, even though we were on the western coast of the island. It has zones, where anchoring is prohibited, and an organised mooring area with a range of buoys for a range of boat sizes. There were supposed to be moorings for 232 boats, according to the brochure given out by the staff, and I have no reason to doubt it, although there were only about ten yachts in the anchorage that day. Each morning the *Capitaine's* staff delivered weather forecasts and collected rubbish and payment from the moored yachts.

The view was breathtaking with mountains ranged around most of the bay, some still with winter snow on their peaks, and the citadel towering above the harbour to the north. The mountains were given scale by the villages on their slopes and a quick look at the charts confirmed heights of over 2000 metres. The atmospheric recession provided a series of two dimensional silhouettes stretching into the distance each higher and bluer than the one in front. At the edge of the sea the yellow sandy beach stretched from the town at the northern edge, to be lost in the distance to the east. Here and there it was dotted with sun umbrellas and beach chairs.

The temperature was nudging thirty with a sky of wall-to-wall blue and no breeze. The day stretched before us bobbing gently with all that view to look at. We lounged in the cockpit with a book each and just relaxed. A blink later and knock on the hull woke us from our reading with a start. An Englishman had spotted our ensign and rowed all the way over from the marina to ask about prices on the buoys. Ann thought he must be a solo sailor desperate for company, 'Why didn't he ask at the marina office?' She wondered aloud. But we accepted his invitation for a drink later, when he'd moved his boat. We picked up our books and looked once more at the view and energetically resumed our relaxation.

Much later we paddled our dinghy the fifty metres to his boat. By now we were getting used to interrogating the people who'd sailed the waters we were travelling through and Ann, the navigator, usually turned up with the pilot, the almanac and various charts to get the low-down on the best ports and anchorages, and so it was that evening. James was another Hans, tall and fit looking with a deep tan that didn't happen overnight, and a penchant for rowing his rubber duck rather than using the motor. He was as good as his word and spent a long time below with Ann pouring over the charts and books while I sat in his cockpit with a wine glass and the bottle, watching the mountains and listening to the hush. At dusk the citadel was bathed in yellow light against a sky and sea of deepening blue.

Next day, over breakfast, I watched C130 Hercules aircraft in the far corner of the bay dropping paratroops into the water. 'James was one of those,' Ann confided. 'He's here on his own and sailed across from the mainland like we did, except he was alone. He was worried a bit about it being illegal, or rather, not acceptable to the insurers so he was hoping they wouldn't find out. He's flying home today though to see his wife, she doesn't like sailing so stays at home with the kids and he comes out for the summer.'

I looked at her a little quizzically, 'Did you get any useful navigational data?'

'He's been everywhere and into every anchorage between here and Sicily and a good many there too.' She'd missed my sarcasm. Just as well. I always feel sad for people whose partners don't share their passions and there are many single handed sailors whose wives won't join them. Ann and I are lucky, we both enjoy sailing, though for different reasons: Ann enjoys it for its own sake, the stoic battling against the elements thing, while I enjoy travelling and am happy to use sailing as a means of exploring new places. Doing this in thirty degrees Centigrade over a blue sea is much more attractive than doing the same thing in the muddy Bristol Channel, which is where home is. Ann learned to sail while at university, sailing Torches on the Blackwater, while I began sailing dinghies on the local lake at the age of forty when I grew tired of flying gliders. Then we went on a flotilla holiday in Greece and the rest followed a predictable sequence culminating in our odyssey.

After the Hercules' flypast we did an oil change. This was a chore we had to do every fifty hours and, no matter how we tried, we could never do it without getting ourselves and the boat filthy with old oil. Today was no different. So to cheer ourselves up we decided to go shopping. This involved taking the dinghy to a corner of the beach then hunting for a way through to the town beyond without going into the marina. The supermarket was marked on the brochure in a somewhat vague way: we knew roughly where it was, but couldn't pinpoint it.

The truth was we were so pleased to have finally left the mainland that chores like shopping and oil changes could not dent our happiness. We felt we'd achieved something more than just the physical crossing, as if we'd joined an elite: the club of exotic *Mediterranean Sailors*, as if we suddenly had *The Right Stuff*. Even our passages to Ireland from Wales, or Falmouth to Milford Haven, or across Lyme Bay, or crossing the Channel had not left us feeling like this. We were *here*. We had *arrived!*

The way to the beach was through a marked channel to a local boat rental place. When we hit the sand Ann jumped out and went hunting for the store while I held the dinghy in place. It was another hot cloudless day and sitting on the dinghy's tube with my feet in the clear water was a better place to be than hiking down a road. At the top of the sand a young couple were all but making love in public. This is what happens in Corsica, I thought. I didn't watch. Ann returned empty handed but looking pleased, she'd found the place but it would take two to carry the bags, she thought.

We did what we could to make the dinghy secure, it's always a target both for kids playing and for thieves who want oars or motors, and the fact that the beach was populated meant nothing. We set off. At the head of the path from the beach was a short embankment capped with a railway line and Ann determinedly set off across it, after that came a large car park belonging to an office, then a main road and finally the supermarket.

'You can see,' She said, 'why we can't take a trolley back with us.'

They had most of what we needed but there was no white wine in boxes. This was an economic and logistic disaster. Normally we refill an empty bottle from a box which is cheaper and easier and safer to store on board. There was no new engine oil either. Nevertheless we happily headed back to where the dinghy should be, laden down with bags and rucksacks stuffed with bottles. There it was, untouched. I mentally apologised for my suspicious nature as we motored back to *Aderyn Glas.* Our first supermarket shopping trip by dinghy.

That evening it finally grew cool enough to contemplate taking the dinghy to the shore for a walk around the town and to explore the citadel. We climbed the hill and entered the old town through a gate in the citadel walls. In the medieval town the streets were narrow and shaded, the homes, shops, restaurants, bars and so on crowded together as if they had grown organically within some restricting skin which I suppose they had. Some houses fitted into the fortified walls and were thus curved where the walls curved, some overhung the streets. It was easy to see why the bastions had been built where they were, from the top of the walls we could see in all directions, out to sea to the north, south and west, and back inland across the bay and directly down to the port below us. It was thronged with tourists, but unlike Saint Tropez, had less of a commercial atmosphere about it. It was welcoming somehow, or maybe it was the glass of wine we had started the evening with.

'Lets stay,' I suggested lazing back in the cockpit.

'Time to go,' said Ann

We loved Calvi and were sorry to leave. This is another aspect I've yet to get used to, along with saying goodbyes to people we seem to be always leaving places I'd like to stay at longer. The weather was calm and so was the sea. We were heading north to eventually round the tip of Corsica and head down the sheltered eastern coast, but today was simply a steady motor along to a town in an inlet called Saint Florent at the base of the Cap Corse peninsula, where we would ignore the marina and anchor for the night.

Saint Florent, Corsica, 1666 miles to Gouvia. Day 27

We headed into the bay with a little anxiety, this was to be our first anchorage in the Med. In many ways it should be easier than off the

British coasts where you always had to contend with tidal heights, tidal flows and swinging room, but here the bottoms were more likely to be sand than the weed we were used to and we had a nagging doubt about whether the CQR was the right anchor for the job.

We stuck our nose into a number of little bays as we motored towards the head of the inlet. The first looked lovely with the kind of water you normally only see on postcards with a clean, white sand bottom, but everybody and his dog was parked there so we motored on.

'Did you see,' Ann was incredulous, 'they were so tightly packed they all had fenders out?'

The next bay was empty and had a bottom covered with weed. This I thought was perfect for us but worried a little about why it was empty. Ann came up with the answer: 'Poseidon grass,' she hissed as if it was some kind of monster. The French love Poseidon grass and are trying to encourage its growth and discourage anchoring. This is why they have no-anchoring zones around the Porquerolles and other such places. Although I thought I could drop the anchor cleanly between two distinct areas of grass Ann would have none of it and emphatically ordered me onwards.

Our next attempt was even more quickly ended, the bottom of the next bay was pretty much all rock. By this time I was getting a little panicky, we had already spent an hour trying to find an anchorage. Strangely the idea of anchoring was so fixed in our heads by then that we didn't even consider the marina under the town.

At the end of the inlet were a number of anchored yachts and a large topsail schooner. We didn't automatically choose the location in the first place because it was pretty much open to long swells coming down the inlet. But we decided to trust the weather forecast and bung the hook in. We followed our usual procedure: I stood on the foredeck and waved my arms about a lot and shouted instructions and abuse and Ann did anything she thought fit and shouted abuse and instructions and somehow we managed to drop the anchor in the right place: which, by definition, is the place we dropped the anchor. Then we hauled it up again because we didn't like something or other and did the whole thing over again with even more shouting. It was all perfectly normal stuff.

'One day,' I whispered as we stood mutually worrying on the foredeck, 'I'll get that intercom set up so we can talk normally to each other then we won't get so cross, will you?'

We dropped our chum weights down the chain and set the GPS Man Overboard Alarm to tell us if we dragged at all. We took some deep breaths and gradually the tension and anxiety evaporated and we looked around us. And it was pleasant. Really pleasant. To the north the inlet ended with a pretty village overlooked by huge mountains with even higher peaks to the south and east. We had plenty of space, the next nearest vessel was a good hundred metres away, she was the topsail schooner *Salomon*, carrying a Swiss flag.

Hot and still a little worried about the anchor we took to the water. This time I determinedly left the dreaded wetsuit in the store and braved the sea with trunks only. The water was warm, as it was supposed to be in exotic Corsica. The CQR anchor had only half dug into the sand so I was only half reassured. We were to learn hard lessons about anchoring very soon, but then, in Saint Florent, we had the advantage of naivety.

We stayed on board which, in retrospect, seemed a little pathetic since the village looked so attractive. But the temperature in the early evening was over thirty and not a breath of breeze, so the effort involved in launching and recovering the dinghy and motor was too much to contemplate. So we stayed on board and opened all the hatches and turned on all the fans and hung out a listless and useless windscoop. We wondered what July and August were going to be like. 'Hotter and crowdeder.' Ann abused the English language.

Despite my worries over the anchor the night was calm and peaceful and we both slept more soundly than we had for a long time.

We left at 10:30. This was becoming a pattern, we always left at 10:30. North-west then north we headed bravely towards the infamous Cap Corse at the northern tip of the island. Capes are always bad. They are the places where different currents meet and the sea is usually chaotic so we were a little nervous about what we might find, was this to be a re-run of our worst passage to date, around Lands End, and that other notorious cape, Cape Cornwall? We counteract nervousness by doing the best preparation we can and so we'd read everything we could find and studied the charts. In Britain we would be worried about the tides but here the currents were small in comparison, and usually predictable. So we plugged the waypoints into chart-plotter Rachel's software and steadily motored across a still sea. There were no waves. There was no life. There were no ports to which we could run if an unexpected hurricane blew. There was no excitement. It was the perfect passage. The bimini shaded the cockpit and we alternated between sunbathing and hiding in its shade. We read, photographed the desolate cliffs and talked. We watched our slow progress on the plotter and kept a lookout for the ever-present lobster pots that were the bane of inshore passages, and dolphins that are so spectacular. And saw neither.

Eventually we rounded Cap Corse in another one of those great anti-climaxes and headed south down the other side of the island. That was it: no overfalls, no crashing waves, no whirlpools, no wrecks, no arms reaching for salvation from the water, no helicopters, no lifeboats, no flares, no bodies. We motored slowly around the corner and went south. To Macinaggio.

Macinaggio, Corsica, 1628 miles to Gouvia. Day 28

We went into the bay and anchored; yes we were now suddenly so polished at anchoring we could do it at the drop of a hat and with only five minutes of shouting at each other. At least this was true for those times when anchoring was a temporary stop while we decided what to do next. Macinaggio was a stop on the way south, a little port with a marina and it didn't look too inviting from where we were, all concrete and rubble with a dredger blocking the entrance and a foul smell of seabottom being scraped up.

'But it's too open to stay here all night.' Ann completely ignored the other three yachts that thought the opposite, 'and we need a shower,' she sniffed me, 'and water for the tanks.'

We pretended we were English and had a cup of tea, like real English people do in times of trouble, and thought about it. Eventually the weight of Ann's thoughts outweighed mine and Ann called the marina on the radio. They spoke English, heaven! Four words were enough: 'Anywhere on the left.' The crackling voice said.

So we squeezed passed the dredger in the entrance and found a place on the quay to the left. Go in nose first, hope someone will catch the lines and pass the sternline over, we were used to this manoeuvre by now. Drop the plank onto the jetty. Plug in the mains and turn on the fans. Put up the sunshades and fit the mozzie nets. Find the office and pay the man. Find out where the showers are and the supermarket and the internet café. What's the forecast? Where's the tourist office? Any other British flagged boats in the marina? We had it all off pat by now, believe me.

At first touch Macinaggio seemed all concrete, but this is largely because of the large new concrete breakwater, at one end of which is the fuel and at the other a small concrete *Capitainerie*. Once we left the quayside and headed into the village, along the cultured cobbled path, the feel changed to one of a small seaside village: fishing shops, cafes, souvenirs, fishing trips, fresh fish caught today sir, no chandlery sir but look in the fishing gear shop, a single SPAR supermarket and a bread shop all in a long curve circling the harbour. Behind the village the road wound up into the hillsides and disappeared towards the blue mountains beyond, the only other road ran along the shore towards the south. I liked Macinaggio but I didn't know why. And it was winter again, the plump, young, female *Capitaine* told us the spring mooring rates didn't start until July, another little bit of heaven.

We bought a float with a long length of rope attached to it, to protect us when we snorkelled, and a plastic slate on which we could record the toilet strokes. This needs some explanation, I realise. My patent capacitive system for measuring the depth of, well – you know the *stuff* in the poo tank – had failed. It had worked in Britain when it was new, and stopped in the canals because, I thought, of the different conductivity of fresh water. But it hadn't recovered in the Med and so was now declared dead. This meant we couldn't tell how much – you know: *stuff* – was in the tank, so the brilliant idea of mine was to record how many pumps of the flush we each made every morning as we deposited, you know – *stuff*. Then we could tell whether the tank was about to overflow down the deck and whether we had to vacate whatever marina we were sat in at the time out of a sense of decency and self protection. So we went looking for a diver's slate on which we could accumulate strokes of the pump up to the magic number of 225.

'Un tablet, sous-marine pour écrive. Comprenez? Je suis plongeur.' Got me nothing but a blank look.

'*Vous voulez un pharmacie?*' After a while the centime dropped, today's wrong word was *tablet*, a tablet is like a pill, you take it with water not write on it underwater.

I tried more words: '*Un panneau?*' A panel, '*Une tableau noir?*' A blackboard.

'*Ah, monsieur etes plonguer. Vous voulez un chose pour écrive sous mer?*' Or something like that. I sighed. It cost an enormous thirteen euros for a small bit of plastic and a pencil. I sighed more. No wonder the guy was happy as we left.

Morning conversations were never again the same: how many strokes did you do this morning? Only thirteen! You probably need more fibre for breakfast or olive oil.

And in the village there was a *laverie*. It was expensive but worth it: even our underpants came back pressed.

We'd moored next to *Dream*, our friend Hans from the Porquerolles, who was due to leave for Elba next day, he'd hired a car with some friends and had toured the island. We were a little jealous, the problem with travelling on a boat is that you so rarely see anything more than quaysides. We said another goodbye, this time to Hans because, although we were going to follow him to Elba, we would go to the south of the island to shelter from the predicted northerly winds. Hans and Katarina would cross to the north of the island then travel south along the Italian coast so we would not see them again until, perhaps, we all made it safely to Preveza. They left early next day and we watched them disappear slowly into the distance for ages.

They'd introduced us to their friends, Elisabeth and Keith, the couple they'd shared the car with: another Dutch couple. The Dutch and the Belgians we'd met seemed unhesitatingly friendly people, I know better than to generalise about a population after meeting so few, and we knew from our travels that all countries had much the same ratio of good and bad, friendly and distant, louts and angels, as did our own country. But we had yet to meet an irritating Belgian or Dutchman. These guys were in fits of laughter at the idea that we were going to Greece. 'Look!' Keith proclaimed, 'you cover your boat with sunshades and turn on your fans at every opportunity and hose yourselves down on the decks, do you not like the warmth? It is hot in Greece, don't you know? How can you go there?'

We stayed two nights in Macinaggio and didn't expect to return. The plump *Capitaine* sold us some wifi and we downloaded a GRIB file for the next week. There was a large monitor screen in the window of her office with continuous displays of the weather forecast and it and GRIB agreed that the winds were going to remain northerly with a maximum speed briefly of twenty knots and more normally fifteen. We would have no trouble. Our plan now was to visit Elba then come back to Bastia and on southward. We'd agreed to meet friends in north Sardinia and daughter number one in Olbia, Sardinia's capital, and this set a timeline for us. So we left next day at 10:00, freshly fuelled and watered, and followed in Hans's footsteps watching the coast of Corsica so slowly recede behind us.

We thought we knew about Elba. The Scots guy we'd met all that time ago in Port Napoleon eulogised about it and told us it was so beautiful we shouldn't miss it. We knew with certainty that it was French, even though all the other Tuscan Islands belonged to Italy, because Napoleon was exiled there, and we knew from the charts that there was a marina, forty-eight miles away, halfway across the south coast called Marina di Campo. The Italian name was not surprising: on Corsica half the place names sound Italian. So off we motored into thirty-five centigrade, blue skies, and calm seas. 'This is becoming a habit.' Ann said referring to the flat calm. I wonder if she remembered the comment later.

A couple of hours later Ann was steering and I was idly looking around. To our left, out to sea, a strange shimmering line crossed from horizon to horizon. I watched it, only mildly interested. It grew steadily in definition and size. I suddenly realised what it was and how fast it was moving: 'Wake!' I shouted, 'turn left now! Now!' Ann looked around a little bewildered then realised there was a wall of water over a metre high rushing towards her like a tidal wave and it was going to hit us side on: the worst possible scenario. The wave was higher than our freeboard and we would be lucky to escape with the boat still intact, especially since all the hatches were open to cool the interior. At the very least the cabins would end up wet and strewn with everything we owned as the boat rolled wildly.

Ann slammed the wheel over to bring our bow around to face the wave but *Aderyn Glas* was turning in slow motion. The wave was travelling at such speed I began to wonder what could have possibly made it but then it arrived. Our bow pitched through the wave and green sea crashed down the sidedecks. *Aderyn Glas* almost stopped in her tracks then threw her bow into the air and reared backwards before crashing down into the trough and burying her bow again into the next wave. Ann and I clung on tight and accepted the spray that cascaded over us. Then it was over. Blue calm sea reflected blue calm sky and that was that. Everything was still attached. Below, in the saloon, a few books and bottles had been thrown around and in the heads the little waste bin had once again leapt into the toilet. But nothing serious had happened. Behind us the wave rushed on towards Corsica where it would crash onto the shore. A wake from nowhere, without warning, stretching from one horizon to the other. We called it our own little freak wave and wondered if it really could have been. Had we but known it was a portent of worse to come we could have run back.

At 13:00 I saw a patch of mud brown water and knew immediately what it was even though I had never seen one before. It was a turtle. I gently took the boat over for a closer look while Ann got busy with her camcorder. The turtle ignored us for a while, its metre long carapace wallowing on the surface and its flippers making swimming motions to propel it towards distant Corsica. Ultimately we must have passed too close because it took itself downwards where we could not follow. Our first turtle.

We photographed Isola di Capraia because it looked like a volcano. In fact more so than most of the volcanoes I'd seen. The conical peak had a beautiful plume of orographic cloud being blown downwind that looked like smoke. The island and its waters is a nature reserve with a single port and we'd considered calling there for a night but the port is on the north side and that was where the wind was due to come from so we had decided to cross direct to Elba instead. It was probably a decision that saved our lives.

Chapter 6

Marina di Campo, Elba, 1498 miles to Gouvia. Day 30

The weather was hot and sunny as usual but for once we both felt weary. We arrived in the late afternoon after a fairly unexciting crossing except for the freak wave and an even more unexciting slog around the south of the island to Marina di Campo where we learned a lot very quickly: we learned that Elba is Italian not French, that the word "marina", which, in virtually every other language we have encountered means a posh yacht harbour, in Italian probably just means seashore. This we deduced by the total absence of anything resembling a *"Marina"*. We learned that the harbour at Marina di Campo is tiny and filled with local craft huddled against a rocky town quay or tied, bobbing, to one of the profusion of buoys crowded into the limited space between the quay and the beach. We looked despairingly for an empty buoy.

We learned the local water taxi-man thought he owned the harbour and was the most unwelcoming, rude and unhelpful person on the planet. He waved us away imperiously when we tried to pick up a buoy, standing up in his dayboat, trying to look tall and shouting something unintelligible and clearly rude. Undecided what to do next, or even what the options were, we drove around looking for help. There was none. It was clear that the pilot books had exaggerated the facilities and that the harbour was not a place for us. At best we could have tied up on the harbour wall but a single glance at its condition told us that wasn't a good idea.

'Perhaps we've been spoilt. The French are better at marinas and looking after clients than the Italians.' Ann was being stoical, as usual. 'Perhaps this is the standard we're going to find all the way down through Sardinia: rude bumptious little men with a taste for authority shouting at us.'

'Sardinia is the millionaires' paradise, they wouldn't put up with this sort of treatment.'

'If you were a millionaire don't you think we'd have a larger yacht?'

So we turned away and contemplated a night at anchor. The moderate swell rolled up the beach as breakers and made the kids squeal with the fun of it all while their parents stretched out on the sunbeds and rubbed oil in each other. For us though swell simply meant discomfort. There were a number of boats, including a few British, so we chose our spot and threw the anchor in. We were in twelve metres of water which was far deeper than we liked, but it was that or the surf zone. It took us a number of attempts before the hook would bite and in the end we settled for less than perfect. We knew the wind was going to be from the north and we would be sheltered, or, at least, if we did drag it would be safely away from the shore. So we stripped off and went for a swim to cool down and have a look at the anchor, it was half dug in and half rolled uselessly on its side. The sandy bottom, it seemed, was too hard for it to penetrate properly. I watched an Italian yacht arrive and anchor near us. He had a viciously sharp Delta anchor which looked like it should bite into anything so I swam over and inspected his too. It had dug in no better than ours.

'What do you think?' asked Ann. It was time for a shrug and the Gallic spreading of hands skyward.

We spent the evening in the cockpit as usual, watching the scenery, which wasn't as good as Corsica, and wondering what our Scots acquaintance had seen in the place. It was a pure holiday village with a run-down harbour and seemingly hostile natives. Sunbeds, umbrellas, ball games and nosy kids in pedaloes, windsurfers and shouting children were everywhere and robbed it of any charm it might otherwise have claimed.

As we went to bed the wind had changed and was blowing into the bay – so much for forecasts. It was enough to worry me, so we set the GPS alarm, the depth sounder alarm and the chartplotter alarm. One or all of these would wake us if the anchor pulled out; but I was worried whether we would have time to do something before we hit the sand. Like I said we're expert worriers.

The swell increased as the night wore on and *Aderyn Glas* moved around until she was sideways to it like she always does, and we spent the larger part of the night awake and rolling. In the morning we felt wretched, tired and queasy. The swells were now really powering into the bay driven by a strong wind from the *south* and the boat was rocking like crazy. We tried to launch the dinghy to go ashore but it was too rough, so we hauled it back onto its davits. The beach that had been so noisy yesterday was deserted. Then Ann looked at me and decided she'd had enough. 'Around the south eastern tip of the island and a little way north there is a proper marina and I think we should go there.' she said. There was no need for debate, we couldn't stay where we were and the forecast was so obviously in error that there was no point in hanging on hoping it would die down.

Once we were moving we both felt better. *Aderyn Glas* rode through the growing swell well enough but threw some spray over the bow and we got wet. Once around the headland to the south we had to turn east and had to contend with the rolling motion and we got even wetter. Far from being northerly, this was a southerly wind and we had to chug slowly into it. We hauled some of the mainsail out for stability and motor sailed. The swells were long enough not to make us feel ill, but I still looked forward to a mooring and a shower, and feet firmly on something that didn't move so much: like a concrete jetty, or a city street, or an Alp.

It took forever. Wet and cold, blown about and, above all, dog tired it took forever. When we turned the corner and headed north the wind picked up from dead astern and screamed at us and we had to take the sail in. My toy wind meter told me this was far above the nicely reasonable force three that had been on all the forecasts, more like a force six. We turned left again and headed into the huge bay that held our destination marina. It was half empty. Pretty pink stone houses and a *campanile* looked inviting and we grinned at each other in relief, we were so afraid it was going to be full.

Porto Azzurro, Elba, 1483 miles to Gouvia. Day 31

Ann has a few words of Italian so she had the job of using the radio. I think she is better at it because she listens more intently and I can never understand the squawking answers, which is why she tried to raise the marina staff while I drove around in the entrance. On the outer mole a group of yachts were being berthed by a guy in a RIB and we assumed this was the procedure. So we circled and waited, feeling hopeful. And we circled and Ann called again. And we circled. And eventually the tinny voice replied and told us there was no room. We were stunned, we were staring at a marina that was patently half empty, but there was no room. 'We're the wrong nationality.' Ann said, but we didn't know enough of the language to argue, this was Italy and we spoke English and a bit of French and those few useless words of Italian. After a few more orbits while we decided what to do next, we left the marina entrance and mentally waved goodbye to showers and cafés and solid stable ground.

'I don't like Elba.' Ann was uncharacteristically despondent. 'Nor Italians.' We were exhausted.

'Going anywhere else now is simply not an option.' I replied to her unasked question.

'First thing in the morning then, let's go back to Corsica.'

'Don't worry, the wind always dies down in the evening, and look at all the yachts here, it must be a well recognised anchorage.

Still it was difficult to find a place where there was room and where the anchor would hold. We tried the north side first but I was not convinced that it would be secure, so then we crossed to the south side and anchored near a British boat close to a hotel's artificial beach which was bounded by rocks. I don't like anchoring near rocks but this was the best compromise. We dug the anchor well in, putting the boat full in reverse and revving the engine until all movement stopped. I guessed the bottom must be mud and weed, such antics at our last stop would simply have had the anchor skipping across the bottom. We dropped the chum weights down the chain.

At least it was fairly quiet, the sea wasn't too rough and we were sheltered from the worst of the southerly wind. Both sides of the inlet were cliffs and above us we could just see the hotel that owned the beach. To the west, further up the inlet on our side, was a boatyard with a pontoon filled with boats, and beyond that were mooring buoys for small dinghies. Then the inlet became land and continued into the mountains as a steep sided valley.

As the evening wore on we jealously watched the marina filling up and wondered if those yachts had bookings or whether they were part of a flotilla, or was it simply that they were Italian? We learned later that while the French refused to take bookings at all in summer, the Italians often expected it.

As evening became night the wind got worse. We watched the waves slamming into the concrete of the artificial beach thirty metres away on our starboard side and sat miserably in the cockpit as *Aderyn Glas* began to roll in the swell. The wind was now howling up the inlet and bouncing around the cliffs. We could do nothing. When darkness came we were entertained by a fierce lightening storm over the Italian mainland which was less than a dozen miles away to the east. 'I'm glad,' I said, 'it's there and not here.'

We turned in early, tired and depressed. Ann slept in our usual cabin in the bow but I hated the motion so much I decided to try and sleep in the saloon on the settee, but it was impossible to sleep anyway. Eventually I took a seasick pill of the non-drowsy type that always send me to sleep, and around three o'clock in the morning I finally started to doze a little. It was Father's Day *and* Mid Summer's Eve *and* we'd tossed a coin to Poseidon so nothing bad could happen.

Ann told me later it all began at nine minutes past five, though I don't know how she knew, it was pitch black. The boat heaved and threw me off the settee as all the alarms went off together. I fell across the tilting floor to the inside steering position and grabbed hold of the wheel for support, thoroughly disoriented. My first thought was that we had hit the rocks and I screamed for Ann to get lifejackets. Then an incredible explosion of lightening lit the world and I could see through the window that the rocks had gone. In fact there was nothing. Just water. Ann crawled around me in her nightclothes reaching for the lifejackets. The noise was deafening. The sky-cracking thunder immediately followed the lightening and the lightening strobed continuously like the flickering of an old movie. Then I saw the rocks. They were the wrong side of the boat and we were swinging wildly towards them.

We had spun completely around. This meant the anchor had pulled out. I tried to gather my thoughts, we still seemed to be in the same place and, most importantly, not dragging our anchor out to sea. The wind was finally from the north. I shouted above the din for Ann to turn on the chartplotter while I started the engine. To survive we would need both, one to drive us and one to give us directions. I tried to look through the side window but it had started to sheet down rain in a tropical torrent. Ahead through the windscreen I could see only a sailbag and those damned bikes and I cursed myself for restricting my view. We swung towards the rocks that my disoriented brain still told me were on the wrong side. 'I can't see,' I yelled into the screaming wind, 'where are the other boats?'

Then we found one: in horror we watched as the British boat that had been next to us slowly blew backwards passed us. He was dragging his anchor. His bimini and awning had shredded and blew horizontally over his stern leading the way to the sea. Worst of all he was travelling through the space we were swinging into. We tracked directly at him.

I jammed the engine into forward gear and put the wheel hard over hoping to push the stern around and steer away from the approaching collision, *it didn't work*! *Aderyn Glas* had no control over the way she was moving. I reversed the engine for no other reason than forward gear hadn't worked, aware as I did so that this was going to put more load on the anchor. Fate or luck or something swung us away from the stricken boat a second before the impact. She slid passed us – a dark figure in her cockpit, hunched low, lit up by the strobe lightning.

The chartplotter, the beautiful lovely chartplotter, was showing us moving in a constant arc around a fixed point and I shouted with elation. The anchor was holding.

The lightening was turning the night into day and the rain was now horizontal. The cacophony of wind and thunder made communication impossible. Ann headed out into the bucking, rolling cockpit to look for boats and the rocks. It was a brave thing to do – and futile, she couldn't open her eyes in the rain. Through the open door I could see our bimini flapping and crashing, half torn from its frame. Our flag was ripped to shreds.

Navigation lights came on around us and I switched ours on. I put the engine into neutral and was driving *Aderyn Glas* from side to side of the arc drawn by the plotter using only the knot of speed that the wind on the bare mast was providing, trying to reduce the anchor load. As we swung to starboard, away from the rocks, I caught a glimpse of another yacht swinging towards us. In the next lightening flash I saw crew on her pitching, rolling deck working with the anchor. She was too close. She slipped away again. Gone.

Ann was back in the saloon and looked like someone had poured a bath of water over her. She held onto a handhold and braced herself against the violent movement. She told me of navigation lights all around us. I asked her when dawn was, how long did we have to keep this up? Another half an hour, maybe an hour? Who knew when the squall would stop. All the while the lightening was flashing every few seconds.

We watched in absolute horror as another yacht crawled slowly up on our starboard side, his navigation lights bright and the lightening showing how big he was. Slowly he crept forward and I knew if he continued he would fill the space we needed to swing and we would hit him. We could do nothing but hope he saw the danger in time. In slow motion he edged forward and in slow motion we swung towards him. Nothing I did with the wheel made any difference to our course. Then he checked. We stopped breathing. Then he slid backwards. By then we knew if we ended up in the water we would die.

We got into some steady state condition. The lightening continued and instantly after each flash: the thunder. The wind still screamed and the rain still battered at us and *Aderyn Glas* still swung around the arc defined by her anchor. But things were not getting worse. We longed for the first of the dawn light, the change from black to dark grey that promised a new day. I didn't know why but it seemed that everything would be better in daylight. In the meantime the storm raged on, the lightening, the wind, the rain and spray. The boats veered wildly on their anchors, the rolling, the pitching, the screaming crashing noise, the shivering cold, and even what smelled like woodsmoke from a fire. I tried to drive around the arc on the chartplotter while Ann held on grimly and occasionally would go as far as the companionway door and squint painfully into the rain. Once she measured the windspeed, which was about fifty knots, but that had not been the highest. She also captured the bimini and managed to stop it destroying itself. After each thunderstorm departed we relaxed a little, but each storm was replaced a few minutes later by another.

And so we held on until some sort of daylight came and showed us the results of the storm. Around six thirty the wind eased enough for a serious look outside. The surface of the anchorage was covered with foam. There were fewer anchored boats than there had been in the evening – the missing boats had presumably wanted sea room and left, or been forced out to sea. Other yachts had sails that had unwound themselves from their roller furling mechanisms and had flailed themselves into a ragged mess. Biminis and canvaswork were in tatters. Anything loose on the decks had been flung far overboard and the sea was littered with flotsam. The rain was still so heavy that the hulls of the boats seemed to be detached from the sea surface: they floated in a froth of rain and spray. Mercifully all the yachts were upright and none were on the rocks. To the west the pontoon of the boatyard had broken in two and each half had a group of boats of varying sizes still attached to it. The only thing keeping the two halves from completely separating seemed to be the pipes and electrical cables that spanned the gap.

Around eight o'clock everything was calming down and so were we. We'd been running on adrenalin for four hours after virtually no sleep for two nights and suddenly I slumped. I think my subconscious decided we were out of danger and switched me off. Ann took over the wheel and stopped the engine. It was still rough but we were going to be okay. Outside was as much daylight as we were going to get and visibility was marginally good enough to see across the inlet to the village. A huge, dirty slick of brown water was spreading away from the land: silt washed down into the valley by the heavy rain. Within half an hour the blue water had turned brown everywhere.

Throughout the morning boats collected their battered belongings and a few tried to leave but they all returned, it was obviously still rough out there. In the early afternoon a yacht motored into the bay with its jib in tatters and jammed around the forestay. The skipper was single handed and it was obvious he would not be able to anchor until someone was able to get his sail down. He motored up and down shouting across to an Italian boat that was anchored not far from us. We could see the Italian make a call on his phone and shortly afterwards two men in a RIB arrived at speed from the boatyard and one of them made a perilous leap onto the yacht. With his help the skipper brought the ruined sail down and dropped anchor. He was close enough for us to see the dreadful state both the yacht and the man were in. Maybe the storm had caught him at sea.

In the late morning a large silver-grey racing yacht was brought in, headed by a coastguard cutter, and slowly made for the entrance of the marina. He anchored and the crew were taken ashore. Later we were to learn that two of the crew had died, washed overboard in Marina di Campo, last night's anchorage.

All day long there was a steady stream of battered looking boats arriving, some with torn sails but mainly just beaten about by the weather. When the rain stopped we could see the state of the boats anchored around us. Compared to most we seemed to have survived well: everything was still attached and undamaged. Most crews were reluctant to venture onto the decks. We had no idea which boats were the ones that had come so close to colliding with us, or who the captain was of the boat that realised the danger he was putting us in and backed off. I would have liked to have thanked him.

In the evening the sea and wind had died enough to think about moving. Some boats had crossed into the marina so Ann tried her few Italian words in a suitably pleading voice on the radio, but got no response at all. So we stayed where we were. One thing we knew with certainty was that the anchor was going to hold. We made bedtime nine o'clock and slept soundly.

'Do you realise that last night was the shortest night of the year?' Ann asked next day, 'And didn't it feel like it?' And after a while she added: 'Happy Father's Day.'

We left Elba at seven thirty, one of my rare early starts, but we couldn't wait to leave. It was difficult to haul up the anchor and we had to motor ahead to trip it out of the ground, it had dug in so well, and when it came free it brought with it a ton of mud and weed. We looked at our weather forecast then threw it away, predictions from a few days ago meant nothing now, but we found Monaco radio on the VHF which gave us a reasonable forecast for the day.

Outside the inlet the sea was still rough but it subsided as the bay opened out and as we cleared the cape it became calm. The wind had also died and we were motoring again, straight back to Corsica. It was a long day. We saw some dolphins about halfway across but they didn't come to play.

As we approached Macinaggio we found ourselves faced with crossing a virtual shipping lane with ship after ship ploughing northwards. Ferries, cargo ships, large multi-deckers all steamed up the coast following each other so closely that we had trouble finding a gap. It was as if someone had fired a starting gun or a traffic light changed and they all set off together. In the end I raced us across the bows of a cargo ship which was a totally reprehensible and dangerous manoeuvre because we didn't have the right of way and I knew from my bearings that if he didn't change course he would ram me. I held my breath, my nerve, and a portable VHF radio in my hand, ready to call him if it all got too close. And it did get close. But at the last moment the helmsman must have tweaked his finger on the joystick and the ship turned so slightly to starboard that it was hardly noticeable. But for us it meant we were through the lines of ships and clear into Macinaggio. I waved a huge wave to the bridge of the ship and we smiled our brightest smiles but we couldn't see if anyone responded.

'They'll lock you up,' said Ann, 'chain the boat to the quayside and throw away the key. Burn your licence and make you a teetotaller.'

'At least the boat won't blow away in a gale then, and anyway, you're captain today and I'm already almost a teetotaller.'

Ann replied with an eloquent expression that had taken years of practice to perfect.

So we returned to Macinaggio having never set foot on Elba after a detour of a hundred and thirteen miles and three days.

Macinaggio, Corsica, 1433 miles to Gouvia. Day 33

'Weren't you terrified?' Pat asked. We were sitting in the spacious cockpit of *Lady Patricia* with Pat and her husband, Antoine and telling them about the storm. 'I would have been,' she continued. She had a soft Scots accent, from the south somewhere.

'We didn't have the time,' my cliché for the day. I looked across to Ann who nodded agreement. 'I was more frightened after things calmed down, thinking about all that might have happened. But as it was happening to us – I suppose we got on with it: coped.'

We'd been walking back from the *Capitainerie* and spotted the British ensign and the Guernsey registration and Antoine and Pat had offered us a beer. Despite the flag they were based in Monaco, Pat was slim and maybe fifty, and Antoine short and round and a little older, a typical motor cruiser captain.

They knew about the storm, it had been all over the news particularly because of the lost crewmen. It had been centred where we had anchored in Elba, but its effects had been felt over a wide area, even Macinaggio. Despite that we felt safe, tied up firmly to the quay and alongside a big, solid protective Fisher.

We invited them for a drink later but they politely declined and looking around at their beautiful motor cruiser I wasn't surprised, they probably paid ten times what I did for a bottle of white and had a special cooler to get the temperature exactly right.

'They're nice.' said Ann, She'd had to tightrope walk across the sternline to get across the gap between his stern and the shore, and Antoine had been gentlemanly and held her hand while I had to leap and carry the shopping.

We told our story again to the couple on the Fisher, Michael and Linda, who kept the ketch *Silver Spray* in Sardinia and lived in Britain. Their holiday each year was to sail these waters from the boat's base near Alghero. This time we were having a rare coffee morning in their spacious cockpit. *Silver Spray* was beautifully fitted out for life aboard, solid but spacious with little homely touches like the cafetiere and saucers for the cups. We had mugs and like it and instant from the supermarket.

Ann, as always, had clambered over the guardrails with an armful of charts and books and Michael was enthusiastically scribbling notes on the almanac: the good, the bad and the beautiful. He was quietly spoken, a little grey suggesting our age bracket, but tall and muscular. Linda was slim and attractive, long blond hair and a little younger. Most of the sailors we met seemed to fit the same description. Even we had become slim, tanned and fit. Ann, who is blond and fair skinned and used to get sunburned if she saw a match strike in the distance now had a lovely golden tan. Obviously living on a boat with it's constant movement and a million physical things to do tones the muscles and nearly constant sunshine makes for an enduring tan. This therapy should be available on the National Health, sick people should be sent cruising. But not on my boat thanks.

I settled back into the cushions, 'Let's stay here,' I said with a smile, 'let's buy this boat and chain it to the dockside and stay here.'

Michael didn't smile but Linda did. 'You can buy the boat,' she said, 'but don't stay here, there are so many more beautiful places to see.'

We scrubbed and rubbed and polished and cleaned and washed and tied things back where they'd fallen from and tied the sailbag tighter and tied the bikes tighter still and didn't move them so that next time I still wouldn't be able to see out. We washed her from stem to stern in the hot blue-sky day and got the salt off and got hot and washed ourselves down. We put up all the sunshades and Ann sewed the bimini and tidied up the trailing edge of the flag that had shredded itself by cutting it off – our flag was now uniquely asymmetrical – the Union Jack tucked into the corner of the red ensign was now passed the halfway mark.

That evening Michael and Linda joined us for a drink. 'I do like this life,' I said and we drank to it. Ann served up crisps and snacky things that I detest because they fall about the floor and make a mess, and two colours of wine. It was lovely to find someone to sit and chat to and we felt relaxed with these two, they were so happy together, content and easy going. We chatted of home and family, Ann confessing she felt such guilt at not being able to return for the Christening of her second grandchild, and me confessing my guilt about the overdue oil change.

Early next morning *Silver Spray* left and we waved another goodbye.

We stayed one more night, then put a single waypoint into Rachel's GPS memory and set off for Port Toga.

Chapter 7

Port Toga / Bastia, Corsica, 1498 miles to Gouvia. Day 36

We sailed and we argued, which wasn't like us. One of the amazing things about being a liveaboard is how well married couples get along. It's typical to see liveaboard couples of our age walking down the streets holding hands and in other ways showing genuine affection for each other. I have a theory which is that natural selection plays a part in this, the couples who can't live together in the intimate proximity that a small boat forces on them simply stop doing it, so only those who are genuinely happy in each other's company survive and those are the ones who walk down jetties holding hands.

And yet, take us off the boat and we argue as much as most married couples. Usually, it seems, over the endless mundane trivia that fills our time at home. On board life is simpler and our days are usually predefined so there are few choices and hence few arguments.

But that day we argued. I wanted to sail and Ann, quite rightly, said the wind was in the wrong direction. In truth it was fluky. It came hurtling down the little valleys that broke up the coast and accelerated *Aderyn Glas* happily for about ten minutes. Then she would languish again and I tried to move her towards the next puff. It was a frustrating process but I was fed up with having a sailing boat and motoring everywhere, so when Ann complained about time wasting I'm afraid I got snappy and we argued.

Finally the argument was ended by the wind swinging around and becoming useful for a couple of hours. When it ultimately dropped I was then able to gracefully offer to start the engine and motor the rest of the way without losing face. Okay, so I was a child that day, I admit it.

We tried fishing. Everyone had been telling us their favourite fishing stories, usually along the lines of how easy it is to catch a tuna, and we'd bought, or been given, a tremendous range of lures and hooks and other things I didn't know the name of all of which were guaranteed to catch us at least a shoal, maybe two. And Ann had been seduced by the fresh tuna we'd been given last year in Port St Louis by a couple who'd caught so much between Sardinia and the mainland that they couldn't eat it all. So we tried fishing. Towing out a line behind the boat with a little pink plastic squid on the end that was guaranteed to catch whatever we wanted because the couple who'd given it to us had travelled the world eating only what they'd caught with this lure and were pretty stocky, but were now heading home to see their offspring's offspring. We caught, of course, nothing.

'I'm sure we should have some bait on the hook.' Ann knew the same amount about fishing as me. Well, perhaps a little more, since she was the one who'd been lured into buying all the best kit by the man in the market back home who saw her coming and was willing to guarantee that with all this kit we would be able to catch dinner every day and probably breakfast too, and still have enough to sell. He'd even thrown in a book on Caribbean species so we would know what to eat in the Med' and what to throw away and what not to touch. We caught nothing.

It's easy to find Bastia, you simply have to look for the ferries. Ferries belonging to Toby lines painted with huge cartoon characters on their sides and bizarre colour schemes that strangely camouflaged their true shapes. I imagined their captains wincing the first time they saw their new vessel, telling lies when their friends asked them what they did for a living. Ferries from the Corsica and Sardinia line painted a dreadful yellow like the ones we'd seen in Toulon. I expect all their captains were ex-Toby men, no-one else would want a ship that colour except Toby men who would find them easier on the eye than what they were used to.

Huge ferries constantly entering and leaving, heading north to France or south to Sardinia, or east to Italy. Ferries that made wakes big enough to set us rolling and the crockery crashing and make the little bin in the heads leap into the toilet again.

Port Toga was north of Bastia but only a twenty minute walk from the city centre, or so the books said. We'd chosen Port Toga in preference to the old port of Bastia because BLOC, the almanac, said it was cheaper but we couldn't find it. We were virtually on the GPS waypoint and still couldn't see an entrance. If Rachel was a woman instead of a robot she'd have been cringing with embarrassment. All we could see was a road along the coast that passed the usual low rise concrete buildings that skirt all cities. A mile south, the commercial port of Bastia from which the ferries sailed. Finally we saw a little motor boat disappear. It motored towards a sea wall and disappeared. We'd found Port Toga and it was the most unpromising place of everywhere we'd been to date with a sea wall easily the height of a house.

This port was one that shepherded their clients to a berth with a rubber dinghy. Ann had had a welcoming response to her request, in French, for a berth and when the rubber duck arrived to lead us passed the huge wall there were two men aboard, one of whom spoke English. The berth was dreadfully tight to enter though, and the *Capitaine* insisted we attach two stern lines, one to each side of the boat. This made the whole operation more complicated since the lines were in a mess on the bottom of the harbour, added to this we had to lever *Aderyn Glas* around and over the lines from the neighbouring boats, it all made for a lot of sweat on a hot afternoon. We looked at the massive wall and the two lines led from the bottom of the harbour to our stern, and looked at everyone else's pairs of lines and, with Elba so much in our minds still, wondered what on earth we'd got into this time. How high were the waves that required all this security?

'Welsh?' said the *Capitaine*, a short stocky powerful looking man of about sixty, in the usual uniform of tee-shirt, shorts and cigarette.

It was the first time anyone French had actually recognised the flag we fly so proudly from our port spreader. We beamed at him.

'I have a Welsh wife,' he added, 'from the north, Rhyl. I used to sail on cargo ships into Liverpool and met Angharad and married her the next year. We go back to Rhyl to see her family many times.'

It's a small world sometimes. We once went sailing in Greece and met a couple who owned a boat on the next pontoon in our marina in Pembroke, we'd never seen them before we met in Greece.

'Angharad is such a great name,' I said, 'do you know what it means?'

He smiled.

Port Toga had many useful amenities like free wifi and free showers but reminded me of a Park and Ride, out of town carpark. There was nothing aesthetically pleasing about it or its surroundings mostly these were blocks of apartments, some shops, a few restaurants huddled around the marina quays, and a *Geant* supermarket across the busy dual carriageway. The *Capitainerie* was like a pink World War II airfield control tower.

The *centre ville* was a walk away through some rather seedy backstreets but we had to go and explore, of course. The walk took us to the *Place Nicolas* that bordered the port and we sat in a café and had a local beer. Napoleon watched over us stonily in toga and laurel leaves with a neck like a rugby player's and in the middle of the *place* was a statue depicting two souls that we simply did not understand. It was hot and dusty, the sky was blue, and the noise of the traffic circulating behind the square and the ferries loading their cargo of trucks and cars, filled the air. Kids played, adults promenaded, even though this was still only late afternoon. There were a fair number of travellers, hitch-hikers and tourists, distinguishable by their backpacks or vacant staring at tourist office maps. Young and old, couples and singles. Dogs ran and fouled where they wanted, ignoring the palm trees – this was France – and everyone who sat down to drain a glass lit a fag. Smoke from the ferries lifted into the air black and still. The air smelled of exhaust smoke and stung the eyes. It was a city.

We went shopping for supplies again next day, and found the Post Office where I managed to upset the woman behind the counter by asking if the postage was more from Corsica to the UK than it was from France. '*Non!*' she said and treated me to a scowl, '*nous sommes un département de la France. La meme que Paris.*' I didn't think Paris was the same as Corsica but didn't want to risk my French starting another war so I beamed at her. She scowled more deeply and gave me the stamps anyway. Ann sent off a disk with her Elba article to

Practical Boat Owner. It had taken her about three hours to write it, edit it, polish it and produce the finished thing on a disk. When I write articles it typically take me three weeks, there is no justice.

'It won't get published.' she said, but we both knew it would.

The old harbour in Bastia has much more character than Toga, and the prices for mooring reflect this. It reminded us of Marseille but on a smaller, more intimate, scale. The basin was surrounded by five and six story something-century blocks crammed together, squashing the streets between them until they were only suitable for pedestrians. The church of *St Jean Baptiste* was crowded in there too, somehow. The view was spoilt by all the yachts that are crammed into the little harbour making it impossible to get a view that did not have an array of modern glittering vertical aluminium masts in its foreground. We were there to get fuel having hurried the couple of miles from Toga when we'd discovered Toga's fuelling pontoon was out of service. We had to get to Bastia before 11:00 because that was when they shut, and we were late.

It was a bad start to a long trip down the side of Corsica to Taverna. The seashore was flat plane, populated here and there with hotels and watersports centres, an *etang* and Bastia's airport. But behind the plane the rugged mountains of Corsica rose to two thousand metres and more. We started off sailing but later flashed up the engine. There was a swell, but we were getting used to it. There were ominous clouds that developed later in the afternoon that looked to me as if they might become thunderheads. Since Elba we were completely neurotic.

Port-de-Campoloro / Taverna, Corsica, 1475 miles to Gouvia. Day 38

"Port-de-Campoloro" is obviously too difficult to say even for the locals so it has an alternative name of "Taverna" which has a pleasant hint of taverns and the things that make life enjoyable. There it ended. Taverna was another one of those places that one stops at because to pass it means another six hours or more to the next place. We arrived on the *quai d'accueil* as another yacht was leaving for its berth. We'd radioed in but as usual, didn't understand the answer through the radio's crackle, so Ann jumped off as the bow touched and went looking for help. While she was gone looking for the *Capitaine*, the *Capitaine* arrived on the pontoon in the form of a slim woman of maybe forty, and allocated us a berth: *'jay six, le ponton cote a la montagne.'* she said. She was very determined I understood she wanted us on the mountain side of the pontoon so she said again: *'cote a la montagne.'*

I learned very quickly: "jay" translates to "G". I'm sure I knew this once. Luckily there was no "J" pontoon or we would have been in the swamp but even getting into pontoon "G" was a nightmare. We basically had to walk ourselves through moored boats, fending off to the right and left in something reminiscent of one of those tight canal locks we'd negotiated the year before. The moorings were all chains and we feared snagging one on our keels which irritatingly stick out at quite an angle. We moored as near to the entrance of the pontoon as we could to avoid having to scuff our way passed too many yachts, but this had the disadvantage later that other yachts had to scuff their way passed us. We did a handbrake turn, hanging onto the stern cleat of a moored yacht, and drew up alongside it where a friendly neighbour was holding out a mooring line to us. We'd thought Toga tight, but this was an order of magnitude on from there. I hoped this wasn't a trend. By the time we'd finished the chores we were both sweating madly. The marina was in the shadow of the mountains and there wasn't a breath of wind to dispel the thirty-one degrees of temperature. To add to the frustration the electricity socket was one we'd not met before and we didn't have a plug for it in our arsenal so no fans.

Ann went off to pay and came back with a plug to fit the electrical outlet, and an American called Chas who was leaving for Elba next day and wanted some info. Tall, athletic, forty-odd, with short hair and the American presence that seems to be taught in the cradle, he hesitated over the beer we offered not because it was too early but because the beer wasn't frozen solid.

'The showers are cold,' Ann said helpfully, 'and cost two euros a time.'

I made an extension cable with the new plug while Ann gave Chas the low-down on Elba and we all drank lukewarm beer. He had the

American's deep voice too and used it with good effect to tell us about his meanderings around the globe. He'd been a pilot, a real pilot, so much so that I hesitated to even mention my little licence. I once read that the epitome of flying skill was to land on an aircraft carrier at night, and this it what Chas once did for a living. That got my respect.

He was travelling with his friend from Paris, Sebastien, who was, said Chas, showing the first signs of Alzheimer's disease. How ever many times Chas told Sebastien which rope to pull he would instantly forget. He also forgot what parts of the boat were called, such as 'cleat' and how to start the engine. Commands such as 'tie the sheet to the cleat' or 'tighten the sternline with the winch' were thus futile. Chas was taking Sebastien to Elba for him to catch a flight home but was dreading it: 'You know, you totally need to be able to rely on your crew?' His accent was cultured, 'I really don't know what to do, I mean, I love the guy, I've known him since we were small. Do I tell him?' It seemed typical of Americans that they can ask opinions about something so personal of someone they'd just met. How could we advise him?

He invited us around later for a 'real beer' and to talk about our plans. 'Bonifacio straights,' he said as he left, 'add at least two Beaufort forces to whatever number the lying bastards tell you and expect a sea state even worse than that.' We weren't too sure about meeting Sebastien though, I think we had this picture of a poor Parisian lunatic shuffling along the quayside biting the heads of wriggling fish and murmuring, "Bells, the bells".

And he was delightful, a small dapper, lithe man who was messing with the dinghy when we arrived and who leapt aboard with a vitality I wish I had a share of, and a grin the size of the Seine.

Ann had had a terrible job climbing aboard *Darling* which, at forty-eight feet, had a high bow. We struggled and pushed and pulled and eventually had to admit defeat. Ann's legs were simply an inch or so too short. Chas was distraught. Never before had a visitor had a problem clambering onto his boat. Then I had a brainwave: the boat that was nudging up against his seemed a little more accessible and was deserted, so we used it as a *passerelle*. Ann was thus able to finally enter the cockpit with a little grace restored and meet Sebastien with Chas and I close behind her.

'I think,' Sebastien said with a sad smile, 'that there is something wrong with me.'

Ann was below with Chas, going over charts and pilot books and Sebastien and I were sharing some wine in the cockpit. We were talking in French mostly and I was feeling really pleased to be able to hold a conversation again. Immersion in the language hearing it everywhere, every day allows it to infiltrate your brain somehow.

'I keep forgetting. People I used to work with, worked for years with, I forget their names.'

I tried to pass it off: 'Me too. I think it's because the world of work and the world your friends and family inhabit are different and so when you stop working you forget your colleagues.' I hoped it would reassure him, though I didn't really believe what I was saying. He smiled again and I knew he didn't agree with me. I felt sad and yet he wasn't the drooling idiot I was half expecting after Chas's summary of his condition.

We ate strange and smelly tinned meat, olives and rough bread and drank too much. The return on the bottle of warm beer we'd given Chas was typical American hospitality. We talked for a long time then climbed back over the bows of the boat next door, a little flushed and wobbly. Chas insisted I check the latest forecast for him, which I had as a GRIB, and call him on the VHF. I had the feeling that he was going to leave next day whatever the forecast, after all he'd been around the world on *Darling* and could land on aircraft carriers at night. We felt sad for Sebastien though. 'Good luck and goodbye. *Aderyn Glas* out.' Were the last words I spoke to them.

Next morning we struggled to get out of the berth. There was a wind blowing across us which would blow us sideways before we could turn in the space available. It would blow us onto the Italian boat which would capture us in his mooring chains. There we would lie stuck until we could somehow get pulled off. The only solution was to tie a line to the next boat upwind and pull the bow around. This was great in theory but when it came to it we couldn't get around enough and ended up sliding into the stern of the

Italian. Not so bad as a full broadside but enough to shake some fillings loose if we actually touched. Luckily the crew of the Italian were all sitting in the cockpit having breakfast so all we had to do was shout a warning in a suitably frightened voice and they would all rush to fend us off. We could then probably get the stern around and motor out of the pontoon.

The Italian crew didn't see it that way though. Obviously to them the idea of interrupting their breakfast solely to protect their stern was unthinkable and all the shouting and pleading I could muster made no difference at all: they sat and they ate. We got closer and they turned away. And we got closer still, until, by some miracle, our bow kissed them and we were gone. One of them waved at us as we motored down the line of boats and made for the sea.

'The Italians all come to Corsica in the summer because Sardinia is too expensive.' Ann said, although she couldn't remember where she'd read that.

I had another rash of mosquito bites that morning, undoubtedly from sitting in Chas's cockpit and not paying enough attention to my bare legs.

'We have ointment for haemorrhoids.' Ann said helpfully.

'They haven't bitten me there.' But she was right, it was a good topical anaesthetic and took the itch away.

Solenzara, Corsica, 1445 miles to Gouvia. Day 39

In Solenzara we had jobs to do. Things by now were starting fail and I had to get the tools out and fix them. The stern gland was fine and we'd long since stopped worrying about it, Toulon was so many bad dreams ago. But the GPS link had played up during the thirty mile run down the coast, and I wanted to move the jamming cleats for the genoa sheets since they made it fairly impossible to sit comfortably on the cockpit coaming. In fact our cockpit was fairly uncomfortable at sea but the folding plastic chair we'd steered from as we travelled though the canals had no place on a sea-going boat.

The run down the coast had been another day of motoring, a little south of south-west for most of the time. The coast was a repeat of what we'd seen north of Toga, flat plain with rugged mountains as a backdrop. Corsica is very beautiful so long as you like the majesty of high peaks, what Ruskin would have called "sublime", and the sea was probably the only place where you get a wide enough view to see it all. We also saw a single large dolphin that rolled across our path. It was so big and displayed so little interest in us that we thought it might have been a whale, so we consulted Ann's *Cetacean Dichotomous Key* and were still undecided between a large common dolphin or a pigmy sperm whale. We saw it roll into a dive and it was gone.

There was less traffic on this leg: the ferries from Bastia steamed well away from the coast which left only pleasure craft, like us, to hurry from one marina to the next. There were always a few of these in sight at any one time, sailing yachts, some doggedly carrying flapping sails and making maybe a knot or two on a day like this, motor cruisers fast and slow creating wakes disproportionately large for their size - and sometimes bloody-minded enough to swing close to us for their amusement - and fishing boats. The motor cruisers came close so that they could watch us getting sprayed by their bow-waves and rattled around by their wakes. After a few of these encounters we developed a strategy which was to turn into their path (at a safe distance, of course) forcing them to alter course, then turning a little more as they got a bit closer until they became convinced of our incompetence and turned their expensive ships away not wanting them to get scratched. When they were committed to a course we made an abrupt turn away from them and motored as fast as we could at right angles to the incoming wake so that, by the time it reached us, it was a ripple, not a wave. This strategy required careful timing and didn't always work but became a game we played to relieve some of the boredom and to fight back a bit. Normally, though if the motor yachts stayed at a reasonable distance we simply turned into the wake when it arrived to take it on the nose.

The last group of boats were fishing boats. These came in two sizes: large commercial trawlers and little bobbing dayboats and neither of them gave a toss about us. The trawlers had to be avoided – by miles sometimes – and the first thing we always did when we saw one of these was to reach for the binoculars and try to determine if he was towing a net. If he was actively trawling he wanted to go on travelling in a straight line at a fairly low speed which had the advantage that his position was going to be predictable for the time it took us to either duck under his nose or make a large diversion around the net he was towing from his stern.

Far more of a problem arose if he was not trawling because then he simply went wherever and whenever he wanted and, as often as not, the man who should be steering was anywhere but in the wheelhouse and the boat meandered wherever it wanted. Then it became a game of tag, we wandering around the sea trying to avoid him and he chasing us zealously.

The little dayboats we treated as buoys. They were often anchored close in and came with a set of plump pink men hunched over fishing poles that sprouted like quills from both sides of the boat. The boats bobbed and rolled with every passing wave but the men remained fixed, staring at the point where line met water. We envied their ability not to get seasick. I suppose they must have caught something, sometime, but we never saw any evidence of it.

'It's just a complicated, ritualistic way of getting sunburned.' I thought aloud.

Solenzara was not a marina, it was a posh *Port de Plaisance* and it also cowered behind a seawall with a single entrance to the south. I think we were getting the picture that storms could well cause enough problems to need the protection that the marinas on this exposed coast had invested in. It gave us a few quiet moments while we pictured towering seas smashing against the wall and spray flying overhead while the boats in their moorings rocked violently. Maybe it was a premonition, we were going to see all that before the end of our odyssey.

But not yet. Solenzara was baking in hot sunshine when we arrived, and it had a beach. We were ignored by the staff so berthed ourselves using the buoys provided for the stern line on the east jetty where there was a collection of foreign boats. We plonked down the plank so that we could get off, plugged in the plug and did all those other things that were so routine by now. The east jetty curved around to meet the land at the north of the marina where it divided quayside from beach, and a short way down the road was the modern *Capitainerie*. This one had free wifi and warm showers presided over by the *Capitaine's* staff who guarded the keys, presumably to stop people from the beach using them so if you had sand in your shoes or kids with Mickey Mouse armbands: stay dirty!

That first afternoon we went to the beach anyway. How could we not? We were hot and sticky and the water was warm and inviting and just a hop away over the seawall where it met the quayside. It was well populated with bronzed bodies of all shapes, genders and sizes and we paddled off into the water and cooled down. There was no marine life. Later with the seat of our shorts wet from pulling them on over wet costumes and with feet coated in sand we sidled into the office and paid for a shower. When we'd finished the cubicles resembled a wet day in the Sahara but we didn't get banned.

In the evening the Swedish couple on the next door boat told us they had gone for a stroll up into the mountains and had been rewarded with some wonderful views along the coast. So next day we rose early and caught up on the jobs then in the late morning Ann and I set off enthusiastically in the general direction the Swedes had indicated and discovered Solenzara. It was a one street holiday town cleaned and painted for the season with careful pedestrian crossings, fenced and lit, but pavements too narrow for safety. It had hotels and holiday apartments and pizza places but it didn't have any character. 'It probably closes for the winter,' said Ann, quite serious.

We soon ran out of energy in the heat. So instead of mountains and views we found a supermarket and hid in the corner near the air-conditioned meat counter until our core temperatures had fallen to something resembling normal. We bought milk to excuse ourselves and returned to the boat.

'But it was only ten kilometres up into the hills,' said our neighbour. 'such a *little* stroll.'

We went back to the beach and soaked our hot bodies in the water again. I pointed out that the heat from our bodies was raising the local sea temperature but no-one was interested.

We'd bought a postcard. It was an aerial shot of a beautiful, deserted bay called Stagnolo which was just a stone's throw from Porto Vecchio and a day in our future.

Chapter 8

Stagnolo, Corsica, 1425 miles to Gouvia. Day 41

The postcard showed a beautiful bay with crystal clear, turquoise water and the hull of a single gleaming white yacht at anchor in the middle of it.

'There must be more than one Stagnolo,' Ann was peering out over the rocky, opaque, dark green water of the inlet in which a couple of boats were rolling gently in the mild swell that bounced in from the sea.

It was disappointing. The entrance had been difficult with enough rocky outcrops to have us bickering with nerves. Ann doesn't like rocks on charts, nor does she like shallow water. She also doesn't like an anchorage if there are too few boats there on the basis that there must be something wrong, even if it's not immediately obvious. In the corner of the bay was an out-of-bounds National Park reserve and there was an obvious watersports area complete with buoys. Ann thought we had no right to be there. I tell her it's too many years of academia: too many rule books. In Stagnolo we had all the things that unsettled her and she was fretting and scratching and snapping at me, which didn't help when I was trying to get through a narrow entrance in a shallow bay with rocks all around, a no-go zone and watersports.

As we got closer and closer to the shore Ann's stress increased. When I asked her to go up to the foredeck to get ready for anchoring she point-blank refused and swore at me, demanding that we go straight across to the Porto Vecchio marina.

I would like to say here, with all modesty, that I simply stopped the boat and waited until we both calmed down. But, unfortunately I don't have that patient disposition and so instead I stormed up front and threw the anchor in myself. We were getting a little too childish.

After a while we looked at each other a little bit ashamed. Later on, when we'd sorted *Aderyn Glas* out properly, we relaxed and looked out over the anchorage we'd chosen. The water might have been turbid but the view wasn't bad with the flat beach climbing into the hills then layer after two-dimensional layer of mountains turned blue and grey by the recession. In the opposite direction was the gulf that connected the sea to Porto Vecchio. There was a large deserted catamaran between us and the shore and a small German flagged boat a little way from us that seemed to be anchored from his stern. The crew were a young man and girl and they seemed to want to be alone, disappearing into their small cabin when we arrived despite the heat. It was peaceful.

Around four o'clock we could see the clouds building. We'd seen some thunderheads forming as we'd travelled down the coast but they had dissipated without turning into a storm. But now they were back, gathering over the hills as we watched. Now and then we could feel the flicker of a thermal wind as the air was sucked towards them.

The German unhitched his strange anchor arrangement and we realised we were too close to him so we moved a little to give us more room – just in case.

Then there was a peel of thunder. Ann gave me a small nod and a worried look that sent me below to start turning on all the alarms. Once again we had the GPS MoB, depth and chartplotter – like Elba – but now I took a bearing on the only safe way out of the bay and wrote the course to steer in big letters on the log. If it did get nasty we had to clear the rocks and boats and shallows and that was the only course that would do it. I checked it twice. What was the possibility of holding a straight course out of the bay in the dark, in a storm, with maybe a side wind trying its best to ram us onto the rocks? It seemed like we wouldn't stand a chance so should we leave now? Another flash and we're counting the elapsed seconds to the thunder roll. Miles away but we worried anyway. What else was there to do?

It thundered and blew little squalls for a while but there was always a good time lag between the lightening flash and the thunder so we stayed reasonably calm and after a while the show stopped and peace returned. A peaceful, gentle, safe, secluded anchorage with no-one too near and no noise. We sat in the cockpit and relaxed, until the mosquitoes drove us to bed.

We had a quiet night. There was no storm and no wind and the sea stayed calm beneath us. It was the first day of July and the official start of that mad season of high summer when all of Italy takes to the water and roars across from the mainland to reclaim Sardinia and to occupy Corsica. It was the day the marina prices started an exponential rise and the day when free berthing places began an exponential fall. And we were going to Bonifacio, the most impressive, mysterious and popular port on the south coast of Corsica, just a sneeze across the dreaded straights from Sardinia.

We'd been warned that Bonifacio was so busy that once you were there you dared not move. Even if you'd paid for your berth, if you then left it you would find it filled when you returned and no refunds and no apologies. There was also a limit on how many days you could stay: maybe one, maybe two. But the attractions of the place overcame the drawbacks and enough people had filled our heads with the desire to see it and with warnings and instructions about how to survive it, that we had to go.

Getting around the corner to reach it involved a more careful plan than anything we'd done recently, so we sat in front of our ancient laptop that was the key to our navigation (chosen because it only drew three Amps from our batteries) and carefully plotted out lines on our even more ancient CMAP software that we had been given during our time in the canals. Our CMAP software dated from 1993 but the islands and the rocks don't move, or so we reassured ourselves, and we had all the latest Pilot books for the detail.

So we drew the electronic lines and plopped waypoints at the crucial points on the route, most of which were centred around the islands at the south east corner of Corsica. In particular the inside passage near Iles Cavallo and Lavezzi. It wasn't deep, it wasn't wide and it had a dog-leg in the middle of it. But given good weather we should have no trouble hitting the waypoint. I'd written a piece of software to transfer the waypoints and routes from CMAP to Rachel, our GPS, so I uploaded everything and set the robots humming. Now we had a chartplotter running on the laptop to give us a birds-eye view of our progress and route and a set of waypoints rolling over on the GPS in case the chartplotter failed. It was also easier to follow the GPS since its display was in the helmsman's view. Ann also marked up the paper charts with the waypoints and all the dangerous bits along the way. This was all normal routine for us when we made this kind of passage threading between islands in narrow channels, but we'd not had to do if for a while.

The anchor was a pig to get up, but we liked that. It meant the holding was good and the boat was safe. We had mud and weed in Elba and that saved us, and we had mud and weed in Stagnolo too. We wondered if the difference between the postcard and reality was the encroachment of the weed as time went on.

So we headed out of the bay and out of the gulf and headed south for the islands, Rachel pointed the way and the chartplotter drew a little squiggle somewhere near our intended route. It was another day for motoring and the temperature was thirty-two centigrade.

There was more traffic than we were used to. Porto Vecchio is a busy and popular place and we were passed by a stream of motor cruisers and the occasional ferry. Sailing dinghies crossed our bow busily sailing from one side of the gulf to the other. They could pinch power from a wind that we couldn't even feel.

The course was south then south west and all along the coast we could see bays filled with pleasure craft mostly motor cruisers. Rachel faithfully followed the route we'd set up happy that we'd done the homework and that it would see us safely passed the outcrops, the shoals and the islands. We were probably a little more careful than we needed to be, other boats were motoring all over the place, but we'd sailed enough to know it's best to be risk averse.

We ran down between the islands through another National Park and into the narrow channel that would take us into the Bonifacio Straights. Boats had anchored all along the mainland in inlets and bays disregarding the prohibited anchoring zones in the *Réserve Naturelle*. Islands to the left and mainland to the right and exactly at the point where we had to turn to make the tight dogleg was a huge plastic gin palace. We grumbled and swore under our breath and complained to each other about the standard of seamanship in this part of the world that would allow a ship to anchor in a channel. When we got closer we could see the British Flag.

'I'm going to go and tell him!' Ann said, but she didn't.

We emerged from the shelter of the island and discovered how right Chas had been, the wind was howling through the Straights. We turned west and into it, taking some odd bits of spray over the bow. The coastline now was high white limestone cliffs carved into strange streamlined shapes by the wind: pyramids, mushrooms, seastacks and layer cakes with grass green icing on top.

We followed where Rachel led but couldn't see Bonifacio until we were almost under it. Perched on an overhanging cliff one hundred feet in the air was the old town of Bonifacio. Circumscribed by battlements were a jumble of rose coloured houses huddled, squashed and glued together, some precariously built out over the sea and beneath them the remains of the cliff that had collapsed onto the shore, all of them seeming to extend the cliff-face upwards towards the blue sky.

We could see the lighthouse that marked the entrance to the *calanque* at the far end of which was the marina and port but the cliffs hid the entrance perfectly. We motored on to where Rachel said the entrance would be. Behind us another huge gin palace was bearing down on us more or less on the same heading and we wondered if he would stay clear of us as he should. Although he was overtaking us and that gave us right of way, all too often at sea the rule is "might is right", and we had no misconceptions about who would ultimately have to change course. But we held on and pointed to where we thought the entrance should be.

As in Toga a few days before it was the traffic that showed us where the entrance was. Apart from our huge shadow, now throttled back and seemingly happy to let us lead, there were a couple of other sailing yachts heading towards the same point in the cliff from the west so between us all we formed an arrowhead that intersected with the cliff at one point and that was the way in.

It was confirmed a few moments later when a gaggle of small craft emerged from the cliff followed by a large ferry. It seemed for all the world as if a traffic light had changed to green but the rush was probably the result of the ferry manoeuvring. Whatever the cause the result was we'd found the entrance.

'Never a moment's doubt,' I lied, 'I trust Rachel completely.' Ann poked out her tongue, obviously unable to take the competition.

The *calanque* was about 150 metres wide at the entrance and traffic came and went in two lanes like a motorway. And so much traffic! We began to realise that this was what the south of Corsica and the north of Sardinia was going to be like in July. Once into the entrance and around the bend we were travelling due east back the way we'd come but separated from the straights by the high neck of land topped with the old town. We trickled down towards the harbour looking for the *quai d'accueil* and following a large sailing yacht with a crew of women. On the left we passed two smaller *calanques* the larger of which had boats moored in the centre with long lines taken to the cliffs from their sterns. On the right we passed the ferry port and quaysides where the long schooners and other huge sailing and motor yachts were moored stern-to. Up above, on the cliff, the massive walls of the citadel dominated the approaches. The *calanque* narrowed to a hundred metres. The yacht in front still led us forwards and behind the ship followed us carefully. After about a kilometre the *calanque* narrowed again and still the traffic ran busily back and forth. It was here that the marina pontoons started and suddenly everyone was funnelled into a width of fifty metres. The ship behind us had slowed and was starting to turn around to reverse to the quayside another half a kilometre in the distance. The women in the yacht in front of us did a handbrake turn towards a hammerhead on the north side and, with much shouting and yelling, demolished a lamppost on the end of the pontoon.

They were still untangling themselves as two young guys in uniform tee-shirt, shorts and cigarette in a RIB came roaring up and shouted to us to follow them.

'How many nights?' one asked and looked uncertainly at his mate when we asked for two, 'You must ask at the office,' he said. At least their English was clear.

They berthed us with some fuss since the boat next door had taken the sternline intended for our berth. They instructed us to tie up to him, a yacht twice our length. They promised he wasn't going to leave next day so we wouldn't be rudely woken at some non-existent hour. I ran along his decks, barefoot, to tie my line to his cleats and burned my feet on his teak. Everywhere was bustle and fuss and excitement and noise: we had arrived in Bonifacio.

Bonifacio, Corsica, 1401 miles to Gouvia. Day 42

It was dreadfully hot. Any breeze we'd felt out on the straights was completely cut off and the sun reflected from the surrounding cliffs and beat the air into a furnace. We covered the boat with all our sunshades, hanging them from the boom, the foredeck, the bimini, and we turned on all the fans but they only blew hot air around. It was like sitting in a hairdryer except it was humid too. We turned the hosepipe on the decks to cool them and on ourselves to cool us. Since the pontoons were all individually attached to the quayside, which was essentially the main street along which everyone strolled, this brought some welcome amusement, and maybe envy to the heat stricken meandering passers-by.

The quay was lined with the normal paraphernalia of tourism, the sunshaded restaurant areas, the *glaciers*, the bars. At the far end of the *calanque* the posh marina office and the tatty toilet block and showers sat next to a dusty coachpark. It was here that the day-tripper boats waited for customers and here that the huge gin-palaces reversed into the quayside. Like in Saint Tropez the humble literally looked up to the rich and we squinted up the *passerelles* to try to catch a glimpse of the wealthy sitting in their shaded and secluded air-conditioned after-decks surrounded by their flowers and flunkies and ice-cold bottles of something expensive. 'Good luck to them,' I said, as we wandered down to pay our fees, 'I want to be rich. Anytime soon will do then I can pay someone to have all this fun on my behalf while I skulk in my study.'

Ann thought I was joking. The lady in the office took pity on us and let us stay for two nights. 'Madame,' she thought Ann was captain, 'do not leave your *place* or you will not be allowed back even though you have paid. *Comprenez-vous?*'

We understood. Outside on a poster there was a picture of a *Grand Dauphin* and an explanation of how they were getting caught in the fishermen's nets and thus were in danger. This cleared up our sighting of a few days ago, we'd seen a *Grand Dauphin*. 'Why can't the French think of a more exotic name for these creatures than "Big Dolphin?"' I thought aloud, but no-one answered.

We wandered around, ate ice-cream, found an internet bar and had a beer and email, started to walk up to the citadel and decided it was best left until the cool of the morning. So we spent the evening watching the restaurants fill up and listening to the kids and the bars and the background murmur of a thousand French diners.

Next morning we climbed the steeply sloping streets into the old town. Already, at ten o'clock on a Monday morning, the heat was enough to make us weak and we were glad when we arrived at the gate in the wall and found some shade. The pile of cigarette ends under foot showed how many before us had stopped here for a whiff of dubious therapy. Through the entrance the streets are so narrow that arches span them like flying buttresses, providing mutual support for the houses on either side. Now and then a small car would negotiate carefully through and pedestrians would cower in doorways and alleys to get out of its way. Underfoot the streets are cobbles or stone slabs, uneven and rustic, but the tall, thin buildings provide enough shade to cool the streets. So much so that in my sweat-wet shirt I was feeling decidedly chilly.

We wandered this way and that, where we could looking south over the straights to our next destination, Sardinia, and commenting on the number of ships and boats moving east, west, north and south along and across the water. We wandered streets full of tourists and others which were empty. Streets lined with tiny restaurants and souvenir shops and streets with houses that looked more secret than private. Whichever way we wandered we found the cliff edge and with it more views to capture with our cameras.

At one point we found the *Escalier du Roi d'Aragon* – King Aragon's Steps, all 187 of them leading a hundred and twenty feet down the cliff to a beach and please pay two euros fifty each if you want to descend. We looked out over the cliff and wondered what was at the bottom of such a staircase – free massage at least? Or a hospital offering free knee and hip replacements while you wait? Or cold drinks and oxygen for the climb back up the 187 steps in thirty-odd degrees of temperature. And did it cost more to ascend, once they'd got you down there? Or did you have to pay for a boat to take you back? No-one came up while we were watching. We looked at each other and sadly shook our heads in unison, we would never know now.

'Legend has it,' Ann read, 'that the steps were cut in a single night by the Aragonese to attack the town in 1420, but they are now known to pre-date that and are thought to have been used by monks to get water from a well at the bottom.' She looked up from the tourist map. 'Can you imagine climbing all that way with a water bucket? On a day like this you would have drunk the lot before you got back to the top.'

'Maybe that's why there are no monks around,' I answered, 'they all died of thirst.'

Finally we wandered around the back of the old town hall and down a ruined road onto a demolition site. We felt we shouldn't have been there but there was no gate and no-one shouted at us. It was a modern military barracks and was in the process of being demolished but nobody was working on it so we poked our noses inside the buildings. That was how we discovered the murals.

We walked into a huge wrecked hall which could have been a mess room, or a canteen. The ceiling tiles had cascaded over the floor which was largely rubble and broken glass. On every wall was evidence of a regiment or squadron or platoon of soldiers, mainly artillery. It appeared as if every time a group of soldiers visited this establishment the artist in the squad had been encouraged to paint a crest, an insignia, or some other mural to record their stay. We walked from one room to the next, photographing them as we went. Some were artistic and well executed, most were French. Some were crude and some were both artistic and crude. Green heraldic dragons carrying a regimental shield juxtaposed with red dragons breathing fire onto a parachute. A hawk with a missile in its beak next to a viper carrying the same. Each was a squadron crest. An anchor carrying a gun and a pine tree, the symbology lost on us, a tank, an alligator blowing smoke rings at a portrait of Bonifacio. Each identified its owner: *Cavalerie*, we understood, but not *Marine Infantry* – did they walk on water? *Batterie*, was easy, and *Section* and *Compagnie*, but not *Peloton*. Blue silhouetted heads, often the black Moor symbol of Corsica, Green gauntleted fists – this crest in German – a Churchillian bulldog in a red cap: French. An Italian missile, a black wolf, an artistic eagle straddling crossed cannon. Many were well drawn, some less so. Some were sexy: a busty cartoon beauty that could have graced the inside of a men's magazine next to a huge tank from the *1st Batterie Royal Artillerie*. Because of the familiar word "Royal" we thought for a moment this was British, but there are twelve monarchies in Europe.

The crests had one thing in common, underneath or alongside were names and ranks. It seemed as if everyone who took part in whatever happened here left behind a regimental and a personal mark before moving on. We thought this must be some sort of artillery training camp, maybe a barracks for soldiers using the ranges that peppered the nearby islands. The only clue to when the barracks had shut was the latest date we found: 1997.

Much later we discovered the camp had once been the home of the French Foreign Legion Parachute Regiment before they had moved to Calvi in 1980, presumably the guys we'd seen jumping from the Hercules into the water. But many crests post dated the move and so, for us, it remains a small mystery.

That evening we returned up the hill to the town, determined to have a meal that someone else had cooked and would wash up after. It would be our last meal in France, tomorrow we would cross to Italy, well to be precise, Sardinia, nine miles away. In the evening the streets were cooler but the crowds still bustled around, poking into everything. We'd learned that the French like to eat later than us so we planned to eat before the restaurants filled up. Ann wore a dress and I discarded my shorts for trousers, it was to be a kind of romantic celebration for reaching this far in one piece and of leaving one country to travel to the next and because we liked Bonifacio and enjoyed being somewhere exotic. Then we saw the prices.

In the end we settled on a restaurant and sat on the terrace where we could overlook the *calanque*, provided there were no cars going passed, and ordered a pizza. Then a family with kids arrived and started noisily overflowing their tables in our direction. Then some friends of theirs turned up and made lots more noise and more cars drove passed so that the pizza tasted like exhaust. Then a cat wandered through my legs. Then the bill came and we had to pay thirty-one euros for a pizza and a bottle of house plonk.

'This is why we don't eat out much,' said Ann.

That night the disco started mindlessly thudding at ten p.m. and finished at three a.m. At five a.m. the local refuse collectors had to make it known that they were working hard. Despite the ear plugs we had about two hours of sleep. This is one of the obvious drawbacks of living on a boat in a place like Bonifacio. Nightclubs are often situated down by the water's edge and boats are not noted for their sound proofing. It would happen again and again as the odyssey progressed.

So we tiredly went where we hadn't been before: Santa Teresa Gallura on the north coast of Sardinia. We left Corsica at about ten in the morning and as soon as we cleared the *calanque* entrance we pulled out the sails and actually *sailed*. Chas was right and the wind was greater in the straights than the general area wind, which is what the forecasters tell you about, and was just strong enough to make it pleasant. We dodged the ferries and the ships and the large motor yachts, that were ships anyway, and the little motor yachts that aspired to be ships and the fishing boats and the sailing yachts and schooners and the ones like us. We'd never seen so many craft on one small patch of water. This as yet was nothing: south of us along the north coast of Sardinia, were the Maddalena islands where, it was rumoured you could walk from island to island across the decks of passing yachts. Maybe this is what inspired that computer game "Hopper".

As we came within sight of the Spanish Tower guarding the entrance to Santa Teresa the wind and the seas picked up a bit as the wind flung itself against the cliffs but we refused to pull sail in happy to put up with the odd wet face. We were sailing from one country to another and we would *not* turn on the engine until we got there. So much determination over such a small thing, but we had such a sense of achievement when we sailed into the harbour entrance.

We slipped under the nose of the huge ferry from Bonifacio that turned outside the harbour and reversed in, and the marina *Capitano* came to meet us in his RIB with his Italian uniform tee-shirt, shorts and cigarette and he and his mate berthed us without fuss. In Italy there are no welcome pontoons, in Italy harbourmasters meet you in RIBs and guide you to a berth.

We felt elated. This was the simplest of our sea crossings but for some reason it reinforced the idea that we were actually moving along our timeline. We would be in Sardinia for six weeks while family and friends came and played and went home, and we were finally, safely here to meet them all.

We hauled down our Corsican Moor and hauled up our Sardinian one, four blind-fold Moors and a cross.

Chapter 9

Santa Teresa Gallura, Sardinia, 1392 miles to Gouvia. Day 44

Dirk and Jennie were friends from Wales who owned an impressive holiday villa a short car ride from Santa Teresa, and we were going to meet up with them. Dirk is a tall, slightly overweight, sixty-something Swede with a little blonde hair remaining about his sunburned red face, a disarming smile and a lunatic approach to driving. Jennie is slim, sleek and golden skinned, with woolly auburn hair, a figure that belongs to someone half her age, and is an actress in her spare time with an actress's outgoing personality. They collected us from the far quayside, laughing and waving and shouting, hanging out of their car windows and grinning inanely, and took us to their home for lunch. It felt so good to get away from boats and water and concrete marinas for a short while. We ate and drank, hiding from the sun in the garden of their villa. The food was native Italian, not tourist Italian, bought in the local shops from local people. I wasn't sure I liked it. Proschiutto comes both *crudo* and *cotto*, dry-cured or cooked, with this came lots of olives stuffed with strange and savoury fillings and Italian cheeses which are, without exception, rubbish compared to French ones. The French cheeses are pretty wonderful: Brie, Camembert, and my own favourite: *Tentation*, (it means 'temptation' and is well named) which is like clotted cream in appearance and tastes like heaven. It should carry health warnings or incorporate statins!

Ann liked Italian cheese though and the bread was much better than in France. In France you generally get a choice of *Batons* or *Baguettes* which are the same things only different sizes, and are full of air and have had every morsel of flavour extracted from them. The bread Jennie fed us needed sharp incisors to slice off a mouthful and sound molars to grind through the grain and even then it was a toss-up whether teeth or grain would be ground down the most. Lashings of local olive oil helped. Ann watched me eating too much of it, 'There'll be a wind tonight.' She said, deadpan.

'You've seen the forecast, have you?' Dirk asked, but I knew what Ann meant.

Now we were in Italy and we were experienced enough to know that our diet was about to change radically once again and Jennie and Dirk had pushed the boat out and given us a taster. I even ate hated tomatoes so that I would live forever.

In the early evening Dirk drove us on a little sightseeing trip that included a visit to the local ice-cream parlour and a chat to one of their neighbours. Jennie rattling away in Italian and us not understanding a word. Then Dirk drove us back through the little town of Santa Teresa that sat on the cliff overlooking the *Porto Touristico* and the ferry port, our first intimate glimpse of an Italian town. It looked, smelled and sounded like a French one. Even in the evening it was dusty and hot with the sun still beating up the concrete and tarmac.

There was one long commercial street. Small shops jostled for space with pavement cafes where chairs and tables spilled out on the pavement amongst open boxes of colourful plastic stools, shopping bags, brushes and other hardware. Fruit and vegetable stalls offered a wide variety of fresh locally grown produce next door to the ice cream parlour or fish merchant or video shop. Suddenly Dirk pulled to a screeching halt outside a very uninteresting glass fronted small building with nothing to give a hint to its function. Jennie sprang out of the car dragging Ann with her, holding a variety of plastic screw top bottles. The bottles were passed to large lady in a white apron who walked to a big stainless steel barrel in the middle of the floor. She knelt near the base and a few seconds later raised an arm to Jennie and a plastic bottle, now red in colour and full of wine, changed hands. This was the local wine shop. The Italian version of 'bring your own bottles'.

Ann was right about the wind, though.

If I need to be fair to the marina it was modern, better than those we'd experienced so far and cheaper too. It had silly little Japanese bridges linking the pontoons to the quay and you could stand on them and watch the fish. The showers were good and there was the usual collection of restaurants and bars which were empty most of the time we were there. We tried to get the staff to look at our paperwork but no-one was interested in anything other than the ships registration papers, and that only to confirm the hull length which is what payment is based on. No need for passports, crewlist, medical cards, insurance, logbook, inventory, radio licence, radio installation certificate, Certificates of Competence or quarantine flag – no-one in the world seemed to care about all this carefully husbanded paperwork. What a highway for terrorists.

On the west side was the ferry port which serviced the ferries that ran many time each day to Bonifacio and other Corsican ports. The ferry port was of great interest to us because it provided free wifi to its clients which we could pick up with our super little high gain antenna. Behind the ferry terminal a flight of steps led up the cliff to the town - we viewed it from the boat with the same feelings as we'd faced King Aragon's stairway and didn't bother getting any closer to it. The delights of Santa Teresa that Dirk had shown us from the car could stay over the horizon as far as we were concerned.

The one thing we could do here was sail away and come back. 'Leave your ropes,' the *Capitano* had said, 'and no-one will take your place.' We decided to leave our plank too, since it had the boat's name carefully engraved in it. So by the time Dirk and Jennie turned up next day the pontoon was strewn with all our old bits of rope (no-one was daft enough to leave brand new ropes) and our prized *passerelle* was ready for doing duty as a placeholder.

Our friends had listened to us and brought the minimum, which for Jennie was packed tightly into a large shoulder bag. 'I only brought what you suggested,' she giggled, 'a hat, sunglasses, towels, two types of sunscreen, after-sun cream, deck shoes, change of bikini, something to wrap around me, a camera and so on.' I wondered who had suggested such a minimal outfit.

Ann gave them the safety tour: here are the fire extinguishers, here is the liferaft, here is your lifejacket – Jennie put hers on straight away but Dirk didn't bother, 'We don't have rules about it,' Ann said, 'only at night or in storms...' I had to smile, was she trying to put them off? '... and this is how to send a Mayday call.' Ann finished.

Finally Ann did the toilet briefing. This always gets visitors, they expect the comforts of home, 'You have to literally *pump* the stuff?' and 'Does it really go into the *sea*?' and, 'What do you *mean*, no toilet paper down the bowl?' Our little board on which we record each morning's strokes of the pump seemed to leave Jennie in a kind of horrified fascination.

And still they wanted to come.

'The weather's not too good out there,' I added, 'are you both good sailors or do you need a pill?'

'We're really good sailors,' said Dirk, 'didn't Jennie tell you we used to sail back home?'

Jennie looked a little more sceptical, dressed in her lifejacket. 'Have you heard all these stories about pirates?' she said, quietly, as if there might be a pirate listening.

I replied with an old joke: 'The only pirates we've met are the marina staff.' it took her a moment before she smiled.

We threw off the ropes and the *Capitano* turned up in his RIB to offer help we didn't need so I asked Jennie to tell them we would be returning, and she might have done so, or she could have told them she was being abducted by incompetent idiots who delighted in polluting the sea. Either way they smiled at her, but what man wouldn't smile at Jennie?

I was right though, outside the harbour mouth the wind was blowing a good force five from the west and the sea was picking up enough to have us rolling until we could turn and run before it. Ann and I exchanged a glance, both thinking that we would have to return into it later.

We pulled out the sails and let the wind blow us eastwards and I put Jennie on the helm. We always put the wife on the helm first when we have a couple on board, we'd found that once the husband gets a grip on the wheel it's difficult to prise them free and they show off which makes the wife a little more reluctant to steer later. Jennie was fine.

After a while we rounded a headland and turned south-east and I got the wind exactly behind us and pulled the sails into a goosewing, one sail to port and one to starboard. It takes a lot of concentration to keep from gybing with a crash, but it's beautiful when you get it right and *Aderyn Glas* seems to love it. Dirk took the helm and immediately lost it, the boom crashed through the sky and slammed up against the shrouds with enough noise to wake the dead and the whole boat shuddered. I felt myself turning white at the though of the damage that might have been done. Dirk seemed to think this was a normal way to proceed. For someone who professed to being a sailor he didn't have a clue.

Thus we went to Porto Pozzo which is at the bottom of a long *calanque* and it was a pleasant sail for us. We found a sheltered spot on the west side and anchored for lunch but went straight in for a swim first. Dirk stayed on deck and Ann and Jennie went off for a quick splash at the stern. I put on my facemask and went to look at the anchor. At first I couldn't understand why there was a smudgy track leading towards the shore from the front of the anchor. Then as I watched, horrified, the anchor started moving quickly across the ground. It was dragging and *Aderyn Glas* was sliding away from the shore and out into the channel and the wind.

Panic set in. I pushed myself up in the water and screamed across to Dirk who was on the bow to let our more chain. A glance under water showed that where the anchor had been there was only a muddy trail. I started swimming hard after the boat which seemed to be slipping away from me. Dirk was shouting something that sounded like 'Where is the winch handle?'

Why didn't Ann see what was happening, she was at the right place to climb aboard and take control. How could I leave Dirk in charge? Why did I think the anchorage was good? *What have I done*? Thoughts fled through my head one after the other.

I made it to the bow and grabbed the chain, gasping for air. Dirk leaned down and repeated his question: 'Where's the winch handle? How do I let the chain out?' He grinned, happy that something exciting was happening. His day out was becoming fun with an added bit of spice to tell his mates. My home was being blown across the inlet and onto the rocks. Why do I believe it when people tell me they've done a lot of sailing?

I felt the cold clammy grasp of fear, the feeling you get in your nightmares when you run and run and can't escape the inevitable.

Everything was happening in slow motion and all I could think of was to pull futilely on the anchor chain.

By now *Aderyn Glas* was well into the channel and the anchor must have been at the point of clearing the bottom. Where was Ann? I made it to the back of the boat and hauled myself aboard, Ann and Jennie were sitting towling the water from their legs and chatting happily. Looking down. Drying their feet. Not noticing that the shore was slipping away. I think I swore.

And, of course, disaster was averted. The engine started and panic stopped. After a while my heart rate returned to normal. We winched in the anchor and went around and dropped it again a little further in, with more chain and more care. But the shock of seeing our home floating away, of trying to swim through the water that was suddenly treacle along the side of a boat that now took three times as many strokes from bow to stern as it had before, of being impotent in the face of disaster, all this trauma burned itself into my subconscious and would make me twitch every time we came to anchor in the future.

Later we drove back into the full force of a Beaufort six. We'd been so sheltered in the inlet we hadn't noticed how the wind had risen and now we were getting wet. There was no question of sailing any more. We drove home. Jennie had thrown off her lifejacket, at a time when anyone else would have been putting one on, and felt liberated in a bikini and a transparent wrap.

Wharrrrrrrg! The ferry *Ichnusa* let out a four-second long blast that shook my fillings and made everyone jump. Dirk and Jennie thought he was honking at us like a fifty tonne truck at an irritating driver, but it wasn't that: we were in the way and he was annoyed.

We'd been trying to get ahead of him for the past twenty minutes. As we rounded the headland into the teeth of the wind we could see him steaming across from Bonifacio and aiming at the entrance of Santa Teresa. All big and white and packed with vehicles, his twin stacks pumping black smoke that was immediately whipped away in the blow. I picked up the handbearing compass and squinted along it, over a period of a few minutes his bearing wasn't changing and that meant we were going to collide off the harbour mouth. The wind was whistling and we were wet and getting a little tired and a bit cold and everyone wanted to get ashore, so I opened the throttle and the motor wound up to three thousand revs. *Aderyn Glas's* stern sank deep into the water as the turbo spun up and the motor started to produce forty-odd horsepower. The spray kicked over the bow and we started ploughing through the waves, but the bearing on the ferry changed incrementally in our favour – we would just beat it to the entrance.

I altered course to take us riskily the wrong side of the harbour entrance buoy and gained a little more. If the ferry held her course and speed, and as long as we kept going in this direction and at this speed, we would beat her. I thought. But it would be tight. And probably illegal.

And so we did, ploughing at last into the harbour entrance with the ferry breathing down our necks, ahead but only just, and probably guilty again of recklessness and that was why the captain of the ferry leaned on his siren for the full four seconds the law demands when making a turn signal. He couldn't send me the five blasts that mean *have you seen me sir?* Otherwise translated as *get out of my way you measly incompetent* because under the law of the sea I was in the right – but he could make me jump out of my skin and, as he turned to the right behind me, he did.

Next morning we said goodbye, another goodbye, and headed out. We said 'thank you' to the ferry terminal for our free weather forecast, and 'thank you' to the fuel quay for our diesel, and 'thank you' to the marina for providing fresh, clean drinking water from the pontoon taps, and 'thank you' to Aeolus for blowing a delightfully moderate wind in the right direction, and 'thank you' to Poseidon and tossed him a coin. We'd been afraid that the wind in the straights might blow so hard that we wouldn't be able to leave for weeks. We were heading now for our next rendezvous in Olbia but before that we had a couple of days to look around The Most Expensive Coastline in the islands: the Costa Smerelda.

The wind blew us over the same track that we'd taken the day before but once around the headland this time our route was east and south between Isola di Spargi and the mainland. Sheltering on the south side of the island a number of cruisers flew above an underlit turquoise sea, the colour of the water reflecting off their hulls giving them the illusion of hovering above the darker sea nearer to us.

The whole of the area was dotted with Islands, large and small, and masses of rocks around their shore line. The whole landscape was a blue canvas, powder blue for the sky with wisps of white cloud well up in the stratosphere, with turquoise and dark blue vying for the base. The islands, white rocks or dark grey and speckled irregularly with green vegetation, reflecting in the sparking water surface as we drew nearer to them. The lone rocks were often darker, poking their noses up through the water surface and creating eddies as boat wash hit against them. Birds circled high up, black specs against the powder blue sky, a panorama to savour, peaceful but austere.

The wind blew us onwards passed them with no time to stop, only to admire. The sun was already hot and we had a long way to go yet. As we put the island between us and the wind its force decreased. Ahead and to our left the large flat island of Isola Maddalena and a channel to the straights. It was like joining a motorway, the traffic crossing from the mainland port of Palau to Maddalena and its neighbour, San Stefano, had to weave through a busy stream of other boats heading across the top of Sardinia to the Emerald Coast. As we were. And as always, the odd fool: this one determined to sail upwind, standing on his rights, and zigzagging from tack to tack in the constrained space like a drunk wandering up the fast lane and everyone trying to avoid him.

Over and over we saw the glowing beauty of the water reflecting on the hulls of boats crowded into the favourite anchorages on the islands. The Maddalena archipelago is renowned for its beaches and is a designated national park, though it wasn't clear from our charts whether the infamous U.S. naval base was still in use on San Stefano. I covered one eye, Nelson-like: 'We saw no submarines!'.

The wind dropped to the point where it would take us seven weeks to clear the islands and we stirred the donkey. Now it would take only a few more hours but we still didn't have time to stop. On we went. On passed the beauty of the Maddalena Group and passed the attractions of Palau whatever they might be.

At 13:45 we heard a pan-pan call, a cry for help one down from a mayday, and furiously scribbled down the details: a forty-two foot motor launch aground in position so-and-so 'Wow!' we thought, keen to see a ship rescued, but when we checked its position on the chart it was back in Corsica near Porto Vecchio, so we responded in the same way as everyone else and continued on our way.

Motor cruisers as big as ships passed us in the narrow channel three, four and five decks, twenty, thirty and forty metres travelling far too fast and throwing up a wake that set us rocking. Our normal tactic didn't work here, the channel was so narrow that neither they nor we had room to manoeuvre. On we went, passed all the beauty and consoling ourselves with the knowledge that we were coming back this way in a week or two with more time to explore. On passed flat Isola Caprera and through the tiny, shallow gap filled with ships whose wakes rolled and flung us about, into the wide Tyrrhenian Sea beyond.

Now we headed south into the sea's swell and immediately the traffic we had been part of dispersed in all directions. After a short while, to our right in a gap in the hillside, The Most Expensive Marina hove into view: Porto Cervo. The cost of mooring here was mind shattering, hundreds of Euros a night for nothing more than a buoy to tie up to. The rumour was that the prices were so high to discourage riffraff. The accumulated worth of the ships and yachts we caught glimpses of was probably more than some country's GDP. Somewhere on the hill above the port the Prime Minister of Italy and the man at the heart of so many scandals, Silvio Berlusconi has his summer villa.

'Nice to be rich,' I repeated my favourite theme.

We motored southeast then southwest passed half-submerged rocks like teeth that would tear a boat to shreds. We grew tired. We felt sunburned and dehydrated despite continuously drinking. We looked at the rocks and felt the swell under us and wondered where we could find some shelter for the night. Ultimately there was Portisco, but that was still a long way and we wanted to anchor if we could, to save a bit of money.

In the end we rounded a headland near Capriccioli and began to see yachts and ships anchored in bays along the coast. We headed on towards a promising looking inlet that was shown on the chart as the Golfo de Conglanus and around the corner from it a resort named Cala di Volpe that seemed sheltered from just about everything.

The coastline rolled before us becoming less jagged and flatter, opening into a broad bay fronted by a long beach of white sand. Almost at the right hand end of the bay a long spur formed a narrow channel which led to a large hotel. We passed a few very large red mooring buoys in the main bay, big enough to hold a battleship, some of them occupied.

And the inlet was indeed sheltered and everyone knew this and it was packed. But we are so shallow in draught we can boldly go where others can't, so we nosed gently into the shallows and found a place in a couple of metres. It was five o'clock in the afternoon, sunny and hot, crowded and noisy, on the breeze a sniff of barbecue and diesel, but it was our shelter for the night provided the anchor held.

Cala di Volpe, Sardinia, 1365 miles to Gouvia. Day 46

As far as we could see Cala de Volpe was only the hotel with a boat park for really shallow boats, like the tenders of the significant yachts moored on the red buoys out in the bay. The shore was a tree lined rocky beach and between us and it were a line of yellow buoys and, at first, we thought these were beach swimming marks. But then the RIBs and other tenders began a high speed parade up and down what was obviously a channel. Once a water skier carved his way passed us toward the hotel. We were enjoying swimming in warm gin-clear sea with white sand beneath, when all this began, and glad that we'd played safe and stayed near *Aderyn Glas*. The boat drivers all tried to outdo one another and drove at a speed that left us bobbing and rolling uncomfortably in their wash.

'Never mind,' Ann said, 'they'll all go to bed soon.' She didn't bargain for the stamina of the young Jet Set who were easily able to find something ashore to entertain them until two in the morning. So until two, every fifteen minutes or so, just as sleep crept up on us, with the roar of an oversized outboard a skivvy in a RIB with merry, young and carefree cargo swept passed and set us rolling. Again… And again… And again…

We left late because we were not going far, only a little further into the inlet to find a quieter anchorage. Once outside the bay opened up into a sweep of white sand covered in regimented rows of colourful beach umbrellas with regularly spaced bars and ice-cream stalls. In late morning it was already busy with families and sun worshipers and the shoreline was littered with pedaloes and canoes. Above the beach the hills climbed away into the distance but these were not the mountains of Corsica. It's amazing how different two neighbouring islands could be!

Before we left we motored around the moored super-yachts and drooled. They varied from the five deck motor yachts the size of small ships to the sailing yachts the size of small ships and were, without exception, glistening and polished, festooned with antennae and carrying liveried crews. At the stern the normal deployment was a large RIB or two, for those runs ashore, and a variety of water toys such as jetskies or ski boats, sometimes kiddies toys such as a water slide and floating playpen. All of this normally lived in a garage built into the transom and covered by a hydraulically operated hatch at sea. At the stern of *Aderyn Glas* we hung our little rubber duck on a pair of davits and were pleased to be able to do that.

'Don't get too close,' Ann was looking intently at the stern of a large motor yacht.

'It's okay, her mooring line is well away and she doesn't have a stern anchor out.' I replied.

'It's not that,' Ann was still watching, 'I'm just afraid they'll close those garage doors and not notice they've trapped us inside with the RIBs.'

Cala Petra Ruja, Sardinia, 1361 miles to Gouvia. Day 47

We went around the headland to the next bay, one of those glittering jewel-like little bays for which the Costa Smerelda is famous. This one was called Petra Ruja and it was brim full of boats. We nudged our way between the throng using our shallow draught to advantage until we were alongside the tiny open sportboats and only then did we throw our anchor in. Ahead of us were a family in a RIB, behind us a motor cruiser with a fat pilot, to our left a wooden ketch that looked like it had circumnavigated the globe before ending up here, and on our right a tiny open boat with an old couple who adored the sun. They lay in it without shade the whole day.

The beach was delightful with none of the paraphernalia of the one we'd just left. The only land access we could see was a dirt track and that seemed to limit the numbers on the beach. We swam off the boat and played and rested, catching up on the missing sleep and when evening came we watched as, one by one, the assembled hoard thinned out. The family left early, the fat motor cruiser followed soon after. The old couple seemed to want to outstay us – how they could take so much sun was beyond me – but ultimately they hauled up their tiny anchor and left in a flurry. When there were only three of us remaining the wooden ketch pulled up his anchor and moved across the bay. Now each of us could believe we owned our own slice of the Emerald Coast. We watched the sun sink, drank wine, listened to the waves lapping, dodged the mosquitoes, and slept like the righteous.

It was even better waking up to the sparkling sea and the empty beach and the early morning gentle sunshine and the birdsong. But it didn't last long, by nine o'clock the boats were arriving leaving tracks across the inlet from the sea or Porto Rotundo or Portisco. Our elderly neighbours returned and parked next to us, stripped off and prepared for another absorbing day.

We left and ran before the wind further down the inlet towards Portisco for a marina fix – fuel, water, supplies and a proper shower. We hauled in the sails outside the marina and Ann tried to raise them on the radio. After a while a RIB turned up with a single young crewmember in it and we followed him into the concrete port. It was largely empty and that should have warned me but I was too busy trying to handle *Aderyn Glas* in what was now a crosswind. In an empty marina the baby *Capo* had a radio debate with the office about which berth to put us in while we drifted downwind. He finally decided on the worst one possible of all those available. Exactly crosswind, which meant we were going to move a long way sideward as we tried to tie up.

We moved a long way sideward as we tried to tie up. The kid in the RIB, who by now had lost any respect I had for his skill and knowledge, had leapt ashore and tried to deal with the bow ropes while I tried to haul the sternrope tight while the stern swung around and the bow crashed against the quay. It was a mess! In the end the only way I could get her straight was to haul the bow rope with the anchor winch and the sternrope with the sheet winch. Halfway through the struggle the kid disappeared and Ann and I were left to sweat and struggle.

It was good that the pontoon was empty.

Ann went to check in and pay money for the night. Unusually I gave her a mobile radio to take with her, perhaps the empty spaces had begun to wave a flag in my brain.

After a while my radio crackled into life and there was Ann in a strange voice telling me the cost for a night was a hundred and five Euros and should she pay? I started slackening the ropes we'd struggled so hard to tighten and started up the engine again.

When she got back she was in tears, 'Is this what we're going to have to pay everywhere? We absolutely can't afford it!' The marina staff had made her feel bad about the whole thing, as if she was welching on a contract that she hadn't even signed.

On the way out we stopped at the fuel pontoon to fill the tanks with fuel and water. I asked the girl in charge if the marina was empty because it cost so much. She told me that in the summer it was full every night and to be careful not to take our dinghy to go shopping or they would charge for the dinghy landing. We left there reeling, more than a little anxious and shocked. From that moment we were suspicious of empty marinas.

But less than a mile away was a perfectly good anchorage with a group of boats already anchored for the night in perfect calm. And it was free. We liked free.

Chapter 10

Portisco, Sardinia, 1356 miles to Gouvia. Day 48

South of Portisco, at the marshy end of the Golfo Cugnana, the anchorage was shallow and the water was green pea soup, but it was well sheltered that night. In the morning the sky was still blue and the weather promised to be hot but the wind had freshened a little.

Each and every morning I have to exercise. Even though living on board a bobbing boat continually moves all the joints in my body I have a left shoulder that is ten years older than the rest of my body and a painful back from too much sitting staring at computer screens. I know from experience that if I don't follow some physiotherapy routines that things will reach a snapping point. The physio routines begin by kneeling and touching my head to the ground and I'm always worried in case someone thinks I'm so desperate for good weather I've resorted to prayer. Today, though, Ann and I climbed out on the deck and did some *Tai Chi*. This is something we are normally far too shy to do in public and will try, instead, to do down in the saloon with hands and knees crashing against the furniture.

That day, in the warm morning sunshine with the water still as a pond and the nearest people two hundred metres away, we exposed our chi to the world and felt all peaceful. 'Let's stay.' I suggested.

'Time to go.' Said Ann.

We had a new deadline: Ann's daughter Sue and her husband Rob were flying into Olbia and staying with us for a week of sun and sea holiday. So we hauled up the hook and sailed back up the gulf the way we'd arrived. Porto Rotundo was off to our right, almost opposite the marina at Portisco, and reputed to charge the same eye watering rate. The village was all pastel coloured holiday lets set amongst craggy grey-green hillside. Anchored off the marina entrance was another cluster of superyachts, seemingly deserted, waiting perhaps for their owners or charterers to return from wherever their business took them. But we had no time to investigate, the wind was blowing us happily towards the sea and a meeting with Capo Figari.

We thought it would be easy and that the wind would drop as we ran behind the shelter of the towering cliffs of Capo Figari. We should have known. 'It's a cape.' Ann said unnecessarily. Have I mentioned that capes are always trouble? Instead of calm the wind and the seas somehow managed to increase until we were pitching and rolling in significant waves of one or two metres. It always seemed so strange to have a beautiful blue sky and a wind like that, but we were still catching the tails of *Mistrals* (or so we were told). And the seas were probably overfalls, we thought, a current running one way hitting a shallow bit under the cliffs, or catching another current trying to get around the cape in a different direction. Whatever the cause the effect was we were getting wet.

A little further and we would round the cape into the Golfo Aranci, behind the headland, and it would all quieten down.

Like hell! It was like hell. The wind was somehow funnelling up the Gulf of Olbia from the mainland, still an hour ahead of us, and the seas were worse again than those around Capo Figari. We had long since put the genoa away and now we hauled in the main leaving only a tiny bit flying for stability. The wind was bang on the nose and had enough of a fetch to build waves that buried the bow and shot spray over us.

The sky was blue. The sun was strong. The wind was high. The waves were fierce. We were wet and fed up and although we could see, and almost smell Olbia, it was taking ages to cross the bay: creeping towards it. On our right, to the north, the great sweep of the bay called Caddinas ended at Aranci ferry port tucked behind Capo Figari and we considered whether we could find some shelter there. Six miles to the southeast the massive bulk of Isola Tavolara looked like the Lost World in the 1960 film rising sheer from the sea. Rachel told me that Olbia was still eight miles ahead.

Half an hour later we were halfway across the bay when a ferry came the other way. Not the piddling little thing that had honked at us in Santa Teresa, this was the grown up version that could take you and your fleet of trucks anywhere in the Med. We turned a bit to aim passed him. He turned a bit. We turned a bit more. So did he. We splashed through the gulf. He powered towards the sea. We rolled and pitched. He was like a moving island. People on the top deck, deck nine or twelve, waving and looking down on us rushed by in a confusion of noise and exhaust smells and wake, and in our saloon the drawers crashed open and the oven threw it's trays to the floor and in the heads the little bin leapt frightened into the toilet again.

We turned through his wake and buried our bow, spray leaping back to coat us in water which the sun and wind dried to a layer of salt in minutes. Then it was quiet for a moment as we reached the wake's centre where the waves had been beaten flat by his passing. We turned *Aderyn Glas* towards Olbia and motored onwards, wet, tired, stoic but now angry as well.

'All it would have taken,' I said, 'was a twitch of his finger on the joystick and he could have missed us by miles.'

'What makes you think he didn't twitch his finger?'

I didn't blame Ann for sounding bitter, it had been unnecessarily dangerous. It was something that we would get used to over the coming weeks.

There is an ancient light that marks the start of the shallow, narrow channel to Olbia town, a two story square building with a light in the tower above it, designed to be conspicuous. At that point we had two more miles to run to the quayside and at that point the funnelling was at its worst. The wind and seas were taking a good two knots off our speed. We could see Olbia and we could see the stream of aircraft bringing happy holiday hopefuls into the airport. Sue and Rob would be on one of those flights and we were really looking forward to meeting them.

The channel was well marked with red and green buoys and all we had to do was drive between them and keep on the right of any approaching traffic. Further into the channel we could see seals basking on the surface, grey-blue, sometimes dark green and, unusually for seals, in militarily precise rows and columns. The seals were anchored to the bottom by unseen cables so that only their heads were proud and were guarding the corners of sunken net boxes ten metres to a side that made up a huge fish-farm that stretched almost all of the two miles to Olbia.

On the right the view opened up to reveal warehouses, slipways, shipwrights, repair yards, cranes, lifts and jetties, behind more precise rows of the bobbing buoys.

Next on the left bare rocks breaking the surface and washed by the waves. Rounded, camel humps of rocks that led to a group of masts that became the New Olbia Marina, the sign welcoming yachtsmen and potential home owners without favour. A clean new marina but not yet for us. We motored on between the markers.

We passed the ferry terminals complete with three huge ro-ro ferries all tied up stern-to, bow anchors deployed, vibrating noisily and smouldering slowly. Black smoke whipped away into the blue sky. A police launch stuck its nose out of a hole on the right and sniffed at us as we motored passed. It made me nervous. A sign for a yacht club on the right and a low, impassable, bridge in the distance carrying road traffic out of the town.

Finally we could see anchored boats on the left, and on the right, the rough, derelict quay that everyone who visits Olbia aims for because it is a totally free mooring in the centre of a major town. Boy it looked rough! Eroded concrete and rusty mooring rings, discarded frayed ropes and torn rubber tyres, hanging from corroded chains, for fenders. A storm of dust blowing along it in the wind. A brightly painted portion of the wall told us where we could not park because that was reserved for a tug. Apart from that there was one remaining space in the line of moored boats so we headed for it. The rings were meant for ships and were too far apart for us and the quayside was too high for us. I angled *Aderyn Glas* towards the wind and sidled in towards the gap. People emerged from neighbouring boats to take our lines and wrap them around rusty trapdoors that covered the disused crane rails. The lines rubbed against the dock edge. One neighbour warned us immediately about rats and pointed to her lines which were festooned with cut about plastic bottles in the belief that rats would be unable to balance on them.

Sue was there, slim, five feet two, thirty-something, red hair and green eyes and a character to match, shouldering a heavy rucksack and grinning whitely. Two metres of her husband - Doctor Bob Dylan but call me Rob - stood behind her looking around with a vacant expression as if he'd just woken, which was probable. They stood in front of a decaying warehouse and must have wondered what we'd brought them to. Here there was no water, no shower, no fuel, no electricity, no proper mooring and a dust-storm as atmosphere, it was also too windy to go anywhere else. But it was free.

Olbia, Sardinia, 1339 miles to Gouvia. Day 49

The only showers were what we had with us and we needed one to get the salt off. So we rigged solar showers and washed ourselves self-consciously, on deck. Later we clambered up onto the quayside above us and wandered into the town for dinner. At seven in the evening the main street was closed to traffic and the restaurants had set out their tables and menus in the roadway. We did what we always do and examined them all then chose the first one we'd seen.

The pizzas were fantastic. I don't usually care much about my food, like Ellen MacArthur I think of most of it as fuel, but these were worth writing about. So I have. Rob said *grazie, prego,* to the waitress which made her laugh.

We wandered around the streets: a small square with a modern-art fountain and roads radiating from it, ice-cream parlours selling ice-cream the richness of which I'd never experienced before, restaurants and jewellers, some apartments. The odd car that had somehow forced the barricades brushing against diners while they ate and move your chair please, so my wing mirror can get through. And everywhere street vendors behind their stalls selling all the things a holiday town sells and more: food and sweets, toys and tattoos, electronics Made in China, lace made by hand. The warm air was full of the scents of food and perfumes and the accumulated sounds of hundreds of us promenading and looking and sniffing, buying commonplace Sardinian treats that we found exotic. Sue happy and bouncy, Rob gazing around like he'd recently woken up,

Ann delighted with her clever daughter, and me: happy they were happy.

We got to know our way around Olbia pretty well in the three days the *Mistral* kept us there.

On the second day we were told to leave by a man in jeans and a shirt with the insignia of a famous oil company, who looked down at us from the quayside. There was a seventy-five metre, many-decker, gin palace coming alongside for refuelling, he said in broken English. We looked at each other then climbed up onto the quayside and looked at the other owners and they looked at each other. Then a tall young Italian port official in the brightest, most ironed, uniform I have ever seen strode around the quayside with a radio squawking in his hand and we all looked at him. He spoke to the radio, he spoke to the oil man, he spoke to each of us. 'Of course, we will move,' we said, 'where would you like us to move to?' When I know we can't win the battle I always resort to diplomacy.

The Frenchman next to us point blank refused to move since his engine was broken. The German guy, Dominik, pointed out that under Italian law they could not send boats to sea in a wind that strong, and his wife Sophie had a damaged shoulder – look at the sling. The Belgian crew of a yacht smaller than us argued forcibly with the uniformed *Capitano,* and the Italian crews all went into their cabins and shut the doors. International comradeship was breaking out, in fact it was becoming a revolt, but a revolt we could not win since we had no right to be on this quay in the first place.

A shorter, rounder, older, and even more sharply uniformed, port official arrived. Weighed down by gold braid he would not carry a radio but he had the younger man to do that for him. He walked up and down and barked a bit hauling himself up to his full shortness and strutting as only an Italian official can. After a while I got bored with watching them pace and prattle and went down below leaving Ann to organise things. A little later an irritated, grizzled, Italian in a yacht was tying up alongside us – a little tricky in the wind and only carried out successfully due to the high level of anxiety each of us in both crews was feeling. Ann had simply gone along the line of moored yachts and selected which one was small enough to tie up alongside us. This simple bit of common sense negotiation sparked everyone else to do the same. The man with the broken engine found that when the officer offered to arrange a tow and charge the cost to the owner, that the boat was not, after all, quite so disabled as he had thought and could be warped along the quay. Within an hour there was enough quayside space for the mega-yacht to fit and a medley of international pairings of yachts hanging off the quay wall.

Our enforced neighbours were rude: they tramped across the decks of our home, to and from the quay, with big dirty boots that left big dirty footprints. You simply don't do that to a neighbour.

We waited expectantly for the thing to arrive. Eventually we got bored and the four of us wandered up into the town to find the cyber-café and return with a weather forecast. When we got back there was the floating hotel and a string of road tankers on the quay.

Near the gate of the yacht club, which was on the posh side of the quay, a group of uniformed stewardesses sat on the grass, talking and smoking, so we wandered over and asked them who owned such a floating mansion. They didn't know. The way it worked, they told us, was that the ship was hired out to whoever had the cash and the girls were hired in by an agency. At the moment the ship was between charters so they had nothing to do but sit in their uniforms and chat and smoke and get paid for it. They were all English.

The road tankers rolled in and waited in line. Then they coupled up and the ship slurped them dry and they left. This went on all the afternoon and all night. Each tanker held 24,000 litres of fuel and we counted twelve before we went to bed.

Next day the wind was still blowing and the ship was still there. We negotiated our way out of the berth, freeing the Italians to do a circuit and take our place and slipping out backwards behind the ship. I gave the wheel to Sue and told her to head out to sea. The holding tank is the receptacle that all toilet waste gets pumped into. It was sized to suit Spanish regulations since they were the only ones that actually put numbers on how much poo a typical crewmember can produce in a day. Ann and I usually get a week at least before we have to empty the tank so we had no idea what Sue and Rob must have been doing to fill it so soon, and didn't want to ask. We had to empty it and that was that, and the nearest place we could even pretend to do that legally was at the lighthouse. Sue has a Masters degree in Environmental Biology and is enthusiastic about saving us all, so I waited for my destruction, but she was calm about it. Perhaps she was happy that we were taking part in a natural cyclic process: tomorrow we could eat the fish from this bit of water.

Motoring before the wind was easy and we covered the two miles without any trouble, but when we had to turn to come back to the marina entrance we caught the full force of the wind and started bucking into the waves. It took half an hour to claw our way back to the marina, but the marina staff spoke English and came to help us berth, what lovely people! The marina was largely empty and we knew now what that meant, but it was only sixty-six Euros for the night. 'Look how easy it is to say the words '*only*' and '*sixty*' in the same sentence,' Ann smiled a relieved smile.

The marina had only opened in May and it was now July. It wasn't even in the pilot books yet. Everything gleamed and sparkled: shining stainless steel bollards and cleats for ropes, brightly coloured tops on bins in discrete groups along the pontoons, ready to receive all variety of recyclable refuse, stainless lampposts. Stainless lampposts! It took my breath away!

The surfaces of the wooden pontoons and fingers, squeaky clean and unmarked by feet, dogs, or trolleys as if freshly scrubbed each morning and newly planted vegetation in pots or beds as yet unblemished by the ravages of sun or wind. Clean air: unpolluted by ferries or the airport that was over the hill. It was the pride and joy of all the staff and they told us so.

So we filled up with stores from the hypermarket down the hot, baking road and filled the boat with water and washed her. And had civilised showers in the brand-new shower block and enjoyed the sensation of a full sized toilet seat and a flush, and throwing paper into the pan was such fun I almost used up a roll.

The marina was largely empty because it was new, but the vessels that were tucked into the deeper corner were at the elite end of the spectrum: *Dionea* was a classical, 1930's style, four-decker motor yacht of about thirty metres, complete with a funnel and full sized clinker lifeboat on davits. She looked like a small *Brittania.* Next but one to her was an unnamed deep blue stealth fighter of a speed machine rumoured to make fifty, sixty or seventy knots depending on who you believed. Darkened windows, bollards, cleats, and so on built into the hull and inside lurked gas turbines. Sections of her sides unfolded hydraulically to make platforms for the crew in harbour. She was here for speed trials according to the Belgian guy next door.

It was blue-sky, baked-hot and desiccated in Olbia marina, the *Mistral* blowing dust and shrieking with laughter in the rigging. But it died away overnight: someone turned off the *Mistral* switch.

We'd made a real mess of our overall planning. When we'd suggested to people that they come and spend some time with us we'd planned to pick them up at one end of Sardinia and drop them at the other. This seemed like a good idea because our family and friends would get a real taste of sailing. Unfortunately neither Ann nor I had taken too much notice of how big Sardinia is so when we actually sat down and looked at the detail we had a shock. Going flat out day sailing we could just about make it from Olbia, in the north, to Cagliari, in the south, in a week. That was on the shorter and sheltered eastern side, on the west it was impossible to get from Alghero to Cagliari in a week. And these were the airports that we'd arranged to collect people from.

We also misunderstood what people wanted from their stay with us. We thought they would want some serious sailing but, in fact, we were to find they wanted more of a complete diversion from the stress of home and work and were happy to bimble around, swimming, sunning and seeing. So when Sue and Rob expressed complete happiness with the idea of touring around the local area and jumping on a train to travel south to catch their flight home at the end of their week, we were suddenly off the hook. To be honest, for us to have sailed to Cagliari would have been a physically hard effort for all of us after the delayed start. Sue was happy not to be physically stressed, Rob scanned the horizon with the half-smile of freedom and didn't care so long as it was sunny and he could swim, Ann was happy they were happy and I was happy I didn't have to frog march southwards yet.

We left the marina, next day in calmer weather, with Sue driving and finally had a swim in a bay near the lighthouse. Then Rob sailed us north across the Gulf of Olbia to another of those white-sand, turquoise-water bays we were getting so used to, where we tied up to a buoy thoughtfully provided by the national park authorities. It was marked on the charts as Porto Porri.

Porto Porri, Sardinia, 1330 miles to Gouvia. Day 52

Rob went over the side with a splash even before the boat had stopped moving. He is a tall man and plays water polo and reaching the shore was no problem for him. Sue went after him, she is a short girl and plays water polo but keeps being thrown out of the pool for fouling. She denies it but has broken toes from kicking people. Reaching the shore was no problem for her either. Ann went after them both. She does not play water polo and took a little longer. She also has wonky toes but these were mainly caused by wearing fashionable shoes and sometimes from kicking deck fittings. I have perfect feet and slipped them into fins and paddled off in the opposite direction to see what fish were hiding in the rocks. Thus I missed out on the ice-cream which Rob bought on the beach with some of the plastic paper money he'd stuffed down his trunks. There weren't any fish either, only other people snorkelling.

The calm, quiet, peaceful night was so good after three days of ceaseless wind. 'Let's stay,' said Ann.

'Time to go,' I replied, 'these guys want a proper activity holiday.'

Rob looked around, as if he'd just got out of bed and Sue smiled her secret smile.

Sue is good on the helm and Rob stands with his feet apart, the wheel in his hands and rocks back and forth for some reason. When Sue is steering Rob seems anxious to get his hands on the wheel and ten minutes after he starts his trick he wants to do something else.

He became our fisherman and caught exactly as much as we had which was nothing.

We rolled out around Capo Figari again and splashed our way through the overfalls northward. The wind took us through the gap south of Isola di Mortorio (which means *Island of Funerals*) where the sand is the whitest and the water is the best around. Then we motored back to Cala di Volpe, Sue adopting the Kate Winslet "Titanic" pose on the forestay for photos, arms spread and flying, at all of five knots. We went there to watch the RIBs and jet skis and chill out and have lunch and to introduce them both to the super-yachts in the bay. But, wiser now, we headed south and spent the night quietly at anchor in Cala Petra Ruja away from all the noise and hustle.

Cala Petra Ruja, Sardinia, 1312 miles to Gouvia. Day 53

Next day was blue sky and hot. In our cabin in the forepeak we had stifled and sweated our way through the night, naked and damp, the hatch open but the door now shut for modesty. Rob and Sue must have been baked, not only was their cabin in the stern much smaller and almost devoid of hatches – only two small vents – but it was next to the engine which, despite the engine extractor fan, dumped a lot of its heat into it. They didn't complain but Rob emerged from his bunk and flung himself into the morning sea.

Aderyn Glas is a ten metre long Moody Eclipse and is described in the sales brochure as a luxury cruiser for two. She has a large heads and shower and an adequate fore-cabin. The saloon is large and the galley well fitted. But when anyone else is aboard privacy is impossible. We became sensitive to each others' need for space and tended to live outside in the cockpit so that anyone wanting to use the toilet, for example, could do so without everyone hearing what was going on. It was impossible not to hear the strokes of the toilet pump though, wherever we were on the boat, and after a while we all began to automatically count them. Rob, the doctor, announced in fascination one morning that he could now 'Poo on demand,' without having to wait for the urge.

'Olive oil.' I told him, thinking that maybe he could write a paper for The Lancet on the toilet habits of liveaboard yachtsmen.

And we'd had to change our diet again. Ann always likes an excuse to try different meals and the excuse arrives when anyone comes to stay. Sue is a vegetarian, so long as you don't mind reclassifying chicken as a vegetable, and so we were eating salads not salami, peppers not pepperoni, humus not ham.

We walked up over the dunes for exercise and to get a different view of our home bobbing in Cala Petra Ruja. We'd rowed ashore then Rob had kindly towed the dinghy back to *Aderyn Glas,* so that the kids on the beach couldn't do all those things that kids do to dinghies, then swum back to the beach. We walked dusty tracks for a mile or more up, over and down to Cala di Volpe, where the super-yachts were anchored, then flopped under a sunshade in a bar for a drink. The beach was littered with sunbeds and colourful beach umbrellas in organised rows, with duckboards running between and around them to prevent people burning their feet on the roasting sand. Children screamed and laughed and cried and ran and adults lounged and ate and talked and drank. The travel brochure sea played the background music as its waves broke onto the travel brochure sand.

Rob turned pink. None of us had thought of what the swim ashore had done to his sunscreen and now he was burning. By the time we retreated back on board Rob was rose. I looked at Sue who was white, at Ann who was golden, and down at my arms, which were brown. Sue told me my skin would wrinkle and sag, like all those Australians, and that I might get skin cancers. She was smiling as she said it - she's a cheerful kid.

Over dinner Rob told a doctor joke: 'An Englishman walked into a pharmacy in Olbia and asked if he could buy some Viagra. The pharmacist spoke a little English but didn't have the word for "dose" so he asked the man what *size* he wanted. After a moment's thought the man held out his hands in front of him about eight inches apart.'

Portisco, Sardinia, 1312 miles to Gouvia. Day 53

That evening we sailed down to anchor south of Portisco, in the green pea soup we'd anchored in five days before. Next morning it was beginning to blow from the west. I had a feeling about that wind and I wanted to get moving back to Olbia before it increased, but everyone was lethargic, not wanting to leave the beauty of the coast for the smuts of the city. But we needed to go and soon.

By the time everyone had done what they had to do the wind had freshened. Why did no-one else see what this meant? We pulled out the sails and headed towards Porto Rotundo, Sue taking us among the parked super-yachts, getting close for a better look.

It was supposed to be a force four, and here we go again. I took the wheel, the conditions needed experienced hands. By the time we reached Capo Figari the waves were high enough to force us out to sea looking for a smoother ride. We watched other yachts and motor cruisers smashing the wave caps into spray and realised that was what we must look like. We could hear the thuds as they hit a wave as clearly as we could hear the thuds *Aderyn Glas* made. Our speed was down to a crawl. I turned us towards Olbia and the worst of the wind.

In the distance Tavolara looked even more like the Lost World than last time we'd done this. The top of the three mile long island was shrouded in grey orographic cloud that spilled down the side like a perpetual waterfall, dissolving before it reached the sea.

We'd thought the wind strong last time we'd tried this. This time it was stronger. *Aderyn Glas* climbed up peaks and crashed into troughs and I began to realise that this was the worse sea I had been in. We've sailed *Aderyn Glas* around Land's End, across to Ireland, the Channel and all the way here from Port Napoleon, and we'd had some rough times, but this was the worst.

Below it was mayhem already. We'd put away all but a flag of sail, keeping only enough to help stabilise us, and we drove slowly forwards on the engine hitting each breaking wave as square as we could.

Ann passed around the lifejackets and strops.

We kept square to the waves because if we turned sideways to them they could roll us over.

I went below briefly and was flung against a bulkhead, cracking my head.

Sue was feeling ill and we sent her down to sit in the helmsman's chair, the most stable place to be.

Rob wanted to pull the sails out and go sailing.

A ferry hove into view directly on our path. I thought he would change his course slightly when he saw us struggling. He didn't. When I realised I was going to have to turn across the waves to avoid him, I wondered if I was going to be able to pull it off. But I'm good: spin the wheel on top of a wave and crab up the next one. Spin it back again and deal with the wake from the ferry.

The lighthouse in the distance didn't seem to get closer.

Rob went below to try and make himself seasick so he could experience it. He couldn't.

Someone off-stage threw a barrel of water over me. It had cleared the bow and the entire boat completely and descended on my head.

Ann laughed hysterically.

There were other boats around us but they were mostly heading in kinder directions. One with a scrap of sail, beating towards Tavolara, his mast rapidly carving arcs in the blue sky.

The noise was terrific. No-one spoke.

Rob wanted to fish.

Chapter 11

Olbia Marina, Sardinia, 1212 miles to Gouvia. Day 55

We said goodbye to Sue and Rob next morning, early. They were going back to the real world and we wouldn't see them again for months. The evening before they'd taken us for a meal and Rob had told us of his boyhood experiences sailing in all sorts of wild conditions with his father. His dad wouldn't go to sea, in the Menai Straights of all places, until the conditions were at least what we'd seen yesterday. And, no, he'd never been sick and would like to understand what it feels like so he could empathise with his patients.

'You don't die from it,' I repeated the old joke, 'however much you wish you could.' I was a past master at vomiting overboard, once retching so hard I burst a vessel in my nose and bled everywhere. The worst one though was on a passage around Land's End at night when I'd been throwing up in a bucket while steering with one hand. When Ann came on watch I put the bucket on the table and lay next to it, and a little below it, on the settee. Then a wave came...

But now they were gone and we had jobs to do: another oil change was due and another software update for the Engine Monitoring System (called EMS, not Rachel) - and wash the salt off everything too.

We waved at their aircraft as it whined overhead.

'Come on,' I said to a sad Ann, 'let's go and find a chandlery. Spending money always cheers us up.' But the only chandler was in town and taxis cost twenty Euros each way.

We stayed another day – to hell with the cost! – and caught up on the chores, cleaning, doing laundry, vacuuming and re-filling the aft cabin with the stores we'd moved to make room for our guests. We spoke with our letting agent at home who complained that a squirrel had drowned in our water bucket and the smell was putting potential tenants off, as if *we* could do something. 'Tell me again, what do we pay an agent for…'

We walked to the supermarket for the air-conditioning but sweated so much to get there and back that it probably wasn't worth it.

And we planned: Our next deadline was Cagliari, down south, where we were to meet number three daughter, Amanda, on 29th July. That gave us a leisurely thirteen days to get there. We fired up the chartplotter and stepped off the route with the ghostly dividers and found four stopping places: La Caletta, Arbatax - which sounded like a cattle disease - Porto Corallo and Villasimius.

The *Capitano* gave us a weather forecast and wished us well but the forecast showed a storm was due in Olbia in a few days. We needed to get some miles under us and be tucked in somewhere far away when it arrived. The Ligurian sea, between Corsica and the French mainland seemed to be getting a whole series of gales that continued right across Italy and into the Adriatic, and these were affecting Corsica and the northern tip of Sardinia. We had not known it at the time but our decision to leave France when we did had saved us a lot of trouble and time.

We set off next day on a calm sea with no wind and popped down to Olbia town because we needed a chandler and I wouldn't pay forty Euros for a return taxi trip to spend twenty Euros on a replacement oil extractor pump, a bottle of gas and a Sardinian courtesy flag. The chandler wished us good luck, and the guy on the quayside, who'd helped us moor, asked if we'd seen the weather forecast. 'A big wind comes. Very bad.' He said.

'For god's sake,' Ann would have stamped her foot but she knew how thin the deck was, 'this is supposed to be the Mediterranean, isn't it? That lovely blue clear *calm* sea where there is never anything more than a gentle sailing breeze in the summer. Just enough to move us around without having the damn donkey making smells and heat and noise, but we're either getting too much or nothing at all!' I couldn't tell if she was angry or near to tears. I agreed with her, but we had no options. We motored back through the bobbing seals and turned south.

Tavolara is a towering bulk of island that forms the south-eastern limit of Olbia Bay. Only when you pass close under its western cliffs and see the toy yachts in its lee do you get a feel for its scale, nearly 600m high and flat on top which is probably how it got its name – *Tavolo* being Italian for table. A spit of sand juts far out into the narrow channel, between the island and the mainland, which makes it very shallow a long way out from the shore. On the mainland side the rusting wreck of a ship bares its ribs to the sky.

Tavolara, clear of cloud today, was on our left as Rachel led us safely through the passage. On our right were several small beaches and holiday towns and yachts in bays. To and fro, across our path, little ferries ran from the mainland to the island's small harbour and other yachts and cruisers, large and small, travelled the same path as us in our direction or the opposite one. We dodged wakes again - it's not a quiet stretch of water.

We passed between Isola Molara and Capo Coda Cavallo, where the bays and beaches were teeming with boats and holiday makers and the turquoise waters clashed with the garish beach umbrellas. Two hours after we'd left Olbia we passed out into the wide open Tyrrhenian Sea and immediately felt the difference in rhythm as the swell rolled under us.

La Caletta, Sardinia, 1186 miles to Gouvia. Day 57

La Caletta was developed into a marina from a fishing harbour and is another marina that gives the impression of dusty concrete. Like so many others it hides behind a high stone and concrete seawall. Opposite the entrance is a long concrete hammerhead and the marina pontoons lie parallel with it, spaced along a central spine. The small town hides behind buildings on the far side of the original harbour. It consists of one main street and a scattering of holiday homes and apartments. The main road runs through it and out along the coast and back into the distant hills. A small flattened rocky outcrop, over a road at the back of the marina serves as the beach. No sand, nothing more than a place to sit and fish or sunbath. The rough rock surfaces and jagged edges are unkind to bare feet and swimmers are few. There was a background noise of sea and people and a few vehicles but mainly it was quiet.

Our radio calls resulted in a young man turning up on the far side of the concrete hammerhead and waving his arms around until we took notice and nosed our way in. We were getting good at all this delicate manoeuvring by now. He passed us two stern lines and insisted we used them both, one either side. We knew what this meant too – this meant the marina was not going to be a quiet, calm haven!

Between berthing boats the *Capitano* and his mate were installing water and power on the quay, so we had neither at hand. But we always travel with a great long length of hose and an even greater, longer length of cable, so we hiked off with both and sorted ourselves out. 'It's always good to have a long extension.' I smiled disarmingly, but I'm not sure Ann understood.

Next day we finished the oil change and Ann was preoccupied and sad, she was missing the first birthday of her first grandchild, and her Christening.

The storm caught up with us in the middle of the night. We were asleep when the bow crashed into the quayside and shook the boat and shook us awake with a jolt. We rolled out of bed to a screaming wind, grabbed shorts and hauled ourselves into the cockpit. We became hunched black shapes like all the other hunched black shapes on all the other boats who were straining to tighten the sternlines, throwing loops over the sheet winches and hauling the mooring lines tight. Our dinghy leapt around trying to get inside the cockpit, blown bodily upwards on its davits. The plank crashed noisily around on the bow and I crawled forward to secure it and slacken the bow lines so that the boat could move away from the quay and gain a bit more space to move. With a shock I found the quayside covered in bodies, dark hunched shapes against the lights of the town, sitting on small seats and casting their fishing lines into the spaces between the boats, ignoring the storm. At the bottom of our plank an old man and his wife stared at me, not understanding – as if we were aliens that had descended on their town. I stared back at them, shivering a little at the thought that while we slept this couple were only a few feet away. I had to move them so that I could tie the plank up and fasten an extra bow line, they stared at me the whole time, standing, waiting until I'd finished then settling back onto their seats.

But there were things to be done. The guy in the boat next door swapped springs with us, lashing our boats together and pulling hard on the winches to stabilise us both and prevent some of the rubbing between our hulls. We took the bimini and sunshades down, mindful of Elba, and lashed on all the kit that hangs on the rails. And all the time the wind screamed and the whole harbour was in turmoil. At the bow, sitting on folding chairs on the quayside, the fishermen fished on, the little LEDs on their floats waving in the water. It was one in the morning.

And at three, and at four, we were up again checking, winching, tightening knots. The wind was ferocious, hurling itself down the valley and through the town ripping away at everything in its path. Frapping, crashing, shrieking. It was a black, hard night.

And a long, hot day next day despite the continuing wind. The peak temperature touched thirty-seven degrees while we were there, the concrete, the roads, the pontoon surfaces too hot to walk far on: the heat burning through the soles of our sandals. Ann went shopping but I couldn't face the heat and went to hide beneath the sunshades that covered *Aderyn Glas* again. It was impossible to think, impossible to do anything.

In the evening we walked to the rocky beach on the far side of the *ufficio* and envied the local families who had camped under the trees above the shore. The grass was scrubby and the children played on it, the trees gave good shade and the family, from great-granny to the smallest baby, sat in the open air in the shade of a tree with tables, chairs, food and wine. The kids laughed and shouted, the adults murmured and joked. Mostly the adults were fully clothed – the older ladies often in black - mostly the children were in swimming gear.

About six-thirty we wandered the paths through the grass behind the beach, visited the ancient Spanish tower – *Torre San Giovanni* - and walked a little way, killing time until the restaurant opened. We walked back a different route, passed the tiny whitewashed chapel of San Giovanni with its proud single bell above the door and a packed service in progress inside. We strolled carelessly, hand in hand across the paved area along the side of the church in front of a

• throng of old people sitting in the shade on a seat outside, and as we did so they all began singing a hymn and fingering their rosary beads. We hadn't realised that the congregation had overflowed and that suddenly, and embarrassingly, we were immersed in an outdoor religious service.

In the restaurant we ate well and so did the mosquitoes. That evening my ankles were bloated and red and covered in Bonjela. Dessert for me was an anti-histamine pill washed down with a glass of white while sleep - in the heat with the unbearable itching - was a thing to dream of.

The tripper boats started early in the morning and drove passed the quayside so close that we were an object of interest for deckloads of passengers as we ate breakfast in the cockpit.

'... and, *Signore*, on your left you see the seasonal flock of migrating lesser liveaboards who stay here briefly to feed on their flight to Greece. They are known to scare fish away by running around their decks in the dark, partly dressed, and to upset old ladies singing hymns outside their chapels...' Their captains were merciless in their retribution and rolled us all around with their wakes, careless of the speed they were notching up.

We were waiting again for the weather. Waiting for a forecast we could live with, and waiting where it was relatively cheap (For *Aderyn Glas* in the summer season it cost forty-eight Euros, Ann discovered it was one tenth that price in winter).

'Welsh boat off my bow in position south of Punta Nera, whose name I can't pronounce, this is Silver Spray, do you read me?' The VHF sprang into life and made us jump. We'd been passing fifty metres from a big Fisher south of Punta Nera when it had turned sharply towards us so we had slowed down to see whether they were pirates and had wanted to board us when the radio call came.

Silver Spray, Michael and Linda's boat. We'd met them in Macinaggio all that time ago and since then they'd half circumnavigated Sardinia and were on their way back to the west and their home port near Alghero. But we were ships passing in the sunlight and we couldn't talk much – just swapping "have you been to…" – and it was illegal anyway to use the radio for non-safety traffic in Italy, but they briefed us on our next few ports as they sailed away.

We were travelling over one of the deep offshore canyons that are close to the shore on the eastern side of Sardinia, over a thousand metres deep. Ann was driving and we were both scanning the water for signs of life: maybe whales in such a deep hole.

'How can we travel so far and see so little life?' Ann asked. 'We've travelled about seven hundred miles and we've seen, what? A turtle, a few dolphin (we saw more in Cardigan), very few fish … so I think we are due a whale.'

It's true we were surprised at how empty of life the Med seemed to be. I looked over the bow and willed a whale to appear for her, but it didn't, only a column of smoke, ascending into the sky from a fire in the hills beyond Arbatax, and blowing into a hammerhead in our direction. It was being bombed by a couple of circling yellow flying boats that scooped up water without stopping. This was the time for the scrub fires which made the international news. We followed the smoke all the way passed the small rocky islands and across the bay to the marina.

Arbatax, Sardinia, 1143 miles to Gouvia. Day 61

Arbatax is below latitude thirty-nine north, we'd crossed a line! It has a harbour, a beach, an anchorage, a huge yard, where they build massive oil rigs and a significant police presence. The *Policia Costeria* stop anyone anchoring inside three hundred metres of the shore, which is the law, and on the fishing quay and in the empty old harbour. This effectively means you must spend the night in the marina. Anyone not doing what they want is liable to have their boat impounded and have to take out a mortgage to pay the fine. So we skipped passed the anchorage, ignored the fishing quay and hovered until the red tee-shirt uniformed staff on the pontoon were ready for us.

'Have you noticed,' Ann said, 'if you look to the left Arbatax is a small, friendly fishing village with a few bits of holiday-making tagged on – a small hotel, a bar or two, the Red Rock Café soon to be opened? But if you look to the right you get an industrial port complete with an oil rig, tall cranes, dusty and not tourist friendly at all?'

'We should put an eye-patch on our right eye.' I suggested, but Ann thought I was being daft and told me so with her expression. I liked Arbatax. The marina was clean and modern and not expensive and the village was interesting.

We met Bob who was from Nottingham and was on the staff though he had started out to do what we were doing, taking his boat to Greece with his wife. They'd got as far as Arbatax, called in for a spare part, and decided to stay one winter because the rates were cheap. That was seven years ago and now he was employed by the marina and lived in a house. Lanky and fifty-odd he smiled and smoked.

I asked him why Italians never give a welcoming smile to strangers. In every country we'd travelled though in Europe, and in America and Korea and Australia, New Zealand, Hong Kong and Singapore, people smiled welcoming smiles at strangers. Not in Italy.

'They're all mad.' He said, 'They just don't do it. It's probably a Mafia thing.' He added enigmatically. 'Look at the way they do their pricing: bookings in this marina and every other marina are way down this year because of the economic crisis, so what to they do?' he answered his own question: 'They put prices up!'

But it was cheap in Arbatax and full of Italians running around the pontoons or riding bikes and motor scooters along them, negotiating and fighting over water pipes and electrical sockets and sometimes simply stealing them. We were okay, we had our own supply right in front of the boat, and when I tried it, it didn't work.

'I'll get it fixed for you.' Said Bob, and he did.

We'd carried our used engine oil from La Caletta because they had nowhere to empty it and now was the time for it to go. With a big beaming smile I opened negotiations with the two girls in the office, the Italian was beautiful with dark curly hair, lithe and slim, twenty something, but her English wasn't so good and she wouldn't smile.

The German, Elisabeth, was younger, pretty, and was hitch-hiking around the world, efficient and fluent in colloquial English she grinned a white grin. She translated my request to the Italian who squawked into a radio. It squawked back.

'You have to wait here,' said Elisabeth with a hint of accent, 'she has called the manager.' I began to feel a little uneasy. In every other country you just have to pour your oil into a container provided for the purpose.

'I can pour the oil away,' I offered, 'no need for the manager.'

'Stay here please,' my translator said, 'it is not so easy you know. It must all be tested and logged.' I was beginning to feel like a schoolboy in the headmaster's study.

'Maybe I can keep it until the next port,' I suggested, 'it's not so important, really.'

'Please wait. The manager will not be long. It has to be measured and logged and tested for water content.' This was going beyond the bounds of belief.

'I'm only trying to get rid of my used oil, it doesn't have to be difficult.'

'She says it is not possible to just pour it away, they will be fined if there is any water in it and it breaks the furnace.' Elisabeth was embarrassed but her Italian colleague was now deeply frowning. We waited, toe tapping and finger fumbling.

The manager arrived and spoke in rapid Italian to the girls. The Italian girl answered and he looked at me as if I was the cause of all the world's problems and more beside. Elisabeth repeated: 'It must be weighed and tested for water. How much is there?'

I held the oily, black plastic container aloft so they could all see. The manager made to take it from me but I pulled it back. 'It's very oily,' I said, 'you'll get dirty.' He was in his best uniform tee-shirt and slacks, his hair combed back and shades in place. The creases in his tanned face were all perfectly positioned and he hadn't upset them by smiling and wasn't going to any time soon. He drew back when Elisabeth had finished her translation, and said a few words in Italian.

'You are to follow him,' she said, 'and you must be sure there can be no water in the container.'

By this time I was completely cowed, like I remember being so many times in so many interviews with headmasters who would stare and utter menacingly: 'You, boy, *you* know what you've done...' and even the innocent would have lied about anything.

'No,' I said, 'there can be no water. This container only had oil.' I felt so guilty under three stares.

The manager abruptly turned and walked off and the Elisabeth signalled for me to follow. By hurrying I caught up with him as he was striding towards the gate. He was slimmer and taller than me and looked down at me.

'*No es facile?*' I grinned in my best Italian that owed a lot to Spanish. He scowled down at me and I wondered if this man had even developed the muscles needed to smile.

'*Facile!*' he said pronouncing it "*far-chee-lay*", which wasn't how the Spanish said the word for "easy". For emphasis he said it again, three times. I was the backward schoolboy trotting along behind the head and destined for further punishment, the poor fool who had all his sums wrong and was wondering what could possibly happen next. I want my mum...

'Here.' He indicated a big oil storage container. I looked at him puzzled but he walked off leaving me to figure it out myself. What about measuring? What about water content? I looked around and sneakily poured the oil into the opening in the top, scared that any moment I was going to be shouted at or kept in detention. I slunk away when the can was empty, depositing it in the recycle container after wiping my prints off it.

'But there *was* no water in it.' Ann said, 'there *couldn't be* any water in it. Oil came out of it last time, and used oil went into it this time.'

'You weren't there,' I said with feeling.

'They're all mad,' Bob repeated when he stopped by for a drink, 'but it's true they get fined.' He told us where the supermarket was and the best restaurants and the way to the *Rocce Rosse* – the red rocks. 'And have you found the little train yet?' he asked.

And so later we found ourselves in the station building, at the junction of the sea and the quay, which also serves as the tourist office, learning about a train journey into the hills to see a little of the culture and sample an authentic Sardinian lunch. We bought tickets for Thursday.

Arbatax is really a single street with pastel coloured homes climbing up the hillside on the south of the village. On the street are the usual collection of shops and bars and a chandlery and a mini-market. I'd grown accustomed to drinking ice tea by the carton, flavoured with peach or lemon, and this place had neither. Rob had said it was one of the most thirst-quenching drinks he'd tried and told me why, but the chemistry was beyond me. I drank it in quantities that was probably bad for me and now I had to wean off it. So we went to the chandlery and spent money as compensation.

Next day we swam off the Rocce Rosse and I had the fright of my life when a black shape the size of a small dog shot passed me in the water. Its speed was tremendous and I had no time to move or even protect myself. *Shark* my brain screamed, I'd seen Jaws three times! Luckily it had no interest in me at all. It was a cormorant fishing!

The area was very popular and was draped with families despite there being no beach, only large uneven slabs of red and grey rock. There is an almost perfectly square hole running through a tall, pointed, red outcrop and everyone felt the need to clamber up to it and walk through to see what was on the other side. On the other side were people peering at the opening from another outcrop to see what was on the other side, which was us. Boys and girls leapt into the emerald green pool formed between the outcrops. It was all very picturesque.

We ate lunch in a café and spent the afternoon on board. In the evening Ann began to complain of stomach ache, and by midnight she was throwing up forcibly. She spent most of her night being sick every hour on the hour, lying in the saloon with her arms around a bucket. I nobly rose each time she was ill to mop her brow and empty it.

So Wednesday passed in a tired daze for Ann and all we did was go swimming again in the afternoon. Thursday we were up at some silly hour and staggered, half awake to catch the little green train, the *Trenino Verde*.

A small, blue, smouldering diesel and four rickety looking coaches seemed just about balanced on the narrow-gauge track. The seats were hard and the backs moved either way and the open windows provided the only air-conditioning. There were few foreigners: a middle-aged German couple who seemed to be in love and oblivious to the rest of us – or anything else really – and a group from the marina who got on a different coach to us. The rest were all Italian happy holidayers on a day out.

After smouldering for the right amount of time the engine groaned into motion and cracked and banged its way around the first curve, the coaches teetering frighteningly. Then it gathered speed.

'Not like the TGV.' Ann said. We were fans of the French high speed train.

We settled down and started to enjoy the experience and the scenery. The track wound up into the mountains around cliff-hanging curves and climbing turns. Through tunnels that filled with diesel fumes, and across viaducts that flew over deep chasms lined with cliffs. At each small station people got on until all the seats were taken. We sat opposite a small Italian boy and his dad who ignored us completely but smiled at each other and chatted happily.

Far away and far below we could catch glimpses of the coast and the sprawl of a toy Arbatax. The sea glinted like a mirror, flickering through trackside vegetation that was lush and green, totally different to the parched scrubby grasses and brush that we were used to seeing along the coast. The air tasted clean.

After three numbing hours we arrived at Seui, which we could not pronounce even after coaching. Only a few of us got off and milled around, stretching aching muscles, flexing stiff joints and wondering what to do. The rest of the passengers carried on in bone jolting, bum-numbing fashion for even more remote places, perhaps all the way to Mandas, where the line ended, almost exactly halfway between east and west coasts. Seui station was all but deserted, only the railway station shop – sometime tourist centre – at the end of the platform had any sign of life.

'You're not *Welsh* are you?' It was said with such a sneer that I couldn't allow myself to speak, if he was trying for humour, he missed. I walked away. Ann was more tolerant, although no more amused. He was with the party from the marina and we were going to spend the day with him. Oh joy! Isn't fate such a joke sometimes? A snob, portly, bald about forty, he smelled of cigarettes and dressed expensively. His second sentence told us he lived in Monte Carlo with his wife, who was a Monegasque of course, and his daughter and here is my wife and my daughter and her friend and our friends who are Monegasques and we have *such* a wonderful life in Monaco…

I was saved from committing murder in the name of our Prince by the arrival of the guide, a wizened, small, skin-and-bone man who could and did smile at us all but spoke only Italian. Since we were to tour the local museums, the town hall and the prison, this was going to be difficult.

Our guide limped away down the station road and we all followed him. It was hot. It's not that I kept expecting places to be cool, but everywhere we went seemed to be hotter than the last place. In Arbatax the temperature was around thirty-three but here in the hills, well above sea level where you might expect it to be cooler, it was hotter again, and airless.

The museum though was cooler, the receptionist collected everyone's water bottles in case we discovered a passion for washing the exhibits. Then our guide lined us all up and delivered his welcome speech. The wife of the friend of Lord Monaco translated into French and Lord Monaco condescended to translate the French into English for us. I hated that we had to rely on him, but my French was not good enough to dismiss his help.

His wife was expensively beautiful and untouchable, like a Lamborghini, and could be relied on to stick unswervingly to the true path should the road ahead ever get slippery. But the two teenage girls were friendly. They wanted to know a bit about Wales, how it was governed, why the prince didn't live there, did we have a coastline and where was it exactly? Some of this we did in French but more of it in English. We told them of the misty Black Mountains and the glittering bays of the Gower, the wild Cader Idris and the deep, black lakes. 'They have a lot of sheep.' said father dismissively. But we liked the kids who seemed to be able to ignore this unimaginative man.

The museum was about mining and echoed some we have in Wales, the history of children forced to work at an early age, the brutal toil of the miners, the poverty and ultimately, the closure of the mines and consequent exodus. In the cellar was a wine press and a display that chronicled the development of the local wine industry since the Romans. We hadn't noticed there was one until then.

Lunch was also brutal. We sat on a table for two in a restaurant above a bar in a side-street. The Monegasques had a table to themselves for which I will ever be grateful. There were a few other diners scattered around a few other tables, but on the whole it was pretty rustic. We were served by a lady of about our age who was unable to smile

We ate: bread, olives, liver, mushrooms, cheese, Proschiutto and melon, and zucchini, and we drank copious wine. That was the first course. A little later the second course was suckling pig, stewed sheep, sausages, crudités, potato-filled Sardinian ravioli… and so it went on. After a while we prayed it would end, our stomachs had expanded to the painful limit and we'd discovered, by experiment, that the wine didn't stop coming when the carafe was empty. Fruit, Sardinian sweets, biscuits, coffee and liqueur finished us. We left, painfully delighted, really pleased with the experience and a bit over-animated but we got our waitress to smile.

Lunch had taken two hours then our guide returned and took us to look at the paintings in the town hall. Someone had stolen the money the EU had given the town to build a small gallery for its art, and so the paintings had to be housed in a far from perfect environment on the walls of the *Palazzo Pubblico*. He had a key to open it for us and locked up behind us. I wondered if someone had stolen the town counsellors too.

The Monegasques went in search of a cool pub but Ann and I wanted a slow stroll through any shady street we could find back towards the station. We were about half an hour early for the train and thought we could wait in the waiting room, but of course it was locked and we had to wait under the shade of a tree. Shortly before the train was due our guide turned up and unlocked the station doors and the door to the ice-cream shop. Then he pulled some levers and changed some points and signals. The stationmaster arrived from somewhere, portly and old enough to retire, but smart in his uniform, and the guide went to serve ice-cream.

We waited in the waiting room with the Monegasques, chatting again to the two girls who were far more interesting, and interested, than their parents. And we waited and waited and ate ice-cream because we were hot even though it made us feel even more bloated. And when the train came we felt a rush of relief until everyone on it got off, made a scrum at the shop then sat on the tracks eating ice-cream. We sat on the train, hot and puzzled, and waited.

After a while it became clear that we were not going anywhere and that everyone else on the train knew what was happening and we didn't. A middle aged Italian woman with two grizzling kids started raising her voice to the stationmaster who was happily chatting to the driver and guard, and we began to recognise enough words to get the gist: another train was occupying the single track to Arbatax and it had broken down. Until it was repaired we could not move. The stationmaster showed the woman with his hands what happens when two opposing trains meet on a single track.

After an hour a phone rang and suddenly everything was in motion. The stationmaster animatedly waved people off the tracks and into the coaches, kids ran, adults hurried, everyone trying to recover their seats and us jammed against the windows by overweight Italians. The driver hurried to his cab and we left, accelerating away down the incline at a speed which seemed more than the train could endure and finally a breeze blew through the heated coach. The train rocked and rattled and scraped its way downhill, flinging itself into tight bends that had us all quiet with the expectancy of a short future. Passed shacks with rocks on their roofs to hold the slates against the wind, passed bent trees, rocking over viaducts with tiny trees so far below. We crossed viaducts where only the noise of the train told us we were not falling.

Silence, then little shrieks in unison from us all as the coach rolled, then silence again and wide eyes and clenched hands as the train clattered alarmingly, high in the sky or clinging to a cliff-face. Still we rocketed downhill swaying violently, knees pressed together, hands clutching each other, the scream of the brakes or the tyres on the tight bends followed by another roar of acceleration as the driver took the brakes off.

And slammed the brakes on, as we approached another viaduct. He leaned on the horn and we all crowded to look out of the window as we slowed. A family was walking carelessly down the track using the viaduct as a bridge.

We arrived back thirty minutes late, we'd left an hour late. 'I wish *Aderyn Glas* could make up time like that.' Ann said, hanging on my arm and shaking a little. 'Let's stay here.'

'Time to go,' I said.

Dominik and Sophie were sailing around the world, they'd started three months ago and had crossed from Italy to Sardinia where Sophie had hurt her shoulder. We'd met them briefly in Olbia, the day the floating palace was refuelled, and Sophie still had her arm in a sling. Dominik told us she'd fallen as the boat lurched and it was taking forever to heal. We'd invited them for a drink in our cockpit.

We'd taken them for a young couple on a holiday and, as is too often true, had started mildly boasting about our brave plan to sail to Greece and how clever we'd been to cross France on the canals when Dominik calmly mentioned that they had both given up their jobs for a year to sail around the world. Dominik was short and wiry, dark haired and bristle chinned, about thirty and gave the impression that he would be capable of hauling himself out of any trouble with sheer muscle power. He was tanned, lived in a single pair of shorts, and was polite. They lived in Holzkirchen, near Munich, which is one of those coincidences that make me suspect that maybe there is some joker watching all this on celestial television and that we're all actors playing out a script. Of all the places Dominik could have lived he happened to come from the same tiny town as a friend of ours.

Sophie was blond and lovely, tall as Dominik and his equal in every obvious way. She didn't drink alcohol and didn't eat meat. They were careful with their funds and had tried to moor against the fisherman's quay but the police had turned up and moved them, so they'd had to pay for a marina place.

'Africa,' he said, 'when we leave Sardinia we're going to cross to Africa and move along the coast to Gibraltar, then the Canaries and Cape Verde islands. And we have to do this to a plan or we will miss the winds.'

We told him the British foreign office was issuing warnings to UK citizens recommending they don't go to Algeria, it seemed there was some new unrest there.

They hadn't had much experience, this was their third month aboard. There was nowhere to sail near Munich and they'd virtually picked up their boat in Italy and sailed it to Sardinia and that's how their odyssey began. I looked over to their yacht, she was longer and thinner than *Aderyn Glas* and festooned with all sorts of equipment, obviously more capable of crossing oceans than our mobile glasshouse. Dominik was particularly proud of all his electronics and solar panels though he didn't have a homebuilt computerised Engine Monitoring System.

Her fenders were hung horizontally and neatly along the sides. 'We're going to do that,' Ann said, 'we bought some hooks yesterday.'

'Make sure they are all parallel with the water,' said Dominik without a hint of humour, 'I'll check.'

Later Ann said how brave they must be to give up everything and sail around the world and wondered if they would write a book.

Chapter 12

Porto Corallo, Sardinia, 1111 miles to Gouvia. Day 66

I stood naked except for a towel in the *Capitano's* office and dripped on the floor. The office was a Portakabin and the *Capitano* was a prim, middle-aged woman who sat with her young secretary on the far side of a desk. She was having a conversation with someone who seemed keen to buy a berth for a year. The air-conditioning was turned to maximum and the cold was biting at my wet skin. They all seemed happy to ignore me. I felt bits of me shrivelling in the cold.

We had travelled down the coast from Arbatax into a southerly force five that was forecast as a northerly, and a pitching sea to go with it. We were supposed to have had a pleasant sailing day with the wind behind us and instead we'd ploughed into a swell for six hours to reach Porto Corallo, thirty-five miles south of Arbatax. The wind was a *Scirocco*, the hot southerly wind from the desert of Africa which brought enough dust with it to turn the horizon smoky rose.

We had crashed and rattled into Porto Corallo with the wind behind us and, with the help of some incompetent guy in the *Capitano's* RIB who couldn't understand that I'd tossed him my sternrope because I needed him to hold me off the pontoon, we had crashed and rattled into the pontoon and we were both angry. 'Uninformed uniformed idiots in RIBs.' I muttered but only Ann would be able to hear.

It was the hottest day we'd seen: thirty-seven centigrade and we were hot and sweaty and wanted a civilised shower. The toilets and showers were Portakabins. Ann slipped into the ladies and the blokes' was next door. There were two German guys already in there soaping up for a shave and I stripped and jumped into the shower. The water was cold but I persevered. Then the flow started to wane a little and I fumbled with the valve and it dried to a dribble. Then it stopped. By then I'd covered myself in soap from hair to toenails.

'I think,' said one of the Germans, who was standing over the sink, stripped to the waist and watching me in the mirror, 'that your need is greater than ours,' and the two of them laughed. I grabbed my towel and headed for the office as Ann in her towel stuck a soapy head out of the ladies'.

'There's no water.' she said unnecessarily.

And so I came to be standing naked, except for a towel, covered in soap from head to toe, in the office of the lady *Capitano* and dripping on her floor. She squawked at a radio and the radio squawked at her. After a while a man came and turned on the a valve. It was the same man who'd let us crash into the pontoon.

'Did he hear you call him an idiot?' Ann whispered later.

In the early evening the wind changed to northerly and the temperature climbed again as it blew the heat from the land down onto us.

Porto Corallo sticks out into the sea remote from anywhere. It has no town, no village, only a huge campsite and a touristy restaurant for the hapless campers on the other side of the main coast road. It was fine for a stopover but there was no reason to stay there. Mostly home to little local speedboats and some trawlers it was mainly empty when we passed through. There is a large concrete hard with a crane and a yard so it might be a cheap winter berth, but we didn't care, we were going to Greece. Actually there is a village: Villaputzu but it's a few miles inland so we didn't bother, for us it was onwards to Cagliari and a rendezvous with daughter number three.

The next day was calm again and we motored. We were beginning to realise that good sailing days were extremely rare and that the normal weather pattern was either too much wind or too little. The route was down passed Capo Ferrato, inside Isola Serpentara, where the dolphin are supposed to play, and around the south eastern tip of Sardinia: Capo Carbonara. A nature reserve covers the whole of the cape area, as far north as Serpentara, but it didn't seem to stop people anchoring in crowded bays. And who can blame them: the water was pure and clear, and I had the overwhelming feeling that I could scoop it up like molten turquoise and trickle it heavy through my fingers and that if I bathed in it I would live forever. It sparkled, invited, seduced, but we motored on by, regretful.

There were no dolphin near Serpentara, nor anywhere else for that matter, there were no capricious winds fluking across the flat isthmus at Carbonara, nor were there any overfalls off the headland. From the east we could see across to the masts in the marina but it took another couple of hours to get around to them.

The guides listed Villasimius as one of the more expensive marinas so we aimed for the centre of the bay and chucked the anchor out. We anchored just outside the line of buoys marking the limit of the swimming area off the beach and worried whether we were far enough out. We'd been frightened by the stories of the *Policia Costeria*, the three hundred metre limit, and the excessive fines. Nor were we being neurotic, across the bay a police launch was tied alongside a yacht that had anchored too close to a small promontory.

Villasimius anchorage, Sardinia, 1085 miles to Gouvia. Day 67

I went for a cooling swim in the glorious molten turquoise, heading for a rock about a hundred metres inside the line of buoys. When I got there I paddled around to the far side and lay quietly on the surface of the water, breathing through the snorkel, getting my breath back. Ten seconds after I'd stopped moving I was surrounded by fish. Big fish, little fish, striped fish, coloured fish, long thin fish and short stubby fish, pretty fish and ugly fish. They circled, mainly in shoals, some clockwise around me and some the other way, in concentric, rotating walls of fish. I took a breath and dived head first and they took fright and shot outwards. I surfaced and stayed still and they returned. I moved slowly, as if there was a current, and they moved with me still swimming slowly around me. This was the magic we'd come for. There was, after all, still some life in the sea.

Ann said she was too tired to swim two hundred metres but this experience was too good for me to let her miss, so I nobly rowed her across to the rock in the dinghy. She had been a SCUBA diver in her time so rolling backwards off the dinghy and snorkelling wasn't a challenge.

The fish came back and surrounded us again with moving walls, we could see no further than a couple of metres for fish. They swam without any effort, hundreds of fish looking at us with hundreds of eyes. Patterns of refracted sunlight danced off striped and coloured scales as they moved.

Half an hour later we were getting cold and it was time to return. There is also only so much excitement you can get from watching fish swim passed and it was getting towards that time when a glass of white held more interest than anything else. Ann might be a certified diver capable of exceptional back rolls from dinghies but she suddenly discovered that she couldn't climb back into them. After struggling for a bit, and with me threatening to leave her behind, we settled on the idea that I would tow her the hundred metres back to *Aderyn Glas*. This I will never do again: I have learned how hard it is to tow a submerged, unstreamlined body through the water by rowing a rubber dinghy, and I couldn't help noticing the difference between the slim teardrop shapes of the fish, and Ann - but I know when not to say anything.

There was, thankfully, only a gentle swell, the anchorage is not well sheltered from the south through to south-west but *Aderyn Glas* always turns beam-on to any swell however weak, and starts rolling. It's one of her less endearing traits. So, for the first time ever, I took the stern anchor for a ride in the dinghy and dropped it in to hold her nose to the waves. Ann took up the tension on board *Aderyn Glas* and promptly pulled it out. We tried again in a different spot, hoping for a patch of softer sand that would let it bite. I dropped it in and Ann pulled it out. We needed extreme measures so next time I followed it to the seabed and dug it into the sand myself. Ann pulled it out. We took the silly little folding anchor to bits and never used it again.

I bolted our ten kilogram Delta to the chain and took it for a ride in the dinghy. I threw it in and Ann pulled it out. We gave up. This sand obviously had no intention of letting us anchor. We'd had a little trouble with the bow anchor when we arrived but put out so much chain and the chum weights that we'd stopped worrying about it.

I'd climbed back aboard and we were sitting pondering what to do next when I realised that we weren't rolling. The anchor was on the bottom, right under the stern, waiting for me to recover enough strength to haul it aboard again and holding our bow into the swell. 'Is that all we need?' Ann asked, a little doubtful, 'A little bit of friction? We just need the anchor to drag itself around on the bottom and that's enough to stop us swinging?'

'Pour the wine.' I said, 'That last coin you tossed to Poseidon must have really pleased him. How much was it?'

Through our wine glasses we watched the sun change the sea from molten turquoise to liquid gold. By sunset there were half a dozen other boats in the anchorage, all well spaced out and all seemingly deserted. Most were at right angles to us and rolling in the swell. We wound down the day, relaxing for the first time in a long time and watching the slow descent until the sea ate the sun.

'We're going to have an energy-saving day.' Ann greeted me next morning.

'Great,' I said predictably, 'I'm going to save energy and stay in bed. Or do you mean I have to get up and change all the lightbulbs for LED ones?'

'Neither,' Ann giggled a girly blonde giggle and smiled with three hundred pearly-white teeth. Then I woke up.

'We can sail today,' said Ann, opening one eye and somehow conveying the fact that it was my turn to make tea, again, 'and save a bit of fuel.'

I used to think this was some magical gift Ann had, this ability to tell which direction the wind was blowing before she'd even got out of bed, then one day I realised that from her side of the bunk she could see the wind indicator on top of the mast.

It was true, the wind was from the south so once we were clear of the bay we hauled out both sails and used free energy to take us to Cagliari. With a boat speed of no better than four knots and less for most of the time, it took forever.

The first thing you see when you approach Cagliari is the small conical hill and the cliffs called *Sella del Diavolo* (the Devil's Saddle) and it's not until you clear this that the whole wide industrial agglomeration that is Cagliari comes into view. It's not a pretty sight. The Marina di Sant' Elmo is new and is squeezed between the older Marina del Sole and the rusting hulls of a tug and a floating dock. To get to the marina you have to motor right through the port until you are at the extremity of the eastern mole and can go no further. Both the marinas are here and to get to Sant' Elmo means crossing the realm of Marina del Sole and we were accosted by a man in a RIB trying to hijack his neighbour's trade.

We'd already booked, in a city we felt we needed to, so waved the RIB away and squeezed into the corner.

Cagliari, Sardinia, 1065 miles to Gouvia. Day 68

'It's very muddy,' I'd forgotten to put gloves on again and was hauling the sternlines the *Capitano* had given me with bare hands. They were fat ropes and liquid mud squeezed out of them as I handled them. They were also covered in some sharp little shells and had the occasional fishhook stuck out of the roving. I was stupid, I should have worn gloves and to prove it I bled all over the boat from a host of small scratches.

The *Capitano* was good though, in his bright white uniform tee-shirt and shorts, and his cigarette, and fixed us up to the electricity. The office staff took our money and gave us a key to the gate, this was the first marina with security that we'd been in since we left Port Napoleon, at the start of our odyssey.

We were berthed right on the seaward end of a pontoon, the first boat any wash would hit, and the view was a rusting hulk or a concrete mole and the smell was of old mud drying in the heat. The city was over a mile away and a motorway roared by with dust and noise half a mile inland. There wasn't anything to recommend this area at all. But that was it: no choices, no options, apart from leaving which we couldn't do until Amanda arrived.

We wandered up towards the town later, to have a look around. But by the time we'd walked the mile along the hot road and found our way to the port, where the bars and restaurants are, all we wanted to do was have drink and recover under the shade of the loggias.

Next day we went early to the supermarket the *Capitano* had told us about to try and beat the heat, but by the time we'd lugged our faithful sack truck to the shop door we were already wet with the sweat of it; when we went inside the air-conditioning made wet shirts cling icily to our skin.

Ann managed to break the vegetable scales then had a deep meaningful conversation with an ancient, scruffy, Italian guy over the broken machine during which she promised to marry him and have his babies but thankfully neither of them knew what the other was saying so the status quo wasn't threatened much.

On the way back, laden with trucks and backpacks full of supplies, we ran into Dominik and Sophie who had snuck into the port and tied up on the free quay. Sophie greeted Ann like a long lost sister, with kisses on both cheeks, and I shook hands politely. All Italian ports are obliged to provide free overnight mooring for twenty-four hours and Dominik was trying to push this into a free, week long, stay.

'If it will not work,' he said, his English a little strange, 'we will come to your marina.' But he must have got away with it because we didn't see them again. No drinks, no time for coffee, just kisses on the cheeks and another goodbye.

'I'm *so* impressed with them.' Ann reiterated but I wondered if she would feel the same if it was our kids heading off across an ocean.

The boat moored next to us was a twenty-six foot sailing yacht with a crew of three, a girl and two blokes, all about the same age as our kids. They were going to Sicily next day. Two or maybe three nights at sea in a tiny boat, were they brave or foolish, or was I simply not daring enough? Would they have signed up with Dominik while I stayed in bed? Do we lose a degree of courage as we get older? Or is it that realisation of our mortality that comes with the accumulation of bad experiences: watching people die for example, and discovering how easy it is and how a simple small error can kill you? Like the friend who pulled the stick back too hard when he was taking off in a glider and spun into the ground in front of me: I still hear the noise.

'So maybe we're old because we're not bold.'

'You're getting maudlin,' Ann said. 'they'll be perfectly safe. The worst that can happen is they'll get seasick or hit a whale.'

'And die.'

We ate out that evening, repeating the walk to the port then heading up the hill into the old town that hovered over the port and looked disdainfully down on it. There were plenty of places to eat, mostly in the road or overflowing into the green spaces, and mostly serving pizzas and pastas. Dogs and birds, mosquitoes and children buzzed around us while we ate and later I had diarrhoea, which after fire, is the most terrifying thing to happen on a boat, especially when the boat is too far to sprint to the marina toilets. Sitting, sweating, aching and making explosive noises and disgusting smells in a space that was so small it was difficult to stand in, while your loved one lies in bed three feet away through a flimsy door and politely pretends to be asleep is the single most disgusting and embarrassing experience that a yachtsman can have.

Next day we had to explore and so armed with loperamide we repeated our climb to the old city. By the time we reached Piazza Martiri at the top of the hill I was already exhausted and soaked in sweat but Ann's sympathy is measured in milliseconds and she was determined, so while I rested against the glass of some expensive jeweller she went off to find the tourist kiosk and get a walker's map. We were in a palm tree lined square at the bottom of a colossal stone wall which turned out to be the historic Bastione Sant Remy which was listed on Ann's new map along with sixty-six other places of interest. My heart sank.

'It is a city,' she said, 'the capital city of Sardinia.'

'Cardiff is the capital city of Wales, which is a whole country, and it doesn't have as many places of interest as this.'

She looked at me a little sadly, 'Perhaps one of these places will be air-conditioned to cool your poor tummy.' That was two milliseconds of sympathy for the day and don't expect more!

One of those little road trains went passed stuffed full of tourists. 'Why can we never get one of those and watch the monuments roll by in comfort?'

'We did, in Marseille, and you moaned most of the way around about the sunburn you were getting and how hot you were.' Sympathy time was clearly past.

The Italians like architecture on a grand scale and the Bastione Sant Remy is massive, a hundred feet tall and clad in sunbleached white limestone. It has a lot of steps up to the topmost level and you enter the piazza there through a triumphal arch, which after climbing a hundred feet in that heat is entirely appropriate. It may also explain why the museum is at street level. The museum, I'm sure, is air conditioned and has toilets, the two things I wanted most, but we never found out because it was closed that day. So we climbed the steps and looked out over the harbour, the ferry port, the oil refinery, the marinas and yacht clubs, the oil tankers and cargo ships, the tugs and pilot boats. We took pictures and Ann recorded some movie and we photographed some other couple with their camera and they photographed us with ours.

Ann unfurled her map and set off purposefully northward then came back to where I waited and set off purposefully westward. This time I felt she had it right so I joined her and we dived down into the tiny streets of the old city which were, at least, cool. They were built for horses and foot traffic so were populated with narrow cars and scooters that appeared from behind, honked, and flattened you against the wall.

The itinerary listed the places we visited, eleven of them, spread around the old city: two forts, two towers – one with an elephant but it was only a carving – two palaces, a cathedral and more.

I realised that I was probably on the verge of cultural overload. We had been inspecting historical monuments since the odyssey began and I had reached that point where only the stupendous was going to get noticed. When we reached the end of the itinerary at the Porta Cristina, where the Museum of the Castle and Fortifications beckoned irresistibly, I went instead for the café and had an iced tea in the draught of the air-conditioner. We'd been walking for nearly four hours and although we'd drunk two litres of water between us we were dehydrated by then.

We walked down the hill towards the station where there was a taxi-rank, Ann's sympathetic concession to my current poor condition. Above us Cagliari splashed some colourful bunting which set off the colours of the sunshades and pot plants and the pastels of the houses themselves. Beyond the street the elephant tower watched over us.

While Ann was in a shop buying some more water a couple of kids ran passed shouting at each other in English. I realised with a shock that it was probably the first time I'd heard English spoken by someone passing by since we'd started our voyage. Their mothers chatted to us for a while then we went our separate ways. Us to the taxi rank and them up the hills to see the monuments.

Amanda arrived on time which was late and it was dark. She stood uncertainly outside the locked marina gate wondering if the taxi had found the right place, but she cheered up and smiled when she saw us tripping along the pontoon to let her in. Quite tall, darkly attractive with long hair that was deep red today but would be different next week, she had dark brown eyes and a smile that flashed white against already tanned skin. She was a qualified sailor, had tried parachuting, windsurfing, gliding and SCUBA diving but now she was thirty and had settled down with James. But not so settled that she couldn't leave her man to come and sail in the Med for a week. *Eeyore* clung terrified to her back and she clutched a small bag that held everything she would need for a week.

Amanda is used to sailing with us and arranged the backpack and her bag in the aft cabin which we often refer to as hers: "*Amanda's Cabin*". She brought us news, something which we are often forced go without for days or weeks: the state of the world, the town gossip, the national and international stuff - disasters and scandals usually – and she brought us spare parts, DVDs of the latest TV series, and she brought us her happy self.

Her flight out was from Olbia and we had the same decision to make as with Sue and Rob, do we play around locally or steam north in a drive to catch the flight. If we stayed in this area and Amanda caught a train to Olbia we wouldn't have to go back up the east coast, we could duck around the bottom of Sardinia and head up the west coast to our next meeting which was in Alghero.

Amanda, bless her, being the sailor wanted to go all out for Olbia. 'Well, at least, we'll circumnavigate the island.' Ann whispered later, 'Look on the bright side.' I determined never to pick someone up from one airport and deliver them to another ever again.

So next day at some horribly early hour we threw off our ties with Cagliari and Amanda drove us out through the harbour. In order to make our deadline with a bit of margin we had decided to miss Villasimius and push all the way to Porto Corallo. We swung around Capo Carbonara about lunchtime and anchored in a turquoise bay for a cooling swim.

There were still no dolphin off Serpentara island.

It was a long hot slog and we arrived in Porto Corallo after five o'clock in the evening.

Porto Corallo, Sardinia, 1023 miles to Gouvia. Day 71

'I have nothing to write in my diary,' Ann said next morning, 'nothing has happened and even the showers are working.'

'I think that sums the place up completely.' I replied. 'Time to go.' For once she agreed.

We motored out of the port at nine thirty and spent another day motoring north. Amanda took photos, which was her hobby, and did her turn at the wheel and we all looked for life in the sea and found none. Once in a while one of us would go and sunbathe on the foredeck but the sun was so hot that we couldn't stay unprotected in it for long. But it was pleasant to get away from the noise of the motor and listen instead to the hiss of the water. Amanda began to despair of seeing a dolphin.

We anchored in a bay near Arbatax a little after lunch time. Ann and I were a bit scratchy with each other, Ann wanted to get into the marina but I wanted to show Amanda some fish. It was depressing to bicker and I think it was the draining heat and the endless motoring that had made us snappy. And there weren't any fish, only muddy coloured things that lay about the bottom.

The bay was full of boats and swell and *Aderyn Glas* rolled around so we left and motored around the headland to Arbatax.

Arbatax, Sardinia, 991 miles to Gouvia. Day 72

I suppose, looking back on it, we should have celebrated in Arbatax because we were about halfway through our odyssey and we'd dropped below the one thousand mile mark. But the truth is we didn't really know at the time, and since we were heading north and still had another guest to meet it didn't feel as if we were actually reducing the distance to go at all.

We were greeted well. The staff recognised us and smiled at Ann when she went to pay so she felt like an honoured guest. Bob came along the pontoon and met Amanda and chatted about the state of the marine industry, the poor summer trade, the Italians in general and the latest Berlusconi scandal in particular. He reaffirmed his belief that they are all mad.

We showed Amanda the sight (there being only the one) and she photographed the Rocce Rosse. Ann wrote the temperature in her log, which was thirty-two centigrade.

We had our first briefing on Sicily and Italy from the tubby Italian next door while he filled his boat with water. His holiday was to sail with his wife from his base in Syracuse across to Sardinia or to Italy and he gave us all the places to go and the places to miss. 'Go to *Siracusa*,' he said with passion, 'The architecture and the museum of art are wonderful.' But it seemed unlikely we would go that far south. 'And *Stromboli*! You must see *Stromboli* at night.' he added excitedly.

As far as crossing Italy was concerned Reggio and Rocella were the only marinas on the western tip and they were reputedly the haunts of thieves and muggers and best avoided. Ann and I looked at each other, if we couldn't stop on that coast we were going to have some long passages and I had hoped that the crossing to Sicily would be our last night passage.

'And the Messina Straights,' he added, looking at us hard in the eyes, 'you must get the tides right. Do you understand about the tides?' We told him we understood about tides but he looked sceptical.

Then his wife emerged from their cabin. She had lost all her clothes and had made a bikini from a couple of her tiny handkerchiefs. They were just big enough to circle her slim body. He beamed at us excitedly and climbed back into his cockpit.

So we showed Amanda Arbatax and showed Arbatax Amanda and neither really had much to say about the other so next morning, early, we left.

It was Dominik who had told us about the *cale* north of Arbatax and Ann had collected a leaflet from the tourist office which had photos of a dozen pretty little creeks and bays, complete with their distances from the port. So we motored close to the coast to find them all so that we could marvel and Amanda could take photos. But actually the *cale* were often too difficult to find, or impossible for us to get close to, or were so popular that we didn't want to get close and the whole thing became a big disappointment. We headed for a lunch stop under the high, guano coloured, sea cliffs aiming for the advertised *Grotto del Fico*, which seemed to have a landing stage and a line of steps climbing the cliff, but as we approached the jetty a guy turned up in a RIB and handed us a leaflet for an excursion. We couldn't land there but apparently he would come to the boat when we'd anchored and collect us and take us to the grotto. We knew we didn't have the time so we headed instead across the bay. As we approached the crowded shore a day-tripper boat came up behind us too fast and I asked him to slow down with a hand signal, but it did no good. He passed us just a dozen feet away and threw us all over the place with his wake. I shouted and waved my fist and no-one smiled at me, no-one even looked.

I saw life in the sea at last. While the girls were changing into their costumes I went up on the sidedeck and was just about to dive in when a jellyfish swam passed. A big brown medusa. I hate them. I cancelled my swim. We cancelled lunch. We pulled up the anchor and headed north.

Chapter 13

La Caletta, Sardinia, 943 miles to Gouvia. Day 73

It was a long hot drag and we didn't arrive until seven in the evening. By that time we were all tired and Ann and I were getting a bit snappy again. I began to wonder whether Amanda thought we were always like that, in truth we weren't, but we seemed to be on each other's nerves a bit since she'd arrived. It wasn't her fault, having Amanda on board was almost normal for us, she'd sailed with us often, and she ghosted around the boat knowing how and when to keep out of the way and knowing how and when do to whatever was necessary to sail it too. Ann and I had been locked up together for seventy-three days and maybe that was the limit. It was also our wedding anniversary and there we were, hot, tired and under pressure to keep moving instead of being in some gourmet restaurant celebrating with a bottle of wine.

'You know your trouble?' Amanda said, I knew she was going to tell us anyway, 'You both want to be captain. You are both so used to having staff to run around and do your bidding that you can't get used to people not instantly doing everything you demand. You need to find some way to work this out before it all goes to rats.'

Being lectured by one's daughter is the first stage on the slope which ends in old-people's homes and incontinence pants. Parents are supposed to lecture children, not the other way around. But Ann and I knew she was right.

We had a free night. No-one answered our radio calls when we arrived and so we tied up to the concrete hammerhead back again in La Caletta. No-one came to collect money, then or in the morning. It was rough at first while the tripper-boats ran in from the day's tourist milking, rougher than the other side of the hammerhead where we'd moored before, but then it all calmed down.

Next day the first of the day-trippers ran passed us while we were in the cockpit having breakfast, steaming too quickly through the harbour and heading out to the breakwater and the sea. On the top deck the tourists hung over the rail and stared down at us with wide-eyed blank expressions ready to yawn with excitement at a moment's notice. Life was normal. Then there was an excited crackle and squawk from the ship's tannoy and they all rushed away from us to the starboard side. Something was going on out of our sight. All around us people were staring, some were pointing, little kids were bouncing up and down in excitement or asking to be picked up. There was a focus, everyone dropped whatever they were doing, moved to the edges of the jetties and looked out across the harbour towards the town. The tripper-boat finally moved away and we stood looking where everybody else was looking and wondering what we were looking for. Then a large glistening wet shape rolled into view on the surface and a gasp and a shout went up, and some children cheered and clapped. Everyone seemed to be pointing and Amanda ran for her camera.

'The poor thing is probably trapped.' Ann said, 'It followed some fish into the harbour and now it can't get out.' We watched the huge dolphin circle then dive in slow motion. People on the pontoons were hurrying along to watch, people on the town quay were lined up. Cameras clicked.

The animal surfaced and breathed and dived and seemed perfectly happy. A fish leapt out of the water in front of it. A man in a little fishing boat skirted wide around it and made for the entrance, the dolphin was bigger than his boat. It rolled to the surface again and Amanda clicked away grinning and happy that she'd finally seen a Mediterranean dolphin and delivered to the door too.

Since he seemed to be content to stay a while I went below and found my homemade hydrophone, a transducer on a broom handle and an amplifier in a box that had once held paperclips. This was my chance finally to try and hear the whistles and clicks that dolphins use to communicate, but all I could hear was the rhythm of propellers and the clank of machinery. I told everyone he wasn't talking and passed the headphones around, but no-one, including me, believed that to be the case. 'Never mind, version three will be better.' I promised.

The inner harbour is only about three hundred metres by a hundred and fifty and the *Grande Dauphin*, for that's all he could have been so big was he, seemed to fill the place. We all watched in fascination, and some in apprehension – was he lost, injured, dying? But he finally found the way back to the sea and life gradually returned to normal.

'Time to go,' said Ann, and so we left the harbour and motored northward. And the sea was blue and the sky was blue and there was no wind and no life but a swell picked up as we closed the peninsula of Capo Coda Cavallo, south of the mass of Tavolara, where every yacht and cruiser on this side of the island converged. After four days we were within spitting distance of Olbia again. It was enough to make me shudder.

It wasn't far and it didn't take long. Tavolara beckoned to Amanda with its cloudy cap and she tried to frame it in her viewfinder but the angle wasn't right yet. We joined the mass of boats heading into the channel between Molara and Coda Cavallo and were immediately caught up in the traffic. Cruisers and yachts and fishers and multi-deckers were all constrained to the narrow channel and suddenly the helmsman had a full time job, not the idle, infrequent pressing of Rachel's buttons any more.

In and around all this traffic were the ever-present RIBs and sportboats who delighted in ignoring any kind of protocol and cut everyone up, with shrieks and yells from the over-excited occupants.

We swung hard left around the cape and into the first bay. What a hope! There were so many boats there that it was impossible to find a spot. It was certainly beautiful, the water was so clear that the boats seemed to hover above the white sand of the bottom, the far away beach was tree lined and coloured with umbrellas, but it seemed to be the most desirable place to go for anyone who could find anything that floated.

We threw out the fenders, that's how packed it was, we put the fenders out because we literally had to shoe-horn our way between anchored boats. We drove gently towards the shore, watching the depth sounder but mindful that we could boldly go places other yachts couldn't because of our shallow draught. It did no good. The boats were graded by draught. From the shore out there were rubber dinghies followed by sport boats and RIBs then small motor launches, small sailing boats and large sailing dinghies after which came small cruisers then the larger stuff, right the way out to the big multi-deckers that didn't need to be too close in because they had garages in their sterns with jet skies and RIBs to take the kiddies to the shore.

We crossed to the other side of the bay and got shouted at when we tried to pick up a buoy. An Italian on a pontoon was going ballistic because we tried to take an empty buoy. He'd probably been doing that all day and had wound himself into a such a frenzy I fully expected him to run unaided the twenty metres across the water surface to us.

Finally we found a small spot behind a raft of three small sport boats. They had roped themselves together and were having a party with music and booze and girls and lots of splashing and shouting, but we thought we'd give it a try and we dropped the anchor as close to them as we dared then let the chain out and ran backwards until we were as near to the boat behind as we could safely be. The captain of that one eyed us with suspicion, it was a clean new yacht and he didn't want it scratched. He lay on the deck and sunbathed and I thought he would have done better to have hung out his fenders. Fenders in an anchorage! How different the world is in the summer, in the Med, in Italy.

The three of us went into some kind of tense relaxation mode. We were surrounded in the beautiful bay by so many vessels that we couldn't take our eyes off those around us. Behind us Tavolara dominated the skyline and beneath us was the molten turquoise and white sand. But we couldn't relax.

Then we noticed that the distance between us and the three partying sports boats was decreasing. We had Rachel keeping an eye on our position with the anchor alarm set and the first thing we all though of was that we were dragging, but Rachel confirmed we were not. In fact logic should have told us that because the light wind, that was holding us and all the other craft pointing in the same direction, was coming over the isthmus and across the beach and try as you may you cannot drag upwind.

The party was getting closer and the occupants of the boats started to take notice and began to shout over to us with glasses in their hands and silly smiles. The gap lessened and I walked despairingly up to the foredeck already knowing what we would have to do. Ann started the engine and I stood on the anchor winch button. As the chain rattled in the party got closer and I thought we must collide. Still they were shouting at us to stop sliding into them. Behind us the man on the yacht watched with a grin but was too far away to shout anything useful to the idiots. I shouted in English to them but they didn't understand.

They came within two feet of us. As they passed by someone finally realised what was happening and they began to separate the three boats. The guy behind was now clambering around his lovely new yacht throwing fenders over and waving his arms about because he was next in line.

I signalled to Ann on the helm to keep us moving forward since we would be able to drop our anchor in the space where the boats had been, but before we could reach the spot the three zipped passed us and got there first.

It was time to go, this was stretching nerves and raising blood pressures and that's not what it was supposed to be about, so we threaded our way out and left. Behind us the status quo was quickly regained: the three boats rafted up exactly as before and the guy on the yacht returned to his sunbathing.

We went about two hundred metres around to the next bay which was comparatively empty and, though it wasn't exactly the best in the world with poor holding for the anchor and a swell whenever a boat passed on the highway through the islands, at least we could get a bit of swimming and all calm down a bit.

Porto Taverna, Sardinia, 923 miles to Gouvia. Day 74

We couldn't stay though, not overnight. There was a wind forecast which would drag us around the little bay and the shores were far too close and far too rocky for safety. The bay was empty because the bay was no good for anchoring. We were lucky to have stayed put as long as we did and in the hour we were there other yachts had arrived and anchored and dragged and left.

So we headed out and tried another. Tavolara has an anchorage at its base and that must be an impressive place to stay with the cliffs towering over you, but it was going to be absolutely wrong that night. The wind was forecast from the south-east so we found our way to Porto Taverna, which is opposite Tavolara on the mainland. I don't know where the name came from because all that was there was a bay full of boats, not a port and not a taverna. But it was late afternoon and we knew people would leave and make room. I took us towards the shore where only the shallow draught boats can go and found that someone had left already so we grabbed the space. We had to negotiate with a couple of kids paddling around on a windsurfer who seemed determined to get in our way, but I was kind and didn't kill them. They went off grinning and Ann threw the anchor in.

As the day ended we stood on the deck and watched as Tavolara changed from blue to a deep purple, the last wisps of cloud deserted it as the sea flashed its parting metallic purple and green pulse, then the rock turned black.

A lot of boats had departed and there was plenty of space but I don't think any of us would have suggested we move again that night. Which was a pity because the wind, as usual, changed direction and blew hard all night from the north which put us on a lee shore and rolled us around so much that we didn't get a lot of sleep. 'Remember the happy dolphin,' Ann said as we lay awake, she always looks on the bright side of life.

That there were rocky outcrops in front of us hadn't escaped my notice when we'd anchored, but they weren't so important as they were next morning when the wind had turned us around. We weren't in any danger – I told people – but we still left early and ate on the run.

We dodged the traffic and crossed the channel to look into Tavolara. Away from the little shelter the headlands gave us, the wind was fierce and Ann and I exchanged looks that said: 'Olbia again!'

Sir Robert Baden Powell was anchored under the cliffs of Tavolara, at least the Belgian schooner of that name was. Tall ships always strike a chord in us, Ann and I had sailed on a couple, Ann more than me, and we'd had some good times with good company and, while I am happy just to recall the memories, Ann has a secret ambition, that she shares with everyone, to sail on a tall ship across the Atlantic. Not me though, I like comfort too much. And wine with dinner. We'd sailed first on *Royalist* in Scotland. I had mentioned over dinner at home one night that each year a colleague spent a week of his summer sailing on the training ship and next day Ann had booked places for us both. The ship is spartan and designed for kids so adults six feet tall tended to have each other's sweaty soles and heels ground into their faces each night as they overhung the cots.

But *Baden Powell* looked good against the backdrop of Tavolara and we snapped away.

We promised Amanda we would return next day and claim Tavolara for the Prince of Wales by landing on it. I think we all knew the wind was so high that we needed a sheltered port for the night and that the anchorage in Tavolara wasn't it. We headed off to Olbia. Again. Into the funnelling wind. Again. And the lumpy swell…

Olbia quayside, Sardinia, 913 miles to Gouvia. Day 75

Amanda is wise and experienced enough to know that we can't dial up the weather to suit but I did feel sorry that we couldn't have done better. I would have liked to show her the walls of fish in Villasimius or moored under the mountain in Tavolara or provided a turtle or a shark or a school of playful dolphin. Instead we had a windblown dust storm on a quayside in a town. She didn't seem to mind, I suppose it was all different from the daily grind of a department head in a school for the tough.

We'd been lucky, the quay was crowded and the first slot we'd tried was guarded by a man who waved us away shouting 'Tug! Tug!' repeatedly until we backed off.

'Like hell.' we thought, but then a yacht pulled away from the wall and we slid into it's berth. The guardian was still waving people away five hours later.

We ate fish in the pizza restaurant and wandered the market with the crowds drinking in the noises and the scents and the scenes and the atmosphere, and went to the open-air free cinema that was laid on for the Italian happy holidayers and started watching a Disney and left because we couldn't understand it in Italian. By eleven o'clock we were ready for bed which seems to be when every Italian holiday maker is ready to start their evening. It's easy to understand: at midnight the temperatures have dropped to something under thirty and everyone has a bit more energy as a result. Only we northern races are silly enough to try to do anything in the afternoon. A huge lunch followed by an afternoon spent asleep is what nature intended in temperatures like these.

When we got back aboard the guardian had gone and the slot was filled with a motor cruiser. What a surprise! I suppose if that had been the only slot we would have tied up and argued that we could move when the tug arrived, then when it didn't we would stay. Or we could have moved later when a slot became available. The free Olbia quayside is an attractive proposition but it's not a guaranteed berth.

Next morning *Baden Powell* was in the corner next to the customs launches so we wandered around and chatted to some of the crew who told us they'd finished a week's diving and wasn't the weather bad – not a breath of wind all week and now the charter is over it blows up nicely. We agreed that the wind was always wrong and that it was probably something to do with global warming. The forecast for the central Tyrrhenian was westerly force seven which would have happily blown him to Italy.

The captain of the catamaran next to us on the quay had had his boat impounded in Spain. The reason we were going to Greece, rather than taking *Aderyn Glas* to Spain as was the original plan, was that Spain has this strange law that requires any boat owner living in Spain for more than three months – on shore or on his boat – to pay a tax of twelve percent of his boat's value as a kind of fine for being so wealthy. The Spaniards, being Spanish, take this seriously and will impound a boat for no reason until the owner can prove he has not been resident in Spain for that period of time. Guilty until he can prove innocence. As well as the fine, sorry – tax, the owner has to re-register the boat as Spanish and has to take his Captain's examinations again – in Spanish. If this is not enough to deter you from ever going to Spain don't say you've not been warned.

Olbia marina, Sardinia, 912 miles to Gouvia. Day 76

We slipped off up the channel, in the afternoon, into the little white capped waves and anchored behind an islet in the bay beyond the lighthouse. It was too rough to go to Tavolara but Amanda and I were determined to find some fish and we swam for half an hour in a last desperate attempt and failed. 'The sea is truly dead.' I said, and we motored back to the marina.

Sad as we were to see Amanda leave next morning, we both knew it was time to do something new. The something new was to cross the top of Sardinia and head down the perilous, exposed west coast to Alghero and beyond. We also knew we were going to kidnap our next guest and carry her away south with us.

We stayed two nights in the marina and now it was summer it was more expensive at eighty Euros each night. We washed the boat and washed our clothes and washed ourselves and filled her with water and shopped and plotted and planned and fixed the immersion heater thermostat and hoped for a drop in the wind.

Next day the weather forecast was giving calm for a week. 'Let's escape.' I suggested, 'Let's escape from Olbia and never return.'

'Time to go,' Ann agreed.

So we left the dusty quayside and the nodding seals and the homicidal ferries and the lighthouse and headed north once more around Capo Figari through the overfalls, that by now seemed familiar, and into the swell where we tried to sail for a while then gave up. Our plan was to anchor somewhere in the Maddalenas – those beautiful islands - then again near Santa Teresa, then route via Castelardo and Stintino, through the scary Fornelli passage and south to somewhere near Alghero. We had this strong sense of finally moving on, of shaking free of all the commitments we'd had on this side of the island. Of meaningful miles that would roll off the chart and take us towards Greece. When we collected Caryn we knew we weren't going to give her the choice the others had had, we were taking her south with us and putting her on a train back. We were rolling.

Or rather sailing.

Actually we were motoring.

But we were moving and in the right direction. Ann looked happier than she had for a while and we chatted happily. No more snapping at each other, we had a common cause. Time to go!

If you want a complicated suicide try sailing around the north east coast of Sardinia in August. And if you really want to ensure your demise try sailing through the Maddalenas in August. We went to have a look at Porto Cervo, The Most Expensive Marina, to see what was to be seen. Anchored off the entrance were two of the three largest sailing vessels in the world: the largest sloop and the largest modern square-rigger, the largest schooner had the day off. But to get close to them meant running gauntlet of the constant flow of motor yachts, multi-deckers and cruisers that came in and out and who all had their throttles to maximum as they passed this small, tatty, old and scratched tubby sailing thing that we called home. Uncaring boats flung their wakes at us, one after another, until we were reeling from the repeated shocks. We, defenceless man-of-peace, had no way to stop them other than by turning and running and we weren't ready to do that.

Mirabella V is the largest Bermudan sloop in the world. She displaces seven hundred and forty tonnes, is seventy-five metres overall and her mast must be a hundred metres tall, but it was hard to judge. She looks like a scaled up racing yacht, which is perhaps what she is, with a low white hull and deck saloon. She has such normal sloop proportions that, as we sailed passed her, we had no real feeling for her size. She could be mistaken for a smaller vessel closer to us.

Not the *Maltese Falcon* though - the beautiful *Maltese Falcon*. There was no mistaking the fact that here was something unusual and magnificent. She displaces 1,240 tonnes has three square rigged masts and is rigged as a clipper. Her yards are not straight, as on the clippers of old, but are beautifully curved and are rigidly attached to the masts. To trim the sails she rotates the entire mast. Eighty-seven metres, three masts plus a stubby thing for the radar and all the necessary domes on the foredeck, two levels of superstructure with a dark blue hull and white topsides. When we motored passed her, her masts were arranged to make a continuous, harmonious, reversing curve from her spars, a double 'S' shape. We were in the presence of beauty.

A passing yacht brought us back to our senses and Ann shouted at me that we were the wrong side of a cardinal mark and we were going to run aground and what was I playing at?

Disharmony in the presence of beauty.

We found more of the uncaring as we lined up our approach around Capo Ferro back into the entrance of the Maddalenas, the narrow, shallow, *Passo delle Bisce.*

Behind us, coming up fast, was superyacht. He was a multi-decked, blue hulled ship and he was going twice our speed. Behind him was another, only a little smaller, and coming towards us in the opposite direction was a third. We were all going to meet in the tiny gap and not one of the monsters was going to reduce his speed. This meant we had to go sideways towards the shallows to let the two behind us through, so that they could move over enough to let the one coming the other way get a bit of sea room so that the arrogant captains who couldn't turn their throttles down a little could safe face. And to hell with that measly little scrap bucket of a sailing cruiser who has no right to be in our water. *Our* water!

The wake nearly destroyed us. The uncaring pig was so close in such a shallow channel that the bow-wave couldn't dissipate at all and a metre high tsunami slammed into our beam. Noise and chaos everywhere. Below decks instantly became a shambles. Above decks all stability disappeared. *Aderyn Glas* wouldn't answer to the helm and was lifted bodily sideward. The mast carved through the sky and we clamped our hands on anything we could find to avoid being thrown around. The yacht stormed passed uncaring. Ann looked white. Probably I did too.

Then came the other one and this time the wake was confused by the arrival of the ship going in the other direction. Now we were in some kind of maelstrom. I opened the throttle and tried to get her to point toward the shore, tried to get some distance between us and the ships to give the wakes some time to attenuate, but some giant hand held the keels and she went wherever it took her. The shore shelved slowly onto a sandy beach and the wakes turned into breakers scouring along the sand. *Aderyn Glas* came back to me: started answering. I thought we should be able to stay in control as long as the sideways thrust of the waves didn't simply dump us on the sand.

Somehow we got through it. The first ship was British registered and I wanted so much to call him on the radio and tell them what I thought of his manhood, but *Aderyn Glas* was still being flung around so that I dared not leave the wheel. And still there were yachts and boats and RIBs and cruisers and ships channelling through the entrance.

A short time later we cleared the entrance and the channel opened out. Why such large ships can't take the extra few minutes to go north of Bisce island, where there is so much room, is beyond my comprehension. Is it going to take an accident before the Italians close the *passo* to ships of that size?

We licked our wounds and changed our plans. We needed to get out of this racetrack and find somewhere nearby to anchor.

It was like bicycling along a motorway, a motorway through the most beautiful scenery in the world. We were in the slow lane and passing us to port was a continuous stream of faster vessels, usually large motor cruisers or multi-decker ships. In amongst us and following their own anarchistic traditions were the RIBs and sportboats. We learned to ignore anything small and fast - they could look out for us - and to concentrate on the large stuff which, on the whole, held to a predictable course, causing us problems only with the large wakes they left behind.

We had one more conflict with another yacht when he decided he liked the look of an anchorage he'd spotted and cut across our bows making us slam the rudder over in a hurry.

All of this was repeated on the other side of the motorway, to the south, as vessels aimed to leave the Maddalenas through the gap. Our chosen anchorage, of course, was to the south which meant we had to cross the lot. We never made things easy for ourselves.

It was a rough ride too. The wakes were anything up to a metre tall and, unlike at sea, the sheer volume of traffic meant the wave period and direction was random so as the bow buried itself in one wave another would hit from a different direction and as *Aderyn Glas* struggled to pull out of that chaos yet another wave might appear from anywhere. What didn't get wet as the bow buried itself got soaked by the spray that was flung up. The bikes and sailbag, on the foredeck, were dunked. The genoa, furled around the forestay, was soaked for metres above the deck. The sprayhood, coachroof and windscreen were deluged. The boat shuddered as she hit, the mast vibrating and the flimsy bimini threatening to collapse.

Waves added together, ganged up on us, one building on another so that instead of weakening with distance they could actually increase in size. It was awful.

But she's a good little ship and we made it through and we were much wiser when we'd finished than when we'd left Olbia.

Chapter 14

Porto Mannu, Sardinia, 887 miles to Gouvia. Day 78

It took us a while to calm down. 'I'm never doing that again,' Ann said but we both knew we had more tomorrow.

Porto Mannu is a little holiday village above a carefully manicured beach with geometrically arranged blue umbrellas and sunbeds and a campsite style shop and club above the golden sand. It's set in a small bay ringed with swimming marker buoys and has a jetty in the corner where active happy holidayers can play action man on jetskies and sportboats. Normally not the place we'd have chosen, it might as well have had a banner saying 'noisy', but it was easy, we fell into it and anchored.

We had anchored at about three o'clock, among a few other small yachts as far in to the beach as we dared which just about gave us shelter from the wakes that still rolled into the bay, though by the time they arrived they were not much more than a ripple. It was a pretty place to moor, the water was clear and the hillside had enough trees to hide the holiday cabins. The beach sent us the sounds of children, of course, and in the evening the club would probably have some music but we had earplugs, so there! After the city the air smelled fresh and clean and there were even a few tiny fish congregating idly around the keels.

Later we had a few drinks on a neighbouring boat that we had met first in La Caletta on the day of the dolphin. I suppose it's logical and almost inevitable that people who circle around an island all summer will keep meeting up. This couple were from Port Grimaud on mainland France and they circumnavigated the islands for their holidays each year. They were a little older than us and rich – they had two boats, the cruiser and a racing yacht, and lived near Saint-Tropez and that made them rich by our definition. But such is the fellowship of cruising yachtsmen that class is left on the shore and we chatted as always about the places we'd been and the things we had seen.

As we left we swapped calling cards, as we always do. 'I don't believe in doing this,' Nancy said, 'no-one ever bothers to follow through and I hate sending out emails and getting no responses.' Since she talked almost non-stop I could imagine her pain when no-one answered her calls.

Ann promised faithfully to keep in touch but her fingers were crossed.

Our weather forecast was now two days old and that was enough to start us worrying. Not about today or tomorrow because we were well sheltered and surrounded by marinas, ports and anchorages while we remained in the Maddalenas. But we had the bit between our teeth and were heading out across that huge bay on the north west coast of Sardinia that looks like an ancient meteor crater, so circular is it: the Gulf of Asinara.

So we wanted a forecast and the only reliable way to get one was to go into Santa Teresa and use the ferry terminal wifi, and that would have been sensible, but for some reason we went instead to Porto Pozzo.

We left Porto Mannu fairly early - for us - in another calm, blue day and headed towards the highway. The rule of the road is drive on the right so we crossed the rushing lines of traffic, from the aquatic mopeds to the aquatic juggernauts, in each direction and tried to relax as we joined the line heading westward.

South of the island of Caprera, where all the traffic funnels into a narrow channel, a fleet of Topper dinghies was making a slow crossing in the light wind from the island to the mainland, crewed by kids. These tiny boats are like plastic tea-trays with a stick holding a colourful sail, and on a good day with a flat sea and a brisk wind they are great fun to sail. I'd owned one and I liked it better than my Laser. But what they were doing was like cycling across a motorway with a flat tyre.

The little boats rolled in the cut-up sea and the kids were scared. More scared was the instructor who was having a dreadful day and wishing he'd stayed warm in his bed. From time to time he balanced on the stern of his little tea-tray and tried to catch the eye of whichever yacht skipper was in danger of running over his kids and, in this, he was being successful. Until, from the east, came a long black shiny ocean racing powerboat, the type with a deep-vee hull, a great long foredeck and a small driver's cockpit in front of immensely powerful engines that would take him three times around the world in a matter of minutes. We could see what was going to happen and had to watch as the movie ran on in horrible slow motion.

The driver of the powerboat couldn't possibly see where he was heading because his boat was going too slowly to plane so his bow was pointing somewhere towards the north star. To counteract his blindness he had put a man on the long foredeck whose job it was to direct the driver. Unfortunately though the driver seemed oblivious to the guy's signals so when the instructor in the Topper stood up precariously in his little boat and started waving and shouting for this monster to reduce his speed and turn away, nothing happened. The man on the foredeck of the racer made some kind of half-hearted signal to the driver and nothing happened. We could only watch as the boat came on, its bow so high we could see under the keel. People on other boats could see the danger and were waving and shouting but nothing happened. It came on and carved through the Topper fleet amid the yells and screams and waving of arms and somehow nothing happened.

No-one was killed.

It passed us a few seconds later and so incensed was I that I left the wheel and stood on the stern quarterdeck and screamed abuse and waved my fists. The man on the foredeck turned and looked around at me, not sheepish, not apologetic, but not uncaring either. I think he realised how close they had been to killing children and was frightened.

Porto Pozzo, Sardinia, 876 miles to Gouvia. Day 79

'So it's not always fun in heaven.' Ann was glad to be away from the islands.

'Sometimes it's hell in paradise,' I agreed, 'but we don't want hell on Costa Paradiso.' I felt clever knowing the name of the coast we were going to sail along tomorrow.

We had cleared the channel by early afternoon and had anchored off the beach in Liscia bay with a bow and a stern anchor to keep us from rolling, but it was too exposed - we could see Corsica - and the swell swept in from the straights and rolled us around anyway. It wasn't a place to stay long. Then a jellyfish *glupped* passed and it wasn't a place to stay at all.

So we motored over to the western corner where there were a whole gaggle of yachts and other craft and tried to find a place which was sheltered by the headland, but the bottom shelved more steeply than anywhere I'd ever been before and within thirty metres of the beach we were in eighteen metres of water.

So we left and motored around the headland to Porto Pozzo where we'd visited with Jennie and Dirk, all that time ago. It wasn't the obvious choice because we'd dragged the anchor last time we'd been there, but the chart said it had some sort of club or marina and perhaps there was a berth for us.

We motored the length of the inlet watching the water get shallower and shallower until, at the southern extremity we found a village, a sailing club and moorings. The village was tiny and touristy, the sailing club was not for us, having only a couple of berths in water deep enough for even our shallow draught, and the moorings were all taken. But outside of the moorings was an area where we could anchor so we did, in two metres of gently shelving water.

Even after all that time we still expected someone to arrive in a fast, noisy RIB and either tell us to move on, fine us because this was National Park, or charge us because he owned that bit of sea. No-one ever did and we never really worked out why we felt that way. Ann felt it more than me, I tell her it's because she was a teacher and is bound up in rules and if it had been left to her the only places we would have anchored would have been those with signs saying: *"It Is Permitted For All Anns To Anchor Here"*, so we wouldn't have anchored at all. She denies it, of course, but it's true.

As we settled down to read ourselves to sleep in the late afternoon sun we were indeed disturbed by a man in a small noisy RIB but we slipped down and hid beneath the coaming and he went away: he was only a fisherman.

After all the fuss of the last few days to find a calm, quiet haven like this was wonderful, and we didn't mind that the water was deep green and murky or that the bottom was covered in weed. Or that the view wasn't so good: low green hills all around us and the fiord leaving for the sea. It was lovely. A quiet, peaceful, sleep filled night.

Another day another start and six new mosquito bites, and we were intimidated by the magnitude of what we were going to do next. Leaving the comparative safety of a coast with plenty of marinas and ports and heading out across the expanse of *that* bay. After that, even more frightening, the west coast of Sardinia. The whole idea should be whispered about with reverence, spoken of in frightened voices. There were only three havens and they were all a long way apart: Castelardo, Porto Torres – which was a big oil terminal – and Stintino on the far peninsula. That was it to cover a crossing of nearly sixty miles.

'Sixty miles? Is that all?' I said, 'Why not go straight across the bay? That's like crossing Lyme Bay. Just eight hours.'

'In this heat, under engine? You won't last half of it. Trust me. You said you wanted small day hops and that's what you're getting.'

'Yes, but,' I thought aloud, 'we don't know how good the weather forecast is. It's now three days old and they can't reliably forecast more than two. Look at the French ones: they even give a probability of accuracy after the first day so even they aren't sure. So maybe a dash is a good idea.' Ann does not look kindly on any questioning of her navigational decisions and is likely to tell me huffily to do it myself, which is too much for me to contemplate. So I've learned not to ask questions unless there is a rock staring at me over the bow. And even then it's wise to be diplomatic: *darling, someone has added a rock since the chart was made*, is usually safe. I shut up and hurried off to do something important like watch a cloud, but there weren't any.

We initially thought we would call into Santa Teresa and stooge about in the entrance while we downloaded a forecast from the ferry terminal but when we got abreast of the entrance there was a ferry heading in and the whole thing seemed too difficult so we motored on passed.

'One day apathy will kill us.' I said.

'Unless lethargy gets us first.'

'I'm too tired to get either.'

It was so hot. Standing or sitting in the cockpit, taking turns on the wheel and drinking more or less continuously, wearing the minimum of clothes and sometimes none at all and it was still so, so hot.

Ann was right. To have tried to go straight across would have been a nightmare. We would have arrived on the other side as shrivelled, wrinkled, desiccated hulks found crouched in the cockpit of a boat sailed by a robot called Rachel.

She telephoned ahead for a berth. Thankfully we were close enough to the shore to get a signal on the phone. Her conversation in Italian was a bit confused but she got her request across and, of course, didn't understand the answer. So we continued along the Costa Paradiso, though somewhat puzzled. Did we book a berth? If they were full there was nowhere else to go.

Castelardo, Sardinia, 846 miles to Gouvia. Day 80

'Ann, he's got to be joking. You booked ahead.'

The man in the RIB took pity on us, Ann thinks he saw the boat's name on a list he had in his RIB but the place was still full. He directed us across to the end of a pontoon where there was a rusting hulk that had once been a boat, and indicated we should tie up alongside it. Since the hulk was on the end of the pontoon this meant we had no way to get ashore except by climbing over it, but at least he hadn't turned us away.

Castelardo is pretty. It is a mix of ancient and modern. Up on the promontory looking out to sea is the castle which is, of course, modern because the ancient ruin has been done up for the tourists.

On the other side of the town is the marina, which is also brand new complete with posh boutiques, a chandlery and small mini-market. Joining the two halves of the town is a road that hikes up and over a low hill that affords really good views of both sides but leaves you gasping and wheezing if you do it in the hot sun.

But the town itself, nestling at the foot of the castle, needs a good scrub followed by thick makeup. We made it to the central square then collapsed into a street café that occupied all of the narrow pavement of the main street. Every so often a car or a scooter would honk and stop outside the door and the waiter would rush out and shake a hand and the car would drive off.

'It's the mafia,' whispered Ann, 'they're palming drugs.' I *think* she was joking.

Across the road a bright little flower shop was attended by a young girl who sat on the curb with a baby. On either side of it were similar little shops that were closed up, perhaps for the afternoon. The square had a temporary stage that suggested some noisy event, an hotel, and a road leading upwards to the castle. People walked purposefully up and down the streets, not loitering like tourists, so we must have wandered away from the tourist trail.

'According to Rachel we've done over one thousand miles.' Ann never really trusts Rachel. In my exhaustion I felt as if we'd walked most of them. We drank cold beer and contemplated the climb up to the castle. Some American walked by and asked the waiter where there was an internet café. We discarded the castle idea until next day and followed him disguised as MI6 agents, sidling along behind him and looking in shop windows whenever he stopped. Turning our faces away so he wouldn't recognise us and sometimes separating, one to the left and the other to the right of the street. We followed him around corners and down a side street, blending into the shadows, and at last he turned into a dark little corner shop. But there was only one ancient computer in a noisy shop full of games machines and it was broken. No internet for us.

As we walked back we noticed kids in the street with laptops and dongles, they used 3G telephones for their access. Ann claimed she knew we should have bought one but I think she was being wise after the event.

The marina was jammed with boats by the time we returned. The *Capitano* was hanging them off the blunt ends of the pontoons. A yacht would arrive, drop its anchor and motor backwards until it could throw a line to the pontoon so it was strung between its anchor and the pontoon. Two or three boats were arranged like this on the end of each pontoon. It made us glad we were alongside a rusting hulk.

Later in the evening, as the sun waned, everyone in the town came and promenaded up and down the quayside. As darkness came the castle was lit up and someone let off a few fireworks. The castle lights and the fireworks reflected in the water and it all looked very pretty.

Next morning we were woken by movement on the boat we were tied to. The *Capitano* had promised us that it wasn't going to move any time soon and we thought it was derelict, all of the previous evening it had pumped water out of its bilges and down the side of our hull.

But now there was definitely some life on board. We dressed and emerged into the gaze of two old men and women. The men scurried around and the women sat in the cockpit and looked at us.

'Are you leaving?' I asked, but they had no English. Ann tried in Spanish and Italian but it obviously wasn't right. In the end we found a common language in bad French and the ladies smiled at us for our perseverance – or they realised how bad the French was.

We had half an hour, they told us, then they were going fishing. More people arrived and looked down at us with pitying frowns. Some of them spoke to me in French, because by then they obviously thought that's what we were, and ten minutes later they started casting their lines off which showed they didn't know the French for half-an-hour. It threw us into a panic, rushing to get the sunshades down and the engine started and the lines cast off and they didn't seem to want to give us a minute more. Did we check the oil, is the cooling water on, did we start the GPS?

'Let's go.' Said Ann, stamping her foot in frustration 'and if they think I'm paying for *that* night they can think again.' We cast off and I waved them a cheerful *'Bon chance,'* with the fishing.

Ann was grimly determined not to pay but the thought of being banned from every marina in Italy for non-payment finally calmed her down. So we fuelled and went shopping, diving the boat further into the marina and tying up for an hour on the quayside. We also got a forecast from the office which showed more of the same: hot and sunny, still and calm.

We skipped Porto Torres five miles out to sea, the furthest we'd been from land since we'd left Elba. Rachel was driving and we were taking turns at watching the water go by. Even from that distance we could see the industry around the port and were happy to stay away. Little fishing boats bobbed around us, a man and his wife, a couple of men, a man and his dog.

As we approached Stintino we worried. If the marinas filled up like Castelardo then what were our chances of a berth in Stintino which had to be the first and last stopping point for anyone going around the northwest corner of Sardinia.

We motored into the harbour, behind the mole, and found the first of two marinas, it was half empty and they wouldn't even acknowledge our calls. So we called the second marina which was in a creek leading to the centre of the town and it was half empty but the *Capitano* claimed there were no spaces. We called the first one again and the second one said there were no spaces there either.

Suddenly we felt frightened, anchoring in sheltered bays among the Maddalenas is one thing but this was an exposed coast with no inviting little inlets and is as flat as they come with nothing to impede a westerly wind or a *Mistral*.

'We should have booked.' said Ann with brilliant insight that started us arguing.

'You had the phone and you claim to speak Italian.' I said in anger born of fear.

We snapped at each other while we searched for somewhere to stop. South was no good, there was a little bay below the harbour but it was rocky and didn't look promising, so we turned north, bickering while we went. What had happened to our harmony?

Eventually we crept into the shallows of La Pelosa and Ann growled about the sandbank that was supposed to be there and don't run aground and mind the windsurfers and the kite surfers and what are we doing here and go back now! And I growled right back. It was time to stop and let pressure levels return to normal.

After a while we realised how lovely the place was. In fact, if you took away all the windsurfers, kite surfers, little dinghies and all the other watersports and the fifty or so anchored yachts and cruisers, so that it became deserted, it would probably have been voted as 'our most beautiful anchorage'. It was not that the water was any better than we'd seen elsewhere, there was simply more of it: the molten turquoise extending to the horizon behind us and to the shores on each side.

We had a figurative cup of tea, breathed slowly and deeply, bit our tongues and counted to three thousand and tried not to spark off each other again.

We stayed for an hour but we were constantly buzzed by the watersports people and swimming would have been dangerous. But the time let us regain a bit of common sense and we studied the chartplotter intently. The wind, such as it was, was westerly and there was an inlet on the Isola Piana, just over there, which would shelter us. The fact that *piana* meant flat and that there was nothing to stop any sort of wind wasn't lost on us, but we were desperate. We managed to get around into the inlet without too much arguing about the depth under our keel and the sandbank at the entrance that was going to claim us. And we anchored and that, I decided, was it for the day! End of argument! The Captain has spoken! That okay, darling?

Isola Piana, Sardinia, 821 miles to Gouvia. Day 81

We argue when we're stressed and tired because we both think we have the only solution to the problem before us and we are both used to people obeying us. We rarely listen to each other when we're in that state and we rarely work together to find the best solutions. Sometimes we compromise and it is painful for us both, but you can't compromise at sea, there has to be a decision made by one person and bought into by everyone.

So when we're stressed and tired we argue and then we anchor the boat and discover that we're going to be alright after all and the anger departs and leaves no scars. Thus it was that ten minutes after we'd anchored at Isola Piana we were in the water with snorkels and happily swimming off towards the scrubby beach on the scrubby island.

In the late afternoon the miracle of home-time happened again and little sportboats and RIBs headed off noisily to wherever they called home, leaving a few yachts and cruisers like us, and a quiet evening that slid into night. We faced west, into a gentle breeze that blew over the island, but behind us was nothing but the empty expanse of sixty miles of bay. If the wind changed this definitely wasn't the place to be.

But the night was calm and we awoke to the realisation that today we would be motoring through the scary Fornelli Passage and into the Mediterranean Sea with nothing between us and Spain but water.

The Fornelli Passage is a narrow, shallow passage between the large Isola Asinara and Capo del Falcone on the northwest tip of Sardinia. It's of interest because it saves a long drag up around the Asinara island which would add twenty-three miles and four hours to our journey. It's narrow, doglegged and studded with rocks on the western side, but given a good chart and a GPS it's not really that frightening. Not like the day we'd gone through Jack Sound in Wales and got the tide wrong, that was nearly an early end of our careers.

So while Ann sorted out the boat ready to leave I sat down with Rachel and taught her a string of detailed waypoints that would tell us where to turn.

Halfway through the passage is a pair of leading line marks for people who don't have Rachels and it was fun to see how close I could get to Rachel's course using eyeball navigation like the old days. The result I will not disclose but I was glad we had her working for us. It was calm and it was easy, if it had been rough I would not have attempted the passage.

We were heading southwards to Alghero which is a large city on the western side of the island. The coastline we were motoring passed consisted of rugged cliffs with rocks jutting out from them waiting a little below the surface to rip the keels from unsuspecting boats. There were very few beaches and if we had a problem there was nowhere to run except onwards or backwards. There were very few boats too, just a motor boat or so and an occasional yacht. If you were to die here you could do it without witnesses.

After a couple of hours we saw a patch of disturbed water ahead. Since it was roughly on our course we went looking expecting some kind of life that might make an otherwise hot and boring passage a bit more interesting, and it was and it did. The flashing tails of thrashing tuna in some kind of feeding frenzy were chopping up the surface, and we had no rods ready since we'd long since given up hope of catching anything. We drove around the patch and through the patch and only after a while did the fish realise we were there. Then they dived and disappeared. And as we headed southward again a little bobbing fishing fleet homed in on the patch of water we'd left. They couldn't see what we'd seen but they saw us circling and that was all they needed.

Porticciolo di Capo Caccia, Sardinia, 789 miles to Gouvia. Day 82

Another cape: there wasn't a breath of wind until we rounded the great pink and white cliffs of Capo Caccia that stretched sheer to three hundred feet, and there was a howling gale and the wakes of vessels plying to and from Alghero which was across the bay in a haze.

So we pulled out the sails and headed to where Michael and Linda, from *Silver Spray* had told us was a sheltered bay and a small marina at Porto Conte. But it was anything but sheltered and there was enough fetch down across Conte bay to have the water picking up nastily. Nor was the marina for us, it was a couple of pontoons for little boats and if we wanted to stop we would have to anchor out in the bay.

So we crossed back to the other side where there should be some shelter and found a howling gale there too. The local geography was generating katabatic winds that came hurtling down the slopes of the tight little valleys that made such good windtunnels.

But we pushed our nose into the inlet where the little port of Cape Caccia – the Porticciolo di Capo Caccia - hugged the western shore. There was more wind than across the bay but, because there was no noticeable fetch, the water was flat so we could motor slowly into the wind and drop the anchor wherever we wanted. It was the first time we had anchored in a hot, violent wind and we scurried below as soon as we were sure the anchor had bitten and turned the alarms on.

Later it died. Katabatic winds off the hills don't last long once the sun starts to wane and by morning *Aderyn Glas* was lazily stretching this way and that while I went for a swim and played with the fish that were feeding off the keels.

The shore was a hundred metres away and I threw myself into a bit of racing crawl, swimming was my sport once, and that was how I found out that life in the confines of a boat saps stamina. I paddled nonchalantly back after a circuit of the rocks, making like I could break into a sprint at any second and was only holding back so as not to show off but knowing the opposite was true. Still it was the early morning, only ten o'clock, and I make it a habit never to swim before noon so that was probably the real reason for my weakness.

The little bay was headed by a small sailing club and was studded with mooring buoys, but they were all marked private. There were six of us at anchor in the morning, well spread out. Above the beach was a hotel and a path led further inland towards a small village. It wasn't hugely attractive and was probably overshadowed in tourists' eyes by Neptune's Grotto back around the corner towards the cape. It was rumoured that you could go ashore in your dinghy and climb six hundred steps to the entrance then another six hundred down to the cave after which you return the way you came – or you could pay for a tourist boat from Alghero. The cape resembled the Eiger North Face, so we nodded wisely to each other and did something more important like sitting still.

Anyway, Ann had been busy on the phone trying to find us a place in Alghero, focussed by the problems we'd had in Stintino, and all too aware that we needed to be somewhere Caryn could reach us. It didn't bother us that we were a few days early, if we could get in then we would.

She tried repeatedly, calling each of the marinas in turn then calling back. The only place she didn't try was the town quay: municipal quays were calibrated in our heads by the one in Olbia as busy, noisy, hot and dusty places. No, we wanted a secure marina berth please and were prepared to pay for it. In the end we were offered a place in Aquatica provided we could arrive before noon. We left the bay with the throttle wide open and the anchor still clambering on board and passed an anchored British boat with a wave.

'Time to go,' said Ann unnecessarily.

Chapter 15

Alghero, Sardinia, 783 miles to Gouvia. Day 83

Someone was whistling the Welsh national anthem and it wasn't me and it wasn't Ann. It wasn't the guys in the *Capo's* RIB either, although one of them was English.

The crossing to Alghero had been a process of dodging wakes. It is a surprising fact that the size of a wake is not proportional to the size of the vessel causing it. Often a smallish motor cruiser can kick up a tremendous wake while a largish multi-decker ship trails a smaller one. Today we had learned that the worst wakes around Alghero were caused by tripper boats that ran to and from the *Grotte di Nettuno* landing stage on the seaward side of the cape. We learned that fact the usual way: by getting rolled around and wet and finding the little rubbish bin hiding in the toilet.

'We're on the town quay.' I said as we allowed the RIB to pull and push us into a hole next to a small fishing boat that the *Capo* had moved for us. Not just the town quay but right in the corner where the bustle was greatest.

'Grin and bear it,' Ann said, 'at least it will be cheap.'

'I bet they saw us coming in and decided we were too scruffy for the marina so offloaded us down here.' We'd passed the marina on the way in, it was a jumble of yachts and cruisers packed unbelievably tightly together and all rather expensive looking with tailored sunshades and darkened glass.

I found the source of the whistling as I lowered the plank. A strange short creature on a bike was rocking slowly in time to his music and looking down at me. He seemed like a teenager but had the face of an old man. He didn't smile, didn't greet, just looked. I made a fateful decision and reached out a hand for a handshake. He looked at it and jumped, like I had taken a swipe at him. 'Excellent,' I said, 'you saw my flag and know my anthem. Do you like rugby?' He took and shook my hand and I don't think anyone had ever responded to him like that before. Even now that I looked closer I still could not put an age to him. He rode a teenager's bike but looked like a short man of forty. I had instant second thoughts and knew that Ann would lecture me about my inability to spot lame ducks and steer clear of them.

'I know all the national anthems.' He said in perfect English and looked keen to talk more so I beat a retreat to the cockpit and busied myself with sunshades and fans, it was over thirty-five and there was no cooling breeze. Every time I peeked through the sunshades he was still there… *waiting*.

Because Aquatica had arranged the berth we could use their facilities like showers and wifi though we had to pay for both. The town quay had water and electricity so we were well enough accommodated but it was as far into the corner of the harbour as you can get and the ferries and tripper boats berthed a stone's throw over there – about forty metres away. But because we were oriented at right angles to them their wash didn't bother us much. There was a strange half-submarine painted yellow that moved like a supermarket trolley with a jammed wheel.

Ann came back from booking us in and climbed on board to the notes of our anthem. 'I hope you ignored that funny little guy on the bike,' she said, 'I think he's a bit – you know – odd.'

'Who?' But she knew, she could always tell. I hoped another boat would arrive and he would go and whistle at them. Maybe a big hearted, motherly Italian lady would befriend him and take him to her bosom, then she could be Whistler's mother.

From the sea Alghero hides behind a wall. A big defensive citadel wall that protected and surrounded the important places of old, the cathedral, the church of San Michele and the palaces of the wealthy. Now the skyline is punctuated by skinny cranes that line up with their backs to the wind and spoil the mountainous horizon. To the left is the new port, stuffed full of marina pontoons and hundreds, if not thousands, of yachts tied to them and jealously guarding their allotted space. To the right is the old port, stuffed full of marina pontoons and dozens, if not hundreds, of yachts... and so on. And a town quay tucked away in the corner and guarded by the massive walls of the citadel. Jammed into the space where the quay meets the nearest pontoon is a white hut that is the Aquatica office, shower, toilet, and bar. The bar is pleasant and the drinks are cold but the view is of a hundred yachts like dogs held back by their leads and waiting to charge snarling at you.

From the battlements we looked down on poor little *Aderyn Glas* who was the littlest boat around and a proper ragamuffin under her drapes of reflective sunshade material and bags full of sail and bike strewn around. Untidy ropes, an odd assortment of fenders thrown over the side and a DIY-shop plank with cross members liberated from Paris Arsenal, nailed on for grip, made the picture complete. Our home!

The battlements turned the corner and followed the quayside towards the modern end of the town for a few hundred metres, and in front of them were the berths for the larger yachts and the tripper boats. Further still were the apartment blocks, dubiously renaissance near the quay, but gradually becoming more modern and utilitarian further inland. Beyond the port was reputed to be a beach but the main interest for us was the old town inside the citadel walls. We also wanted a laundry.

'I bet that whistling guy knows where the *lavanderia* is.' Ann said. I shivered a little and looked around furtively.

The *Capo* staff knew where the tourist office was and the tourist office knew where the supermarkets and the laundry were and knew all about trains and busses from Oristano so that we could sort out Caryn's return.

It was dripping hot in the streets. We hiked up the noisy *via* Sassari to the supermarket and the laundry and cooled ourselves in the one and overheated in the other. We walked back through the tiny scented streets of the old town with the, by now familiar, tall buildings creating shade. They were filled with tourists, tourist shops, tourist restaurants and ice-cream parlours for tourists, but there were quieter alleys to the side and we muddled our way through those until we found the main cobbled concourse where the renaissance palaces of the *signore* sheltered behind the citadel wall. It was all very clean and decorated with greenery and the tourists made it colourful and noisy. Through the gate to the quayside we could see *Aderyn Glas* stuck to a glass sea but the ice-cream shop caught us and wouldn't let us go until we'd bought one and dripped most of it down ourselves. Local dogs waited in the shade, tongues poised ready.

Sat on a bike by our plank a strange creature whistled a tune I knew. Ann smiled and climbed on board tugging at my sleeve but he'd started talking and I'm not rude. I wanted to say: *leave me alone,* but instead I waved the bags at him and said: 'See you later.' Afraid that I would.

We ate ashore. One of our rare meals off the boat and it cost seventy odd Euros for a bottle of wine and two fish suppers but Ann said it was good and the pain of parting with all that money does wear off, and it's only Euros, not real stuff. The crowded old town at night is the place to be and we wandered the streets until we came across a piano recital in a church. Liszt, played by a local hero *maestro* dressed in black and introduced by a middle aged lady Italian who wore too much make-up and talked for too long. People sat on the steps, on the floors, on the benches and pews and stood: leaned against the columns or each other. A mother wandered in with a baby that squealed and she was scowled at until she left. Children were frowned into intimidated silence. The town had come to see and hear and the town sat in the hot fanned silence and absorbed every note.

The brash noise jangled through the night and the stamping feet had the sound of beaten carpets. The crowd on the quayside stood around a group of Red Indians who stomped and rattled drums and played pan pipes and sold CDs and collected money from the audience until someone unplugged their amps and the lights and music died abruptly. This happened a few times and at eleven o'clock they gave up and we all went to bed. When we climbed back on board we discovered the mains failure had happened all along the quayside and our fridge temperature alarm was going nuts because no-one had reset the quayside circuit breakers.

'Would you like a glass of warm yoghurt topped with sweaty cheese and washed down with hot white wine?' Ann said enthusiastically, 'I know I would.' We switched the fridge to battery and made sure the charger was on – to hell with inefficiency and saving the planet.

The high, thin whistle of the national anthem woke me next morning and I shuddered in my bunk and buried my head under the pillow. He was waiting. Hunched over his bike at the bottom of our plank. We were trapped. We would have to stay on board all day.

There was a break in the whistling shortly after breakfast and we made a run for the citadel. Ann has been a teacher for most of her life and knows how to deal with the strange people most of us know as adolescents. 'Just talk to him as if he is normal and don't get involved.' Was her paradoxical counsel as she strolled along unconcerned. I kept looking over my shoulder and hurried to the gap in the wall where the ice-cream stains the pavement while trying to seem normal.

'You think he's a kid then?' but she didn't know. Then I saw him in the distance, weaving through the crowds on his bike, heading towards our boat, and I put my head down and sidled into the tiny alleys. The look on Ann's face was somewhere between amusement, disgust and pity, but I could live with that.

A man and his wife came and taught us how to fish. We'd waved cheerily at him as we left Porticciolo di Capo Caccia, apparently, and they had taken the bus across looking for information. Eddie and Debbie lived in a cave in Spain and sailed in the summer.

The cave is wonderful, they told us, and they were in the process of extending it. The temperature is so constant, cool in summer and warm in winter, but the view wasn't so good in most of the rooms.

We gave them tea and information and Eddie told us how to fish for tuna: how to set the reel, how to attach the little plastic squid, how to strike and how to reel the fish to the boat. Then how to haul it aboard and how to kill it by pouring alcohol into its gills and

Debbie added how best to bleed it so that the flesh stays white. I needed some alcohol poured into my gills by the time they'd finished and we went along to the marina bar so they could use the wifi. 'Who's the funny bloke that keeps whistling?' Eddie asked.

'Why don't Italians smile?' I asked Marco that evening. He and Sara were our new neighbours and had just climbed back on board, after an evening wandering with their children, and we were all drinking too much wine in our respective cockpits. They were young and educated, handsome and beautiful and sailing a bigger yacht than we had. 'You must have a sense of humour,' I added, 'you elected Berlusconi.'

Marco smiled at us and Sara beamed, 'You are right,' she said, 'it is something Italian. We have travelled so much now we know that everywhere else people smile much more than we do to strangers. People like us who have gone to the university or who have travelled and met people from other countries, we will smile and be friends, and say first names, but those who have lived only in Italy they must live by the rules their families have given them.' She sipped her wine and stretched her long lithe body back over the coachroof and I had to smile.

'You see?' Marco said, 'you smile so easily. It is because we are friends, no?'

'We must go to bed,' said Sara but she went with Marco.

Next day they left early and Caryn arrived late and kissed us on the gangplank.

A screech of bike brakes and the front wheel missing my leg by an inch. I ignored him, he was a kid and Ann could handle kids. 'Hi,' she said, 'is this the way to the chandlery?' Ann beamed at me, I was a man again. He rode off whistling some unknown tune.

Caryn had arrived at nine in the evening as I was checking the circuit breakers on the quay. I looked up and there she was, bewildered. She walked over and hugged me, glad to be safely where she should be but a little surprised that she'd made it.

Caryn is short and could be fifty but I've never dared ask, short red hair, cut for sunshine and hot weather, and has a pleasing smile. She was an experiment: we didn't know her particularly well but she was keen to try something new and we were keen to see if we could live with comparative strangers on board with a view to perhaps chartering in the future.

She told us she'd read our crewnotes and had brought exactly three pairs of knickers and a couple of sundresses so as not to fill the cabin. Despite being thus prepared a look of disappointment flitted across her face when she saw how small *Aderyn Glas* was. She sat in the cockpit lit by the quayside lights and listened to the thumping Red Indians and drank a bottle of red wine. Then she kissed us both on the lips again and went to bed. Ann looked at me with a 'Did *you* invite her?' question in her eyes.

I looked back with an expression intended to convey: 'I was drunk at the time.'

The fishing boat woke us while it was still dark, banging along the hull inches from where we lay sweating. The banging was followed by shouts and the sounds of the catch being thrown up onto the quayside. We lay in the hot dark until it was quiet again and when we next awoke Caryn was already munching breakfast.

A boat had arrived and tied up in the very corner of the quay. This was the space reserved for boats claiming their free twenty-four hour stay which all the Italian ports are obliged to provide. The police came and visited him and I thought they would come and check our papers too, but they didn't. Later on, when the shift changed, the police checked his papers again.

The day was reserved for showing Caryn around and she dressed for the occasion in the shortest sundress I'd ever seen. We took her through the old town and along the *bastione* and walked off to find the hotel she was going to stay in when she returned. We lunched on board and tried to teach her a few knots and explain what life on board was all about. That evening she took us out for a meal then wandered back with Ann to watch the Red Indians close up while I walked around the citadel enjoying the atmosphere and the crowds and clicking away with my camera.

Tomorrow was a saint's day and a holiday so everyone was promenading cheerfully in the bright artificial lights that led the way around the walls. I strolled into the old town and found the *Chiesa del Carmelo* and wandered inside. It was calm and peaceful and cool with only a dozen people moving around. I normally look for renaissance art in churches but in the centre of this one was an ornate rococo altar in white marble and in front of it a golden couch topped with a crown of gold above an ultramarine canopy. Lying on the bed was a full sized effigy of the Virgin dressed in voluminous white robes and veil. At her feet a platform had been erected and worshipers moved slowly across the platform and touched, or kissed, the shoes the mannequin was dressed in. For mannequin it was and when I climbed respectfully on to the platform to look, the Virgin had the bland face of a large plastic doll. Tomorrow it would be carried through the streets so that everyone could take part in the ceremony. There are times when I think I understand religion: when I see a towering Gothic cathedral built by the sweat and skill of generations of craftsmen for example. Or look at a Renaissance altarpiece by Duccio or Lorenzetti, or hear a choir of monks in Assisi, but not when I looked at the plastic doll.

I went to watch the Red Indians stomping and fluting and found someone had stolen a fifty Euro note from my pocket.

It was morning and time to leave Alghero. The boat in the corner was being checked for the third time by the police. Whistler was absent. Caryn was ready to try sailing but still struggling with her knots. Ann and I had had enough city and wanted somewhere quiet. It was blasting hot and it was time to go.

Outside the harbour there was a breeze and we let it blow us down the coast for a while to give Caryn her first taste of sailing. From the sea to the south ancient Alghero looks impregnable, the bastion walls dip their toes in the blue sea and protect the low buildings behind. The wind blew us and Caryn steered with a little help from us. We tried to instil a sense that lobster pots were dangerous and need to be watched for but didn't succeed. 'Give it time,' Ann said, but I was doubtful. Some people simply can't do it.

After an hour we turned and headed north again back towards Capo Caccia and Porto Conte where we planned to stay. Caryn was not so good when it came to windward sailing. 'Give it time,' Ann said, 'it's brand new for her.'

Porto Conte, Sardinia, 771 miles to Gouvia. Day 88

How different the bay was this time. There were no katabatic winds to deal with and nothing coming over the flat lands to the north, the water was glassy. We motored up the length of the inlet and turned towards the shallows off Porto Conte and had an almost empty bay to anchor in. The water was only a few metres deep and the holding looked good. We found our old friends on *Silver Spray* lying happily at anchor and they waved at us as we passed by. We anchored about a hundred metres from them. On the photograph I took of them the reflections of the mast are almost as straight as the mast itself.

We went swimming. Caryn told us she could swim and snorkel but the hundred metres was too much for her and she paddled around the boat while Ann and I went calling.

That evening Michael and Linda picked us up and took us ashore to the bar. They had a big rubber duck that would seat seven but the fuel pump kept playing up and Michael had to keep squeezing the manual one or the motor stopped. We'd been right not to try and get into the marina. On the face of it, it looked possible but there wasn't much shelter and, for fun, there were a few scattered concrete blocks just below the surface exactly where you might want to turn.

It was good to see our friends again and we sat in the evening sun and sweated a little and swatted a lot at the mosquitoes and Caryn turned red as the sun sank. We talked about places we'd all been and things we'd seen and the things we'd missed. After the city the calm blue of the sea and the view of the distant hills was relaxing.

But we were keen to get on. We'd told Caryn we were going to drop her at Oristano and she wasn't very pleased but we were well aware of time running down and we needed every day we could pinch if we were to meet our haul-out date in Greece. We saw Michael and Linda for the last time next morning when they came over for coffee, then they said goodbye and left. Heading south. Away from the flat hills of Alghero and towards the mountainous western coastline of Sardinia.

Around two in the afternoon the wind was blowing about fifteen knots from the north and the sea was picking up a little. As we rounded Capo Marargiu the wind stayed the same but the sea picked up and threw a few whitecaps around. Caryn had been reading on her off-watch and was now feeling queasy, we were also getting some spray over the bow.

We spent a lot of time looking for Bosa, and coming from the north it's not easy to find, you have to trundle along the base of the steep hills to the north and be stoic until you reach the coast. Rachel was reliable as ever though and we found the harbour entrance which is south of the river and we rocked and rolled in through the gap and put on the brakes once we were in the shelter of the breakwater.

Bosa, Sardinia, 751 miles to Gouvia. Day 89

Bosa marina isn't really a marina – it's the Italian sense of the word again. It's a couple of jetties behind a breakwater and most of the yachts sheltering behind it were at anchor off the beach. One left as we arrived and hit head on into the waves that were rolling in through the entrance kicking up a cloud of spray and crashing down into the surf. Because the seas were behind us we hadn't realised how rough it had become.

We'd been told dreadful stories of Bosa. Moor in the wrong place and get your boat untied. Take your dinghy up the river and tie up on the quay at your peril. Pay up front or get set adrift. The two *Capos* who helped us moor looked like contenders for the Italian rugby team front row and it may have been that, or it may have been the stories, but I have never seen Ann disappear off to pay for a berth so quickly. The office was in the bar, a kind of ramshackle building leaning against the breakwater that also housed toilets, if you dared, and showers.

'Are you Robert de Niro?' I looked up to see who Caryn was talking to ready to cringe with embarrassment. She was standing in her shortest dress with a glass of wine and looking across two boats to our right where a couple of Spanish guys were tidying up. I cringed with embarrassment and wondered if I could slip unnoticed down into the cabin.

'Are you?' she persisted. The Spanish guy was trying hard to ignore her but Caryn won't be ignored. She drank a little and smiled and she has a friendly smile so the Spaniard – who looked like Robert de Niro – had to smile too. Then he brought us a great slab of bleeding tuna which was, he said, too much for them to eat so would we like some.

Caryn smiled again and took another swig of wine. Ann congratulated her and I went off to sit still until my embarrassed face was replaced by a more normal one.

The Spaniards had arrived that day from the Balearics and had caught the tuna on the way. It's so easy they told us. You throw out the hook and they eat it. Caryn decided she would show us how to fish next day.

That night I went walking up to the local shops. The boat had grown smaller and I needed a bit of space. The mosquitoes bit me.

Bosa is a beach and a harbour and a town. The beach and the harbour sit behind the breakwater and all the local families and tourists come and swim in the relative safety of the lagoon. To the north of the marina is the river Tenno and if you follow it inland you find the town of Bosa on Serravalle hill. Above the town is the twelfth century Malaspina Castle and in its courtyard is the Regnos Altos church with its fourteenth century frescos. I knew all this because I had read a brochure, not because I went walking.

The fun thing to do in Bosa is to take the dinghy three kilometres up the river and climb to the castle, but next day the sea was still a too rough and the forecast was for worsening wind and sea. Ann had found a friendly Scots couple on a small cruiser a few boats away along the pontoon and had made the usual information swap.

They'd told her about the busses so Ann and Caryn went to town by bus and I did a software update to the engine monitor which was much more exciting.

In the afternoon I swam and later, when they returned hot and tired, I swam again with Ann while Caryn showered on the deck. Caryn had opted out of the castle but Ann is a determined woman and decided to see the views from the top. It's worth it, she told me and showed me the pictures to prove it. Caryn just seemed knackered.

That evening the ladies dealt with the bloody tuna while I hid on the foredeck, I'm not much good with blood. Caryn told me I was squeamish and later added that I was finicky with my food because I didn't like tomatoes.

'Ann I've done sixty stokes of the toilet thing but nothing is moving.' I nearly fainted, two hundred strokes filled the tank, fifteen usually does what's necessary. Ann disappeared down below and found the valve in the wrong place. While Ann was below Caryn slapped her daily dose of sunscreen on and splattered the decks then got it all over the cockpit grab handles.

'Did you, by the way, close the hatch in your cabin?' Ann asked.

'I didn't know I had to.' Caryn replied.

'It's to stop the sea coming in and sinking us.'

Caryn disappeared below to wipe sunscreen on the cushions and close the hatch. 'I told her.' Ann said. 'I told her twice at least.'

But I knew that. In the corner of the cockpit three pairs of knickers were hung on the genoa sheet.

'Give her a chance,' Ann said, but didn't sound so convincing this time.

Next day the wind had died and the sea had calmed down so we could head south again. Ann looked at the blue sky and told us we now hadn't seen rain for two months and hardly a cloud either. She sounded a bit worried about it. The temperatures kept creeping upwards, yesterday it had reached thirty-three in the shade. We were also not sailing more than about ten percent of the time, the winds were either non-existent, too strong, or in the wrong direction. We took weather forecasts wherever we could get them, either "Metal Martha" – she was a disembodied metallic woman's voice who repeated the Italian weather service forecast in English on VHF – or a GRIB file from the internet. But neither service took account of the local influences of geography, katabatic conditions and sea breezes so forecasting for our inshore passages became an art and one that we never quite mastered. So we became used to being caught out and every time we set off in calm conditions we expected and subconsciously planned to arrive in a howling gale. This had been true in Porto Conte, when we first arrived there, and in Bosa. But today was dead flat calm. So far.

South of Bosa the coast is flat with villages and towns, beaches of sand or rock, a few sandbars and islets. We were heading for Tharros on the Sinis peninsula for a bit of Carthaginian history then on to Torre Grande which had a marina where Caryn would leave us on a bus bound for Oristano. Caryn was now spending all her off-watch time on the foredeck with a book, seemingly disinterested in either sailing or scenery.

'She's doing her bit, though.' said Ann, but when Caryn steered she'd taken to sitting on the rear step behind the wheel and from there she couldn't see anything more than the compass so either Ann or I had to stand peering ahead, looking for the dread lobster pots. 'But she's good in the galley,' Ann was trying hard. Caryn seemed to like picking on me at mealtimes because I didn't like the same food as her so I wasn't in the mood to agree.

A couple of bottlenose dolphins rolled by just to cheer me up. Caryn, sitting on the step, missed them which made me feel good. Then I felt guilty.

Chapter 16

Tharros, Sardinia, 726 miles to Gouvia. Day 91

Carthage owned much of the Mediterranean seaboard about 250 BC and that included Sardinia and Corsica, and Tharros was one of their cities and that was where we were headed. The Carthaginians lost it in the Punic wars, which was careless of them because we found it easily just around the headland of the Sinis peninsula. The Gulf of Oristano is big and open and a swell rolls in on the calmest of days but close to the coast, under the ruins of Tharros, are a number of buoys for yachts to use, which is handy because it's really deep there. We found one and introduced Caryn to the skills of picking up a buoy.

'Who made the Tharros ruins?' Ann asked.

'No-one,' I said, trying to be clever, 'but the Carthaginians made the town.'

Ann gave me one of those looks that transmitted the phrase: 'You're trying to be clever but are just boring.'

'And time or the Romans ruined it.' I finished sheepishly.

'Actually,' Ann said, 'it was built by the Phoenicians eight hundred years before Christ and lasted until the eleventh century A.D. – so there! It has lots of *tophets* which contained the ashes of burnt children.' She was reading a brochure. 'They had baths and water towers and temples and roads and a bookshop.'

All we could see from the sea were two tall columns, a lot of fallen masonry and a bookshop by the entrance gate on top of the hill.

So we launched the dinghy and got the outboard working and set off for a mile along the coast to somewhere we could go ashore. The somewhere was a white beach with lots of other small boats and dinghies bobbing gently in the turquoise water. We stepped overboard when the motor's skeg hit the sand and waded ashore towing the dinghy until there was only an inch or two under it, then we buried its little anchor and, for luck, tied it's painter to a nearby buoy.

Despite having our feet in the sea the sun felt awfully hot. We waded ashore through warm water and started up the dusty path towards the site's entrance gate above us. We reached a dirt road lined with parked cars and two or three café-bars. On the sea side of the peninsula was a popular beach packed with near naked happy holidayers doing what they do best in the shade of beach umbrellas. Caryn promptly decided it was too hot to continue walking and took to the shade of the nearest bar. 'I don't think she has much stamina,' Ann whispered ignoring my puffing and wheezing progress up the hill. By the time we reached the gate I was a sodden wreck. I took my wet shirt off and put it over my head like a headdress.

Ann has determination as well as stamina and we covered every inch of the site trying to make baths from stone piles, temples from heaps of rubble, dead children's graves from circular ruins. The black basalt roads burned through our sandals and the blue sea looked inviting but we had to walk uphill again to the exit and the ice-cream shop.

We found Caryn in the shade with a beer and she took one look at us and bought us one too.

We had decided to stay on the buoy that night. Looking at the swell I thought this was a bad decision but Ann was captain that day, we were taking it in turns again to try and head off some of the little arguments that we were having, and Caryn was siding with Ann which made discussion futile. We were cooled by a long swim and by the time we hauled ourselves out of the water the ladies didn't want to motor the hour to Torre Grande. It was a pleasant enough setting, under the headland, but I knew it was so exposed we were going to get a swell all night long. We ate tuna and salad and drank white wine in the quiet evening under the columns of Tharros and the homes of the rich while the sun dipped and died turning the sky purple and flashing green across the water an instant before it fell into the ruins.

Torre Grande, Sardinia, 720 miles to Gouvia. Day 92

Ann set Caryn a compass course which would take us across the bay towards the south east. Although we ultimately wanted to go north to Torre Grande we had to empty our holding tank and that meant getting offshore at least a couple of miles. The day was another blue day and if that sounds as if I was getting bored with them, well maybe I was, or perhaps I wanted to head for Sicily and Italy and Greece before the season began to close down. I didn't want storms, but the baking oven of Sardinian August was sapping all our stamina. The sun had made Caryn pink and the heat had made me short tempered. Only Ann seemed unaffected.

She was doing duty standing over Caryn as she steered the course. Now and then Ann would remind her to look at the compass and bring *Aderyn Glas* back on course. I went below and played with Rachel's GPS, adding a waypoint that Caryn would be able to aim at once we'd dumped the tank.

After half an hour we pumped out and turned north. Ann went below and I pulled up a GPS display that was simply a big arrow and asked Caryn to steer so that the arrow always pointed upwards. It was futile and frustrating. Caryn seemed to have no idea that what she did with the wheel affected what the boat did and thus what the arrow did. At first I tried to give her gentle reminders but after a short time I realised that she just steered blindly and waited for me to correct her so I stopped. I suggested she had a look around and I pointed to where we had to go but this didn't help either. So I left her alone to sort it out herself. After another half hour we were heading straight back towards Tharros and I couldn't take it any more. I stuck my head down the companionway and in a kind of hysterical fit asked Ann to take over. Caryn, to me, was a lost cause. I learned there and then that some people simply can't control a boat, something that had never occurred to me before. And from that moment life became easier, I no longer felt frustrated because I no longer had any expectations. If Caryn wanted to learn to sail it was going to be someone else who would have to teach her from scratch. Amanda could do it in spades, Sue took to it like she was born to it, Ann could do it with her eyes closed and so could everyone else we'd ever had on board. Caryn couldn't.

'Fish farms,' Ann said and looking out ahead all we could see were corridors of fish farm buoys. Which buoys marked the channel? After a while the pattern formed like trees in a plantation and we could see the corridor right up to the marina entrance a mile away. It was the shallowest approach we'd encountered, a series of dog legs and if we ran aground there was no tide to lift us off.

Our nerves weren't settled by the fact that boats leaving were taking a completely different direction to us, going far closer to the peninsula. I slowed right down and watched the depth sounder. As we rounded the breakwater and entered the marina there was less than a metre under our keels, but we made it.

Ann, by now, was very good at raising the *Capos* on the radio and we were shown to a berth on an inner concrete quay. The marina's style was concrete blockhouse and the still air was heated by red hot cement. No-one moved on any of the moored cruisers and yachts. It was the first time we'd found the water in the quayside taps was not potable and the electricity needed a man to fix something somewhere before it would work for us. We shared the showers with some amazing insect life and by the time we'd walked back from the shower block we needed another one.

We found brief comfort later on a bus to town. Caryn was treating us to a last supper and the bus was air-conditioned and comfortable. Torre Grande was a linear strip of beach backed by restaurants which explained why the bus conductor looked puzzled when we asked him to put us off at the town centre – there wasn't one. We were too early for the restaurant so we sat outside, had a drink and fed the mosquitoes and Caryn and I amused ourselves taking photos of the sunset and silhouettes of people on the beach.

'What are you doing next, Caryn?' I asked.

'Actually, I'm off to South Africa on a whale conservation program and while I'm there I've signed up to do a competent crew qualification.' Somehow neither Ann nor I choked on our drinks but it was close.

In the morning we said goodbye to Caryn. Ann had given her the bus and train times and she'd elected for an early departure for whatever reason. We all hugged briefly but I think we all knew Caryn's experiment with sailing hadn't been a happy one for any of us and any thoughts I'd had of chartering to strangers left on the bus with Caryn.

Back on the quayside we had a war with an Italian neighbour who objected strongly and vociferously when I detached the hose running from the only potable water tap to her boat. Italians seem to claim a tap and are likely to run a hose from it to their boat where they leave it attached for the duration of their stay. She had the potable water and tough luck to everyone else.

'*Cinque minuti, solo cinque minuti*,' I said, but she screamed at me anyway. Finally her screams woke the young guy on the next boat who crawled out into his cockpit in nothing but a towel and he calmed her down then borrowed the hose after I'd finished filling our tanks.

'You see,' I said to her as I reconnected her hose,' international co-operation is the European way.' But she didn't understand.

'Buggerru next.' Ann said with a glint in her eye, relishing the word.

'*Ooo*, you cheeky monkey!' I camped it up.

'Buggerru. We're free!' she laughed, 'Buggerru and Carloforte and Sicily and Italy and Greece.' and we laughed together and hugged and kissed, freed from chains of family and friends, free to take on the sea, the ocean, the world! If only we'd known.

'Okay, calm down. The pilot says Buggerru's too shallow even for us.' I said.

'There's a bay. Completely unsheltered but shallow enough to anchor.'

I didn't like the sound of "unsheltered" but there wasn't much choice. Buggerru or bust!

We fuelled, waiting while the fuelling station filled its own tanks, a process that seemed to require that all the staff and the tanker driver sit around and do nothing for half an hour before actually starting work. By the time they'd all had their fags there was a considerable queue of little bobbing boats strung out behind us.

The water was shallow. As we left the depth sounder unrolled to the point where we should have hit the bottom but then started to increase again as I was about to go astern. Off the entrance a big French yacht had not been so attentive to his instruments and was wedged onto the sand right where you would expect the channel to be deepest. He was busy setting out a kedge and wouldn't accept a tow from us. 'Probably afraid we'll claim salvage.' Ann said, 'Time to go.'

So we tip-toed away from Torre Grande, sailed across Oristano gulf and south down the Costa Verde which was called green but was actually a line of cliffs interspersed with rolling sand-dunes big as mountains. There was little sign of habitation and few holiday beaches, obviously most of the holiday resorts were in the north of the island with a few on the east and south coast. Eventually we rounded Capo Pécora, which I didn't think stuck out enough to be called a cape, and motored into the bay across from Buggerru off a holiday village called Portixeddu. It was all very open and enough of a swell rolled in to make us want to deploy the stern anchor to keep us pointing into it.

Buggerru, Sardinia, 690 miles to Gouvia. Day 93

Buggerru is where we chopped through our stern anchor rope because I was too lazy to put the dinghy in the water. Ann dropped the bow anchor where I told her and started paying out the chain while I motored us backwards. When we had twice as much chain out as we would ever need I nudged the boat forward to stop it and told Ann to lock the winch. Then I threw in the stern anchor and everything happened at once: Ann screamed that she couldn't stop the chain running over the bow and I glanced into the water under the stern and saw how shallow it was. I admit I reacted without thinking: Ann was shouting, the water was too shallow and we were going to hit and break the rudder, so I jammed her into full ahead. After a second there was a huge bang: we must have hit a rock. The engine made a strange noise and I slammed it into neutral. That was the only sensible thing I did in the entire episode.

The truth dawned on me slowly. With the boat still moving backwards because of Ann's winch problem and me going full ahead the suction had dragged the stern anchor rope into the propeller and bang I had heard was the rope cutter (God bless whichever previous owner had fitted it) cutting the rope.

Now we had no engine: I didn't dare turn the prop again in case it was damaged or the shaft was bent, even worse the engine may have been thrown off its mounts. Nor could we use the power winch without the engine running.

So, tired and angry with myself for being so slow thinking (I'm supposed to be a steely-eyed pilot – best not to fly with me!) I cranked the anchor winch by hand and managed to take up the tension and lock the winch. So long as the anchor didn't decide to drag we were safe.

Ann and I occasionally argue, mainly over trivial things, but when something serious happens we work together. In went the dinghy that I had tried to avoid launching in the first place, and I followed with mask, snorkel and a knife.

The rope had wound all around the cutlass bearing, shaft and screw and was lashed into strands, but I worked at it. It hurt my lungs and my heart was hammering: saw a little, surface for breath, saw a little more... Over and over I nearly smashed my head as the boat, lifted by a wave, dropped on me in the trough. Trying to hold position with one hand around the prop shaft while sawing with the other was killing me. But in the end I had sawn through it and when I turned the propeller by hand it all looked well, I nearly drowned with the relief.

Then I found the anchor which itself was a minor miracle – there was a lot of sea it could have been in. It was deeper than I expected which says a lot about the water clarity. What I had thought was a metre or two was actually about five metres and that's a lot when you have to dive down and do some work. I knew I would not be able to stay long enough on the bottom to tie a rope so Ann went looking for a hook and came up with a huge snap shackle that we used on the chum weights. It worked like a dream: dive, snap, surface and strain the sinews to haul the thing up. Then all we had to do was tie on another length of rope and use the dinghy to deploy it – which is what I should have done in the first place.

'The idea was sound,' Ann said, 'it should have been okay to reverse and drop the stern anchor then pull forward again.'

She was being kind to me. 'It's my fault,' I admitted, 'I threw it in before the boat had stopped then panicked and used the engine. Even if it had all been chain we might still have slid sideways and hooked it.' I went cold at the thought of what chain around the prop would have done. 'We got away with it.' It could have been such a disaster but the shaft and the screw and the engine were all okay and tomorrow we could move on.

In the evening a disco played but it seemed a pathetic place to spend a holiday.

Buggerru – which, with a name like that it should be in Australia – is set in the mouth of a steep high valley on the south side of the bay and has a lot of derelict mine buildings which hang poised above the marina and form a bizarre backdrop to the holiday town. We read that the caves and tunnels, that were clearly visible in the mountainside, once provided obsidian and other minerals and are now tourist attractions. In 1901 its population had been over five thousand and twenty years later it was half that. It was evocative, we wondered about its history and wanted to know more.

'We'll add it to our list of places to visit,' Ann said, but the list is already so long we would need another lifetime. I mentally waved it goodbye and told Rachel to take us south to the island of San Pietro and the town of Carloforte and we hauled out the sails and settled down for a howling, rocking, spray-filled passage to our last port on Sardinia.

Carloforte, Sardinia, 671 miles to Gouvia. Day 94

The wind howled and we scooted across shallow waters that led to the entrance to Carloforte. Ann was worried about the depth and kept looking from the chart to the sounder and worried even more. The ferry came out of the entrance and turned into the dredged channel but I steered us recklessly onwards across weedy water that was a shortcut. Ann gritted her teeth and I knew she thought I was being an idiot but I had a secret. For some time, when she was below, I had watched a large sailing yacht taking this course and thought that if he could do it so could I.

It was one of those better days, a good breeze from behind and a sea that wasn't yet so rough as to be uncomfortable. It was all blue sky and blue sea and a passage that wasn't too long. Then we entered the harbour and suddenly the wind was blowing us sideways and if I took my eye off the ball for a second we were never going to get *Aderyn Glas* to come around again and we would pierce our hull on the anchors of the posh yachts tied up in a line and pointing at us.

There are three marinas and although no-one answered Ann's calls a couple of *Capos* turned up in a RIB and pointed to a berth. We needed them. The wind was a handful. In fact they learned that a boat like ours, which doesn't have a bow-thruster, will not always bend to the whim of a *Capo* however much he waves his arms around so we ended up in different berth where the wind deposited us and we hit the pontoon with a thump. But we were all happy in the end. Welcome to Carloforte, windiest place in Sardinia, I thought. And how the hell would we get out again if the wind didn't drop? We'd need a tug at least.

The pilot book has a lot to say about Carloforte and if you plan to go in there you need to read it. There is a little harbour to the north of the main breakwater that is not for the likes of us, and the main harbour boasts three marinas, one to the south and two to the north. The trick is to be as far from the ferry wash as you can get which means being inside the northernmost of the marinas and on the northernmost pontoon. We didn't get lucky and the RIB that turned out for us was from Marinatour Mamma Mahon but the good news was we were positioned on the north side of their pontoon not in the ferry basin. Their advertising claims the pontoon is well sheltered from the *Mistral* and southern winds. It isn't. There were no toilets, no showers and non-potable water but they did have wifi.

Carloforte is another town built around a ferry port and by now we were pretty much disinterested in one more Sardinian town. All we wanted was a supermarket, a chandlery to replace the rope we'd chopped up, and a café for a coffee. We bumped into *Margaret-May*, with the Scots couple we'd met in Bosa, and they pointed us in the direction of all three.

The first chandlery wanted seven euros a metre for the fourteen millimetre laid rope, and we wanted twenty metres of it so we left. The second and the third all wanted the same so we left them too. The supermarket was small and had no meat nor iced tea, but the café had coffee that was reasonable.

The marina staff were friendly and helpful and showed us the weather patterns for the next few days on their computer. Ann took one look and decided we had to leave. 'Tomorrow.' She said, 'we have to leave tomorrow or get stuck here for a week.'

I looked out at the wind that was blowing the flags rigid and picking up little whitecaps in the harbour and wondered if it would be at all possible.

Back on board we prepared for our longest crossing. The weather window we had seen on the computer would let us leave in the late afternoon next day, which was what we wanted. That timing would give us an early morning arrival off the Sicilian coast after two nights at sea.

'You do realise,' I said, repeating myself, 'that it is actually shorter to cross to Tunisia and then on to Sicily? That would be two single nights at sea rather than two nights in one passage.' Ann could tell how keen I was to commit ourselves to two hundred plus miles, who would save us if something went wrong?

We rang Amanda at home and told her of our plan. She is the contact in case we have to use our EPIRB – our satellite rescue beacon. We checked everything, then checked it again. I changed the engine oil and fed some waypoints into Rachel. Outside the cabin the wind was still howling when bedtime came.

Next day it was still howling. We worried. We checked the forecast and worried again because we knew about forecast accuracy by then. To try to calm our nerves we went and found another supermarket but when we returned we found our nerves waiting for us.

Ann made sandwiches and soup and put the sandwiches in the fridge. She arranged all the warm clothes we would need for the nights – *nights* plural, I shuddered – and checked the EPIRB, and the torches, the harnesses and the lifejackets. I checked the radar, the three GPSs, the chartplotter and the spare computer, the three VHF radios and the navigation lights. I strapped the dinghy tighter to its davits and checked we could launch the liferaft in a hurry. Then we both walked around the boat and worried about everything again to ensure it would work when we needed it.

We planned to leave at four thirty and left at two. We couldn't stand the waiting. It was a stupid thing to do because once a plan is made for sound reasons it shouldn't be changed on the basis of emotion. The wind was too high.

'But what we'll do is call the *Capo* and he'll come and haul us off.' I said, but Ann couldn't raise them and I had a go too and also couldn't raise them.

'We shouldn't go then,' I decided, 'the wind is pushing us onto the jetty and there's no tug to haul us off. Even if *Aderyn Glas* goes backwards in a straight line, which will be a first, we then have to turn side on to the wind and if we're not travelling fast by then we'll get blown onto this line of boats and rip out all our stanchions. We must wait'.

'Okay lets go.' I was hyper and so was Ann, we'd worked ourselves up into a gung-ho state and that was that.

I briefed Ann. She would be on the foredeck and would release all the ropes except one bow-line. I would rev the engine backwards to get some flow over the rudder and when I gave the word she would release the rope and we would fly out of the berth without hitting the posh sailing cruiser on the left or the posh motor cruiser on the right both of whom were moored stern-to so had nasty looking anchors exactly where we would pivot.

I dropped the stern line and watched it fall.

'We're hitting the pontoon.' Ann said with a note of fear in her voice. I clunked the control into slow astern until I was sure the line had sunk then opened her up. Ann decided this was the signal and let go the bow line far too early and my shouting didn't help.

Aderyn Glas crept backwards against the pressure of the wind and I had no rudder control at all. Then she began to turn to the left as she was halfway out of the berth, then swivelled violently sideward as the wind caught her. I put the control to full forward, we were going to be pushed sideways into the sailing cruiser and I had to try and prevent his anchor chewing into our hull. It was imperative I stop the boat or we would get ripped apart. At a stretch I could just reach him and leaned over to push us off. Suddenly the wind accelerated us forwards and we swung violently back into the berth we'd just left. Now I had to go full astern again to stop us ramming the jetty. I was working on instinct, having no clear idea of why the boat was behaving like she was, it was as if we'd been catapulted back into the berth.

Ann was screaming from the foredeck: 'Go! Go now! We're all lined up, it's perfect, go!' I didn't even look around, I trusted her judgement and slammed us astern. We shot out without even kissing either of the boats alongside us and I turned her and kept going flat out astern into the basin at the head of the pontoons. Only then did I dare breathe. Only then did I turn into wind and stop the boat and take a deep settling breath. Then we turned again and headed for the exit. The *Capo* arrived in his dinghy and asked if we needed help. We had arrived in a wind, it blew all the time we were there and we left in a wind.

We held a post-mortem trying to make sense of what had happened, of we had seen and what we had felt under our feet. Ann had let go too soon but she always does, every time we try that technique, I should have been ready for it. As we came out the wind caught us and pushed us sideways enough to hook the stern-line of the boat next door on our keel, this had the effect of catapulting us around, first backwards then, as I changed the throttle, forwards back into the berth. When Ann screamed at me to go astern we had already cleared the line and were perfectly aimed and she was right. We'd been lucky. Looking back as we left the marina we could have been looking at two damaged cruisers and a destroyed dinghy. The anchor from the sailing cruiser would have torn our saloon, broken stanchions and shattered the port windows.

'It can only get better then.' I smiled. All the tension was gone now that we were actually moving. We tossed a coin to Poseidon but it wasn't going to save us.

Chapter 17

Capo Sperone, Sardinia, 671 miles to Gouvia. Day 95

The dolphins shot horizontally out of the front of the green curling waves. They took it in turns, flying from the front of the wave and curving down to enter the water without a splash. We were two hours into the passage and near the southern tip of Sardinia and the wind had not moderated much and the seas were well over a metre which is how the dolphins came to be flying from the front of them as they curled.

And we were sailing.

'Forty hours of this?' I asked. I hoped the note in my voice sent a clear message to Ann, 'we can't even use Rachel, it's too rough.'

'If it continues once we're around the cape we can always run up to Cagliari or Villasimius but then we lose our weather window.'

'What weather window?' I grumbled.

The dolphins kept playing then got bored and disappeared.

I hate voyages that hang about waiting to start. This one wasn't going to get going for six hours, that's how long it was going to take to round Capo Spartivento, the southernmost tip of the island, and only then could we set course for Sicily. Meanwhile the deck twisted and bucked under us and we had to take turns at the wheel.

Flying fish scampered over the surface. Ann was below and missed them. They had appeared from the sea as a group and dived back into the water twenty metres later leaving a brief pattern of ripples like raindrops on a pond.

It was rough and it was chilly and we were apprehensive. For a long time we'd been used to warm winds and flat seas and this was neither. Also nightfall was getting earlier as September approached and so the nights were longer and the watches more dreary. I wore long trousers, the first time for months.

We took down the genoa and started the engine as the sun dipped, and lit the lights and warmed up the radar. I heated up a ready meal, something I have never done before at sea, usually feeling too queasy when the seas are rough. We must be becoming more tolerant of the movement I thought. Ann didn't like it and threw most of it away but I enjoyed the warm feeling in my stomach. A yacht was heading north towards Cagliari and it took an effort of will to keep steering east.

After sunset the seas calmed down enough for Rachel to take over steering and so, by default and without a word, the decision was taken to continue to Sicily.

Around midnight a target appeared on the radar and soon afterward I saw the lights of a huge ship heading our way, travelling down from the northeast. Ferries and cruise ships are festooned with lights, so many that it is often hard to see their navigation lights, but this ship was almost dark and I guessed at a tanker or a container ship, one of those huge things that could run over us and not even notice that they'd killed us. I knew all the stories about tanker drivers who didn't ever look out of the window and all the stories about how little a radar echo a yacht like us had even with a reflector.

The little white radar blip came closer, dodging inside one range ring after another and I tried in vain to remember how to plot a track on the radar screen to see if it was going to collide with us. It was hard to tell. But I could see that his range kept decreasing.

Out in the air it was equally hard to tell. At times I thought I could see both his sidelights which meant he was pointing at us, at other times only his red one, which meant he would miss us.

Finally I could see the bulk of the huge ship. He took form around his navigation lights and the radar blip told me he would miss us – but not by much. He rolled passed, his bridge a kind of green glow, his hull black against black accompanied by a thumping noise and a smell of exhaust. The radar said he was a hundred metres away but I felt I could touch him.

Then he turned. I watched his progress on the radar as he turned around my stern. This was indeed the kindest captain I'd ever even heard of. I always expected a ship this big to set a course and go wherever he wanted and tough luck you little boats get out of the way. This guy actually seemed to have deliberately avoided us and turned around our stern. Out in the air again I watched his port side light swing around behind us but then he continued southward and, after a while, it blinked out.

There was a new moon, but it wasn't bright enough to dim the Milky Way or the shooting stars. A whole heaven of lights arced above us as we swapped watches. I hope I never get used to the magnificence of the night sky seen from the sea. The immensity of it all strikes me every time: a hundred thousand million stars in a hundred thousand million galaxies. How can we hope to comprehend it?

To the north the lights of Sardinia stayed with us for hours eventually dimming as we travelled.

I felt exposed. I felt remote from land and help. Ann was much more positive than I was and I'm not sure that I had a premonition, it was probably simple anxiety.

Next day was bright and sunny and *Aderyn Glas* purred across a flat sea all alone. No land, no ships, no dolphin, not even a bird. We saw nothing all day long. Only the sea, the boat, and each other. Ann read and I caught up on the Formula 1 races I'd missed playing DVDs that Amanda had recorded for me.

We tried fishing. Eddie had told me I needed a steel trace for my fishing line so I made one by cutting a length of insulated steel wire that I had on board. In the process I speared my finger and started bleeding all over the place. Ann loves playing doctor so she wrapped up the hole and told me to sit with my hand in the air for ten minutes which made my arm ache so I couldn't feel the cut any more.

'See,' she said, 'it works.'

My steel trace was a masterpiece of home engineering and was so thick it could do duty as a spare tow line.

'Don't you think the fish will see the trace and go somewhere else?' Ann is always able to put her finger on the smallest miscalculation.

'We won't need a weight.' I pointed out.

I put a swivel between the trace and the line, like Eddie had told us, and tied the pink plastic squid on the end. The appearance of more bright red blood suggested I had speared my thumb with the hook. This meant another ten minutes with my hand in the air and a plaster which promptly fell off when my thumb got wet.

After an hour I noticed a strange thing, the fishing line was tying itself in tight little knots.

'Look darling,' I said, hoping to head off any critique of my technique, 'the line is *hockling*.' This being an American word used to describe the DNA-like twists inside twists that cables make when they are spun I thought she would be impressed.

'It looks like it's twisting to me,' she said, 'that swivel isn't working is it?'

I started hauling in the line and trying to untwist it as I went. Every time the tension was relaxed the line tied itself furiously into ever tighter knots and in the end I had to admit defeat. I hauled the tangled mess over the side and recovered the little pink squid then cut off the mess and stuffed it into the rubbish bag.

'Well we didn't need all that line anyway.' I said.

About halfway through the day we realised we were travelling too fast and slowed down. This was a psychologically hard thing to do, the desire to arrive as soon as we could was strong in us. But we had calculated on the basis of five knots and were doing six and had hit seven in last night's winds, so we would arrive in the dark, at four in the morning. Even with Rachel that was not something we liked to do. We'd been caught out by our planning before and should have learned a lesson.

The second night was rougher. We knew there was going to be a wind and had planned our course and speed to miss the worst of it - and then left too early and travelled too fast. It blew from the east so we met it head on, ploughing into increasing seas with the main up for stability and the speed down to about three knots because we were still far too early.

It was in the middle of that night I noticed the bright glow of an indicator lamp on the dashboard, the one that lit up when the alternator wasn't generating enough electricity. I revved the engine a little and it went out. Then it came back. It didn't register on my tired mind, for some time, that we had an alternator failure. Then I checked the battery voltage and had a shock.

Suddenly we had a crisis. If we continued to burn amps the way we were we would kill the batteries long before we arrived off land. We started switching things off: the radar, the computer, the radio, the internal lights, we thought about the nav lights and the fridge but left them for the time being. And we left the GPS on. The alternator light stayed on.

'NASA, we have a problem.' Where was Tom Hanks? All Apollo 13 had was a fairly trivial *"main B bus undervolt"* while we were losing bus A and bus B and every other bus in the depot.

We travelled, miserable, towards a dark, unknown landfall in a wind that chopped up the seas and threw us around. On my watch a light appeared that had to be the forbidding, island-strewn coast of Sicily. I turned us a little north to give it safety distance and immediately suffered as the seas began to roll us about mercilessly.

Ann took over for a while but I couldn't sleep, the boat simply rolled too much and I was too worried. The little indicator light burned brightly but the battery voltage had stopped its plummeting. I suppose it was cool enough that night to stop the fridge running too much.

I took the helm back and sent Ann down for a sleep, there was no point in us both being exhausted and she sleeps through anything. In the distance I saw a large ship lit from stem to stern against the blackness and altered course a bit more to the north.

Now I saw little lights on the shore to the south that were far too close and turned away again. Ann had worried about there being an island to our north but without the chartplotter I had no idea where it might be. The GPS wasn't helping me, it showed we were off track by miles. We could and should have plotted our position on a paper chart and I don't know why we didn't, I suppose we were simply too tired to think straight.

We saw a string of lights where the shore would be and they were too close: a fish farm. Again I turned away northward. I saw ships and boats and harbours, pontoons, breakwaters, buoys and lighthouses. I saw houses and factories and busy roads… and I saw nothing. I wanted dawn to come. Most of all I wanted the rolling to stop and the noise and spray; and I wanted the hot summer sun to return and warm me through. And I wanted someone to tell me it would be okay and he would have the alternator fixed in ten minutes and the batteries were undamaged, and here, have this lovely warm breakfast while you wait. And welcome to Sicily.

When dawn came, it brought crashing disappointment. All those things that had driven us north because they were so close were miles and miles away. The ship was an apartment block, the pontoons and harbours streetlights on a distant coast road, there were no lighthouses, no buoys and no breakwaters anywhere near us. And now, because I had turned so far to the north, we faced another couple of hours slogging towards our destination on a sick boat.

San Vito, Sicily, 447 miles to Gouvia. Day 97

We couldn't miss it. The rock towering over San Vito lo Capo rises fourteen hundred feet straight up from the coastal plain and looks like Gibraltar. The town and its marina lie on a bay at its foot and a hook of land protects the marina from the north, though the bay is open to anything with north or east in it.

We sailed into the marina and tied up at the fuel pontoon, pushing our way into the mass of fisherman that thought the fuel jetty was for them. The attendant was the usual non-smiling Italian and as a welcome for a boat that had just crossed an ocean there was a certain something lacking. He told us to call the marina on channel sixteen, there were two, he said, so there would be no problem.

There was no answer from anyone. We drove around a little hoping that a RIB would appear with a couple of welcoming *Capos* but none did and after one foray towards a space on a pontoon the propeller started vibrating so I gave up and took us outside the marina to anchor in the bay.

The day was warming a little though it was still only nine in the morning. I went for a swim to investigate the propeller and found it wrapped Christmas-present tidy in a gill net.

We had breakfast. It seemed the civilised thing to do. I looked out over the bay and my gaze met the horizon in a broad sweep from north to east and I knew we couldn't stay anchored in such an exposed place.

We tried again, this time aiming at the pontoons on the southern side. There was a space on the far side of the first pontoon and I tickled our way towards it. By now we were in the mood to be forceful: there was a space and we wanted it. I put Ann on the bow with a boathook like a blonde warrior queen.

There were boaters everywhere but no-one bothered to help us at all. Then a guy from a yacht the other side of the pontoon leapt off his boat and came running across to take our lines and hand us the stern-line. He was Italian but smiled and spoke English so must have been a bit less parochial than the others around.

'They're all mafia,' Ann whispered. 'We didn't know who to pay so the Godfather told everyone to ignore us.' I wondered if there was a grain of truth in what she said, after all, this was Sicily.

The boss turned up in livery with a side-kick and told us we couldn't stay. Our new friend argued with him. The boss said he had a booking for five boats and couldn't guarantee a place but that we could pay him anyway. Our new friend said in that case we could have his berth because he was leaving. The boss grumbled and went away with his sidekick following and took up guard duty in a chair where the pontoon ramped up to the breakwater. Our new friend told us all would be well and we would be okay now and not to drink the water and the showers had mosquitoes and the toilets were like an oven.

But we didn't care - we were in Sicily. The longest passage of our careers was over. The longest passage we had to make to get to Greece was over. Our last night passage was over. All we had to do now was find a way to fix the alternator and we could continue. Naivety is wonderful!

Despite the wind it was hot, thirty-three in our cockpit and all the shades and all the fans didn't help much. The Italians on the pontoon washed themselves down with water from the taps then washed their boats and washed the pontoon. They were happy and chatty amongst themselves but didn't talk or smile at us, we began to feel less like foreigners and more like aliens from some remote star.

We charged the batteries with the mains charger, although it would add a bit to the heat in the saloon, we had little choice. At least we had no power issues until we moved again.

It's a sandy place, this San Vito lo Capo. As soon as we set foot on the breakwater our ankles were assailed by wind-blown sand and the concrete underfoot was covered in miniature dunes that broke up and reformed as the wind swirled around. We walked into town and visited the museum, bought an ice-cream and found an internet café. I went looking for an alternator on the internet and found I could have one couriered overnight from Britain if I was willing to pay a lot of money.

'Lets see if there is a Volvo agent in Palermo,' I suggested. Ann is always ready to spend money to fix things but although the parts are far cheaper in the U.K. the cost of shipping them is often high. 'There must be a shop in Palermo that will sell us an alternator and if not, well, it's still going to be easier and quicker to get one shipped to Palermo than to this little halt.' My logic was unassailable so I ignored all comments and we went fishing for a fishing shop to buy a fishing trace wire so we could fish.

Ann knew the word for "hook" and we read the words for "fishing line" off a packet, and we looked up the word for "between" and so put together *"fra il gancio e filo da pesca"* and the man didn't have a clue and found us some swivels, so we drew a diagram. We also bought some lead weights and another octopus. Boy we were equipped, we were going to empty the ocean of fish and never buy any again!

Back on the pontoon the Italians were having a party with beer and dancing – well, tottering really which is about all you can do on a narrow pontoon – girls in bikinis and men with fat guts. We threaded our way through and were as polite as we could be but *Aderyn Glas* still seemed like sanctuary when we climbed on board.

We slept for Britain then, next morning, left the rock behind. We motored in a straight line to Palermo and every half an hour we noted the battery voltage. We had nothing but the fridge drawing current, and the solar panels could just about provide enough Watts to maintain it. 'We're going to be okay.' I smiled at Ann to reassure her and because I was still so happy that we'd done the worst bit of the odyssey, 'In Palermo we'll find an alternator. Probably any one will fit from any engine, maybe even a second-hand one.'

It was a long passage on a hot day under a blue sky and windless. First there was a large bay to cross then a rocky, hilly, coastline to follow. We passed an airport on the coast and watched flights landing and taking off and concluded that we must be close to Palermo, but we were wrong. Finally we turned right around a headland and onto our final course. It took six hours and whenever we rounded a headland and expected to see Palermo in front of us someone put another headland in the way and we had to motor on.

At one point yellow flying boats swooped down from the sky and scooped up water, then flew away and presumably dropped it on a fire. There were two of them and they took about ten minutes for each cycle of filling and dumping.

At last we found Palermo. It has a marina at the north end of the harbour which we'd been warned against: too far from town and too expensive, so we motored on passed the great long breakwater to the entrance at the south. We raced a yacht into the harbour, I'm always afraid that the yacht in front is going to take the last available space, then we motored into the industrial heart of Palermo's port.

There were ferries and cruise liners and gargantuan blue cranes and machines we couldn't even guess at. There were cargo ships and police launches, pilot boats and tugs and little coracle fishing boats in the middle of it all. There were floating drydocks, one with a ship in it, and an oil rig parked in a corner. On a rocky cliff, above the port, an ancient castle and on another the trappings of modern society: a host of aerials. Inland, beyond the port, enigmatic minarets and towers, Romanesque gates and renaissance palaces. And behind it all the backdrop of high mountains.

We turned left again, towards the forest of masts, following our pilot book. Another breakwater formed an inner harbour and behind it were the small craft: the cruisers and the yachts like us. Hundreds of them. We ploughed our way further and further into the marina looking more and more despairingly for a space or for anyone willing to help us, because we really needed a berth this time – somewhere we could sort out our alternator. But there was nothing and no-one. We tried to manoeuvre into a small space at the end of a pontoon but it was too tight and too shallow so we headed reluctantly back out, away from the town, with no idea what to do next.

Salvation came with a shout and a wave from the shore. We were passing the Club Mediterraneo and a *Capo* was waving us into a berth. It was dirty and full of floating litter in the knee of the breakwater, and next to a gaggle of small fishing boats, but it was wonderful.

Palermo, Sicily, 412 miles to Gouvia. Day 98

A smiling *Capo* took our lines and handed us one for the stern. He was grizzled and looked like he'd been around the world a few times but he didn't speak English. Ann asked if we could stay two nights because we had a problem and did he know where we could buy an alternator. He grinned widely and took her away to the little office where he plied her with iced water. By the time I'd finished plugging in the mains and erecting the sunshades they were both back and both grinning and having a whale of a time though neither was sure what the other was saying.

'He knows a man and he's already made the phone call. The engineer will be around this afternoon or maybe tomorrow and he will either fix it or sell us a replacement.' She said and the *Capo* grinned widely.

'I though you were going to ask him where there was an agent we could buy one from.' I said under my breath while returning the *Capo's* grin. The thing I hate most is having no control over costs and now I had no control over costs.

'Things kind of escalated,' Ann said, a bit sheepish, 'and before I knew it they'd called the guy and set everything up.' She brightened, 'Don't worry, I'm sure it won't cost much and we've had nothing go wrong yet.'

'Kiss of death.' I grumbled, but I was reluctantly happy that I didn't have to traipse around in the heat looking for a Volvo agent who might not even exist.

Then, suddenly, I was very happy. The whole immensity of what we'd done kind of kicked in and I couldn't help but hug Ann and she grinned and I grinned and the *Capo* grinned and life was wonderful again.

Ann showed me the club's brochure. It was beautifully produced on plastic to avoid it dissolving in the wet and claimed, in English, it had been:

"Founded in the 1965 from a group of loving friends of the sea and all the connected sports to it: sail, peach and activity marinare, the our club be one association without scope of lucro".

It went on but we were already lost in giggles and wondered what the loving friends did with the peach. It also showed the island Ann was so afraid of hitting when we arrived in the night, it was thirty-five miles to the north.

'Not a great chance of hitting it then, not inside seven hours sailing anyway.' I rubbed it in a little.

Once in a blue moon, because of some bizarre bio-chemistry, I need a BigMac and chips. I think that McDonalds must inject their food with some kind of *come again* hormone that makes you return for another burger some time in the future. I also think that the chemical never leaves your bloodstream and is triggered by the presence of a McDonalds restaurant within a five mile radius. I had to have one. So I dug out Rachel version three – the car sat-nav – and found a McDonalds on the other side of town, just about inside the hormone's detection radius.

'More likely you can smell them,' Ann said when I shyly explained my needs to her, but she likes them too so when evening came we headed off to the city.

The area around any dock complex anywhere in the world is not going to be pretty and it was true of Palermo. We'd been warned by a couple who'd been there about the shady people hanging around the end of the breakwater, about the rubbish and the general disrepair. We'd been warned by Ann's son who'd visited Palermo when he was in the Navy and had spent most of the time ashore in a running fight with the locals. And, in truth, the area around the docks was not somewhere we would want to spend time but we didn't feel particularly threatened as we walked across the main roads and headed towards the city's commercial centre. But the trouble with sat-navs is that they take you the most direct route and Rachel took us through some dark backstreets that night and that's where we started getting an itchy spine. People live in the backstreets of Palermo. I have this rosy view that people don't actually live in cities but in manicured housing estates on the outskirts arranged so that you never had to trespass on someone's home turf. So when Rachel started taking us through backstreets - populated with kids playing soccer and people talking on corners, people gossiping in doorways and lovers smooching - I felt as if I was intruding and that someone was going to come and sort us out.

'Relax,' Ann, ever the optimist, 'and smile.'

'I'm holding a sat-nav in the backstreets of a major city not half a mile from the docks and you want me to relax?'

'Think of the BigMac and chips.'

Ann's phone rang, Sue had moved into our house and were we okay? Great, I thought, we're wonderful, now they know we have a posh phone too.

In the end we reached the bustling centre perfectly safely, just as Ann had promised, and got our fix. But we took a taxi back. After the driver had found the boat's location on his sat-nav he stayed on the main roads.

Next day it was thirty-seven centigrade in our cockpit and a small dripping man arrived to fix our alternator. He took it off in three seconds, tore the back off it in two, diagnosed a regulator failure in one, put it under his arm and left me with a pile of screws and bolts, a fading Cheshire cat smile and a few words of Italian that I had no chance of understanding. It was some seconds later that we realised that a complete stranger had taken away our alternator and had thus completely disabled our boat. We didn't know who he was or when we would get it back or how much it was going to cost.

'Don't worry,' said Ann, 'I'm sure it will be alright.'

We found a chandlery and bought the cheapest fourteen millimetre rope in the western hemisphere, sold by the kilo, and how many kilos for twenty metres please? But they knew that too. 'And gas?' Ann asked, but we had to return for that later after the delivery had been.

We walked miles and miles looking for a supermarket only to find one no more than half a kilometre from the boat, but in our walk we found historical wonders and vowed to return next day.

The man with the alternator brought it back about five o'clock and signalled that it had been *il transistor* in the diode pack that had overheated and burned out. He pointed at our charge regulator and shook his head so I disconnected it which earned me a grin. He fitted the cover in a second, replaced the alternator in two and had the engine roaring in three to prove it was all okay. Then he wrote me a bill on the back of a notepad for two hundred and something euros, about the cost of a whole new alternator in Britain. He grinned again, I blinked then grinned and to hell with it we're back in business thanks and you're a wonderful guy and so are the *Capos* and Ann was happy too and we all had a glass of wine.

Late that night we discovered the quayside was covered with fishermen. They would set up a stool and lean their kit against the "No Fishing" signs then cast carefully between the boats.

Occasionally a hook would catch on something and someone would scramble onto a boat to free it.

'I'm not going to bed,' I said, 'what if someone climbs on board. We're only feet from where they're fishing.'

Ann walked down the front of the boat and pretended to tidy something and said *'Buona notte.'* to the nearest fisherman who said the same to her. Later we heard him climb on the boat next door: then it was morning.

Next day the *Capos* expected us to leave because the boat was fixed but Ann negotiated a couple more days so that we could go sightseeing. Palermo was seeping into us slowly.

Chapter 18

Palermo, Sicily, 412 miles to Gouvia. Day 100

'It's day one hundred,' said Ann as she filled in her diary. 'congratulations.'

'Congratulations because of what we've achieved in a hundred days?' I thought it was pretty impressive.

'No, congratulations because you still have me as your wife after one hundred days of being locked up on a boat together.'

I could laugh at her joke but some people wouldn't still be together after one hundred days in each other's company in a space ten metres by three in temperatures consistently over thirty. Ann saw the look in my eye: 'Don't think too hard about this.' She said. So we went out.

I think Palermo must be one of the undiscovered gems of Italy. Sure there are places that are run down and you could probably be mugged or robbed as quickly here as in any other capital city, but for anyone interested at all in architecture or art it has some amazing locations. It also has a great long street of rather posh shops called *Via Roma* so we stayed away from there and I clamped my hand on my wallet in case it had ideas of its own.

Instead we went looking for some culture. In the shady little garden square called Piazza Marina, not far from the port and where the supermarket hides in a corner, is the Palazzo Steri. It is a pre-renaissance palace built by one of the ruling families of the time, the Chiaramonte, the last of whom was executed outside the door, and that's a nice thought as you stand waiting to pay. But for me, as a one time student of renaissance history and art, it was wonderful to see a set of preserved frescoes in a place I never would have expected them. In the seventeenth century the cruel Inquisition met here and the walls may have rung with the desperate pleas of the condemned before they were carried down the stairs to the prison or death. In the meeting chamber a gaily painted wooden ceiling incongruously depicting chivalrous, courtly life.

What was also amazing was how much Italian we had absorbed in the six weeks since we arrived in Sardinia. The guide spoke only Italian and there was only the two of us and her, so we couldn't hide away in the back of a crowd like we usually do. But we understood her and were even able to ask her questions. It seemed as if we had achieved what everyone always wants and had learned some language simply by being immersed in it.

When I mentioned this to Ann she poured a little lukewarm water on my idea: 'Ah yes, my dear,' she smiled, 'but don't you think knowing a lot of French and some Spanish helps?' I didn't argue. The thing is it hadn't helped so far and I liked my idea better.

Okay, so art history is not everyone's cup of tea and neither will the cathedral be which was our next stop straight up the Via Vittorio Emanuele and dodge the lure of the shops and feel the tug in the wallet when you cross the Via Roma. Pause at the Quattro Canti, the strange crossroads with sculpted and be-statued facades, and around the corner the Palermo version of the Trevi Fountain where the water is noisy but cool.

The cathedral is ornate and impressive, as most cathedrals are once you get outside Henry VIII's dour Britain, and we visited it and followed the throng and drank a lot of water in the heat, and grumbled about the Japanese. But we didn't stay long, there is a better gem in Palermo, it's called the Palatine Chapel and it's in the Royal Apartments.

We had to wait outside for twenty minutes while someone got married. This, without doubt, is *the* place to get married anywhere and must have cost a fortune. Strange that Sicilians wear black for weddings, but you could tell it was expensive black. The bride carried red roses and wore black and white.

Dating from the twelfth century the little chapel is a blend of Arab, Byzantine and Norman and is the most glittering little chapel ever built. Every millimetre of wall and ceiling space is covered in mosaics depicting scenes from the Bible and most of the mosaics are gold.

That night we ate out with the mosquitoes in the Piazza Marina.

'David,' Ann said quietly, poking at her red beef, 'I don't think this meat is very well cooked.'

'Ann,' I said equally quietly, 'I think we've discovered what *carpaccio* means.'

I ate the raw meat quickly and tried not to think of tape-worm cysts. Ann poked at a raw mushroom and decided to stay hungry.

Later that night we drank a glass of white in the cockpit and watched the flickering of a hill fire in the mountains beyond the city. Later still a thunderstorm crackled and the air temperature dropped from thirty-four to twenty-three in a few minutes, but there was no rain.

Palermo is lovely. It has some wonderful places to visit, it is cosmopolitan and the natives seem friendly and at ease with foreigners. Or: Palermo is untidy and parts of it need some money spent on it simply to clean it up. Palermo has everything you might need, if you can find a space to moor. To entertain you it has fishermen who launch their luminous lines between you and the boat next door when you want to sleep in peace, and fishermen who launch nets from little coracles in the outer harbour to encircle the fish but catch nothing. I caught nothing either, no sign of a tape worm and I really wanted a pet.

Next day Ann said: 'Time to go,' and we gave the *Capos* a bottle of wine each because they'd been so helpful and friendly and *nice*. Then we said goodbye.

Cefalu, Sicily, 381 miles to Gouvia. Day 102

We had brown skins and bleached hair. We were fit from the constant movement but had no stamina because of the constant sun and the heat. It was difficult to think and talking wasted energy. We wore sunglasses, a hat, a pair of shorts and Ann wore a shirt. We lived in the cockpit at sea because the temperature in the saloon was so much higher. We hid from the sun but it found us anyway, bouncing off the sea. At night we lay naked on a towel and tried to sleep.

The day was flat and it was windless and so hot. We motored to Cefalu from Palermo and we tried to stay out of the sun. We sweated, we drank continuously, we never peed. We squirted water over each other from a plant watering spray. We had no appetite and no energy. This was the end of August and the heat was killing us.

Cefalu is a town built under a volcanic plug, and approaching from Palermo the most obvious thing about it is the huge cathedral that seems to grow out of the mountain. But we motored on passed and found the inlet with the marina but anchored across from it near some rocks. The town is the other side of the headland and we had no interest in going there, preferring to swim in green water and watch the few fish we could find. A hydrofoil service for foot passengers runs out to the Aeolian islands, as far as Stromboli, and to Palermo, and the ferry kicks a bit of wash around. The anchorage is also a bit exposed and I wouldn't want to be in such an exposed and rocky place if there was a swell from the east.

When the day ran down and the temperature dropped as much as it was going to we sat in the cockpit and contemplated the next legs of the odyssey. Vulcano and the Messina straights were already determined, but the ports along the southern coast of Italy's toe all had a bad reputation – thieves and scoundrels, vagabonds and wastrels. Then I heard myself say something fateful: 'Why don't we just go for it? Why don't we just go to Greece from here? Why bother with the mainland at all, we can do it in two nights.'

Ann grinned like this had been her plan all along and she had been waiting for me to catch up.

So the die was cast. In fact we planned two one-night passages with a brief stopover in a place called Crotone and we would start from Milazzo, which is on the Sicilian coast south of the Aeolians. That was the plan. I had completely thrown away the idea of never making another night passage and had volunteered to do two, on consecutive days. I think the heat had fried my brain or did I hope that Greece was cooler and let's hurry up and get there?

But first we had to go to Vulcano for Ann to see a volcano.

Vulcano, Aeolian Islands, 332 miles to Gouvia. Day 103

We fished our way to Vulcano because that's all there was to break up the monotony. We'd seen boats congregating around a patch of sea and we'd seen a few dolphin so we decided there must be fish to be caught and we caught the same as always: nothing.

It was a long day too and we left the driving to the tireless Rachel. It was made worse by the view of the islands that hovered in the distance and never seemed to get any closer. Vulcano, Lipari and Salina are about fifty miles from Cefalu, but Stromboli, which is supposed to provide a spectacular show every night, is twenty miles more and too far for us. Ann had settled for Vulcano. When we arrived we headed for the anchorage on the western side and milled around for a while in the crowded space before dropping the hook in three metres of clear green water.

Above us towered the volcano but it didn't do much. It smouldered and sent a little steam up into the atmosphere but was otherwise unimpressive. It was grey and black and had a white cap like snow and was sometimes streaked with yellow. It had a little path that wound upwards with tiny figures that gave the view scale. I had a great fear that Ann would want to climb it because she likes challenges and doesn't like to miss things.

'Simmering and smouldering is better than spewing out molten lava or hurling rocks and ash.' I pointed out. It smelled authentic though, there was enough sulphur in the air to make our eyes sting.

The anchorage had a beach and the beach was noisy and had shops and cafes and a host of other seaside buildings, and joyfully noisy Italians on holiday. The anchorage was busy too with jetskies and speedboats, RIBs and pedaloes but it was the only sheltered spot around apart from the port which seemed less appealing. The water was blue and warm and clear and we lazed in it for ages soaking the heat from our bodies until we were completely relaxed. Ann discovered that the next boat was a charter and the family was from Yorkshire. You can travel to the most exotic and remote places on the globe and the boat next door will be from Yorkshire.

In the early evening a small cloud appeared, the first we'd seen for weeks, and a high haze formed around the sun which gave it a pink and purple aura with rays radiating upwards. The cloud was backlit and dark with a rim of bright light which formed a beautiful backdrop for the silhouettes of the rocks at the entrance to the bay. *Click click* went all the cameras. Later the sun dropped below the cloud and lit the sea with a gold street that stretched to the horizon. *Click.*

A slight swell appeared as we were eating and all the boats swung around. I worried that the anchor was now lying in the wrong direction and hoped that the chum weights and the chain were enough to hold us. I trusted the forecast which said no wind for days, but the swell was rolling us like a pig. We couldn't put the stern anchor out because there was no room to turn the boat in the crowded anchorage so we had to put up with it.

It became so bad that I tried to sleep across the double bunk and Ann curled up in the saloon. It was making me feel sick and all I wanted to do was shut my eyes and hope that it would die out soon. I didn't even want to get up and put the mosquito nets on the hatches but I thought we were far enough from shore to be safe and it was probably the end of the season anyway so there wouldn't be any around.

Next morning I had eight new bites and the swell was still there. When we pulled up the anchor we had to motor around in a semi-circle because we were pointing the wrong way. There was more steam from the crater and it curled and hung on the steep ash slopes but Ann was disappointed, she was expecting more and she wanted to climb it.

We motored around to the harbour on the west side of the island and discovered a motorway of boats and ferries and hydrofoils which carved through the usual raft of little fishing boats and RIBs out for a day's fun. We wondered if we would have been better off anchoring on this side and nosed in towards the beach and through the laid moorings for a look. But the bottom was twenty metres deep and more right up to the shore so the question was moot: there was nowhere we could have anchored. In any case the swell was worse.

The smell was worse too. The hydrogen sulphide rolled down from the crater above the little town and made our eyes water. 'At least now we can say we've sampled a live volcano,' Ann said, smiling through the tears.

'When I was a boy,' I said, thinking that so many conversations started with these words now, 'we used to have a firework called Stromboli which was shaped like a cone and would erupt in flaming pink and make lava which rolled down its side. That's what I call a volcano!'

'We must be wimps.' Ann added, 'to have come here and not gone up to the crater, just because the boat was rolling a bit.'

'We can lie about it,' I pointed out, 'when anyone asks describe that place in New Zealand to them, where the geysers were and the mud pools. Where I was ill and you made me go to a Maori folk evening in the freezing cold.'

'And they made you chief and you had to rub noses with all those men in short skirts.'

'And if I so much as smiled they would have killed me for the insult. Believe me when a huge rugby playing New Zealander dressed in a skirt and holding a spear wants to rub noses with you, you don't want to laugh!'

But there was no nose rubbing to be had on Vulcano so we headed for the mainland, for Milazzo which was to be our last port on Sicily. Our last port before the Messina straights and fabled Scylla and Charybdis who would bite off our heads or suck us down into the depths.

Milazzo, Sicily, 306 miles to Gouvia. Day 104

'It's September,' said Ann and punched me. I think she had wanted the excuse. We ran parallel to the peninsula north of Milazzo where the view is of boats bobbing on unprotected moorings backed by a beach and apartments climbing up the hillside to the walled citadel above.

'Oh goody! Another walled citadel. And blue sea and blue sky,' I said, sarcastically.

The harbour is industrial and to the east is a huge oil terminal with unloading jetties reaching into the bay. The fuel jetty we needed was closed though. On the right, inside the entrance, a raft of trawlers and on the left a ferry port with huge ro-ro ferries. Ahead a marina, a raft of pontoons, but only the first was empty enough for us to berth against. Ann had called on the radio and a *Capo* waited for us. When I tried to go bows-to he motioned for me to turn and come alongside. I wondered why. It was the first time I had done a British style, alongside berthing, since Marseille.

The concrete pontoon was too low for Ann so I leapt off, barefoot, to tie the sternline and burned my feet. The *Capo* laughed at me as I scrambled back on board, but it was good natured. The air temperature was thirty-five but the concrete was much hotter.

There seemed to be only the one stretch of pontoon for visiting boats and we had the last slot. When a German boat arrived later we thought he would moor alongside us, which would have been inconvenient but perfectly normal, but the *Capo* waved him away.

'Aren't you suspicious?' I asked, wondering about the berthing arrangement.

'They know what they're doing,' she said absently.

In the heat of the day, while the engine was hot, we changed the oil. We needed fresh oil to see us to Greece but we ended up so hot we had to hose each other in cold water afterward.

The lady *Comandante* had to give her permission for us to stay for two nights. Tall, forty, full bodied, rouged and dressed to kill in diaphanous layers she smoked a cigarette in the shade amongst the potted plants on the green plastic grass outside her office, her staff literally sat at her feet. I was afraid to speak. She waved the cigarette, 'Of course you can stay two nights, this is not a problem.' But the *Capo* who had berthed us had a strange look on his face.

We told her we needed fuel and she said she would arrange it for next day. She waved the cigarette at one of her men and he nodded. I had the feeling that if we'd asked her to arrange for good weather she could have done that too.

'Mafia,' breathed Ann afterward, looking around as she said it.

'Oh my God, do you think she's the Godmother?' I asked equally quietly.

Milazzo is two towns separated in time. Before nine in the evening it's a grimly industrial place and, alright, it has the restaurants and the shops and the ice-cream palaces and the bars but it's a bit like walking through Birmingham with added sea. After nine the place to walk is northwards where traders have set up stalls amongst the palm trees and the town turns out to wander and promenade before eating. Up above, on its rock, sat the citadel and Ann wanted to climb up to it because that's where the best restaurants are supposed to be but I was worn out by the heat and a bit scratchy. The other place we didn't walk was across the peninsula, which is only about half a mile wide, but we did find a little side-street restaurant with tables laid so as to block the passage of anything larger than a scooter and where the Police Chief and a couple of his men were busy eating. This seemed like a recommendation so I grabbed the last available table, moved the dog with my toe, jammed a paper napkin under the leg to stop it wobbling on the uneven surface (the table, not the dog) and ate with the mosquitoes.

The food was good and the setting had atmosphere and after the litre of *bianco* we finally felt relaxed. On the way back an orchestra was setting up on a stage so we found a park bench and waited. A grizzled old guy leaned his bike against a rail and sat on the other end of the bench and complained that the concert should have started at ten. It was ten thirty and the audience were still trickling in and taking seats. Behind the stage the traders were still blasting out music from their stalls and promenaders were still strolling in the warm night air.

The concert began at eleven and all the seats were full. The traders had turned off their CDs and the air was filled with classics and cicadas. Tomorrow it would be hot again and the streets devoid of people but here and now the warm night was filled with real music and the town was full of life.

We motored across to the fuel pontoon as early as we could next day. The *Capo* had arranged for someone to be there at ten and we wanted to beat the heat. The fuel pontoon for small yachts is outside the harbour in a shallow bit of water with great boulders on the bottom ready to trap the unwary, but the water is always clear enough to see them.

Back in our berth we discovered finally why there was so much emphasis on alongside berthing and why the German had been turned away. We were sitting in the saloon when the boat gave a huge heave upwards then rolled violently and crashed down with the noise of splintering wood. Then she rolled the other way and rose upwards again, trapping a fender which screamed in pain. Ann and I hung on and watched the inevitable crashing of plates and pans and books onto the floor and heard the little wastebin in the heads throw itself into the toilet again.

The rolling stopped and we climbed outside. The pontoon was full of bemused crews from neighbouring yachts looking hard at their hulls and at each other. We'd lost a fender, it had been ripped open, and the step we hang over the side when the jetty is low had splintered but the hull was okay. Like everyone else we started tying on extra ropes and checking the ones already in place and, like everyone else, we didn't think it would help much. Wherever the wave had come from – and there were no obvious culprits – stopping the boat moving fore and aft wasn't going to help.

Next door a German-Canadian decided he would leave. He'd been around the world a few times but hadn't seen that sort of violence inside a harbour before. The crew of a plastic cruiser had found extra fenders and tied them on. Since we'd already used all our fenders and ropes the only strategy left was to worry harder but this, we felt sure, would help.

It's ironic that with a huge oil refinery down the road the only oil we could find for the engine was really expensive manufacturer's stuff from a chandlery. Things change as you move from region to region and what you can buy in a supermarket in one region you won't find in the supermarkets in the next. This applies to food, of course, but also to things like oil. It also applies to the internet and in Milazzo the internet hides away in a Western Union office opposite the ferry terminal. So we discovered that the weather was going to change and switch from no wind to too much wind in a couple of days time.

'We should stay,' I said, looking at the screen.

'Time to go,' said Ann, 'we can make it through the Messina Straights and get all the way around to Crotone before this weather window closes. We might even get across to Greece.'

So Ann dug out the tide tables that we hadn't used this year yet and checked the tides for Gibraltar, which is how you decide when to head through the Messina straights.

'If we leave about seven in the morning,' Ann said but my mind shut down at the thought of it and I missed the rest.

Messina Straights, Sicily, 285 miles to Gouvia. Day 106

Beloved of classical adventurers and frightening enough for the Admiralty to put a comment in their nineteenth century Pilots, a passage through the straights seemed to fit with our little odyssey as well as Homer's. In fact, once Ann had decided not to go by way of Africa, the passage through the straights was inevitable. She'd been reading a magazine article: 'This silly man tried to go through the straights northwards and met a wall of water. I bet he got the tides wrong.' I loved her confidence. I read it a different way: it's possible to get the tides wrong and mess it up.

We were going north to south and I'd already fed waypoints into Rachel and dire warnings into Ann: 'Do not cut the corner!' On the mainland Scylla waited to bite our heads off, the six headed beast that ate Odysseus's crewmen, and on the island the giant whirlpool of Charybdis was waiting to suck us down. 'Do not cut the corner – it's very shallow over there.'

We'd had a hot day so far, five hours of motoring across the top of Sicily, cutting through blue water with Rachel in charge. But then the land dropped away to form a flat plain and a mile away stood the third highest pylon in the world built to carry power three kilometres from the mainland and now preserved in its red and white stripes. 'Why would you want to preserve a pylon?' Ann asked, 'look at it, it's an eyesore.' And she was right.

A cargo ship came down from the north and we followed him sticking carefully to our waypoints and away from Charybdis. We were excited. Hoping for a little fun and a bit of safe terror like watching Doctor Who from behind the sofa. But after half an hour we realised nothing was happening. Scylla must have been asleep and Charybdis plugged.

I sighed.

Then the water churned up, Rachel squealed and I grabbed the helm. All around us little waves chattered and spat, breaking their tops and turning white. The sea boiled. Was this what we'd been looking for? Ann spotted a smooth patch: 'Over there!' she said, but I didn't like the look of it: maybe it was an upwelling and maybe it was dangerous.

We travelled on making more than ten knots over the seafloor. Then the water got rougher with defined waves like a wake that sprang into being from nowhere. Behind, on the beach, people were playing in the surf, didn't they realise they were going to be sucked down any second?

Then it was calm.

Then we hit a wall of water that dropped our speed to five knots.

Then it boiled again and white circles formed around us and little waves chattered at us.

Then the speed increased and *Aderyn Glas* dug in deep and churned southward.

Behind there was a bizarre sight and I thought Scylla was chasing us but it resolved itself into a swordfish catcher. These boats have a huge long bowsprit about twice the length of the boat on which a man stands with a harpoon searching for sleeping swordfish.

The radar screen showed thirteen targets inside a mile and I photographed it. Ferries ran across the straights and cargo ships through it. A yacht was trying to sail northwards and getting nowhere: just wet. Then Charybdis grabbed the keels again and twisted us sideways, but she was spent. Her strength wasn't what it had been. We grinned at each other, enjoying the fun. Poking our heads above the sofa and poking out our tongues at the Daleks.

In Messina port the biggest ship I had ever seen. This was no mere floating hotel, this was a floating holiday resort, complete with golf courses and airport. It dwarfed the ferries around it. We counted ten decks of superstructure above the hull.

But the straights were not done with us yet and caught and twisted us a few more times before we were free. And Charybdis was still tickling our keels an hour later as we set off down the coast of the Italian mainland.

'Time to go,' we were laughing and happy and had no inkling of what was going to happen next.

The one thing we wished we'd known, when we set out, is that there is a place on the toe of Italy that is so flat that it doesn't impede the weather at all.

We trundled onwards towards Crotone which sits at the edge of the Gulf of Taranto. Once we'd turned the corner, south of the straights, there was a wind and we'd hauled out the sail to go motor sailing. There was also a swell which wasn't surprising since the only thing south of here was Africa.

The shore was fairly mundane and the occasional port of no interest to us. We were spoilt by now, we'd seen so many beautiful places that this was simply not exotic enough to stimulate us. And we were on a mission. The lapis lazuli waters of the Ionian islands were calling us.

Because we were motoring we decided we should get some fuel before we set off for Greece. The plan now was to go into Crotone and get fuel then head off straight across the Ionian sea to Corfu. The timing was right for this, we would arrive in Crotone after a night at sea then arrive off Corfu the following morning. Ann kept grinning at the challenge but I must have been mad to go along with it, and yet it was me that suggested it.

Darkness was falling but it was calm enough, a slight breeze blowing on the mainsail to steady us. We started doing our night watches, looking at the stars, checking the radar, keeping an eye on

Rachel, nibbling at brunch bars and drinking hot chocolate from a flask.

So eventually when we reached somewhere called the *Golfo di Squillace*, we were happy and contented and we didn't bother to check what the name meant.

Chapter 19

Golfo di Squillace, Italy, 250 miles to Gouvia. Day 107

The Gulf of Squalls. The wind from the whole long fetch of the Tyrrhenian sea funnels southward across a plain between the mountains to the west and those to the east so if there is a gentle northerly breeze somewhere near Rome there is a howling amplified gale in the Golfo di Squillace. We didn't bother to check the Tyrrhenian forecast because we were in the Ionian and because we didn't know we had to.

Here we are again! I thought. The deck bucked under us and solid water shot over the bows. The night was black except for the lights of houses and the odd vehicle moving in total safety along the shore.

'What do we do? The wind is in the worst direction for us and the seas are reaching for us straight off the beach five miles away. If we point towards our next waypoint the boat rolls like a pig and it's all too frightening and we might get rolled over. We have to try to turn but which way?' I wasn't sure if I'd spoken the thoughts out loud but no-one answered.

Further out to sea the lights of another yacht showed what a dreadful time he was having too, his mast light bucked and pitched across the sky. That's what we must have looked like to him.

'Not that way then. Let's do the unthinkable and head towards the shore, we should get some shelter sooner or later.'

We were wrapped up in lifejackets and wet weather jackets and any bits of clothing that were hanging around but we were cold and soaked. This was the worst yet. Ann was happy to let me steer and I steered almost back the way we'd come. The sail was reduced to a handkerchief and the speed was two knots. Once more I wished daylight would come but it was hours away.

We didn't stand a chance of sleeping. Ann was sick, just once. All over the dodger. Had I not been busy steering I would have been too.

I even contemplated calling the coastguard. Did they have lifeboats? Was there anyone who could tell me what was going on and how to cope with it and when it would end? We pitched and rolled and the sea roared at us and the spray flung itself at us and the boat screamed and we were forced backwards a lot and struggled a little bit towards the shore as well.

'Rachel is lying.' I said to Ann. Rachel was telling us we were pointing directly at the next waypoint which was ridiculous. My numbed brain took a while to work out that the antenna was travelling east-west as the boat rolled, much faster than *Aderyn Glas* was travelling north and that had fooled the GPS.

It continued for ages. We were heading towards a dark and unknown shore hoping to find shelter and there wasn't any. We were going backwards, back to where we'd been, back to Messina and Sicily.

We hung on. Hoped something good would happen.

The boat out at sea had gone.

After maybe an hour the wind and the seas shifted infinitesimally and we could start to pinch a few metres in the right direction. Mostly we had to keep pointing the wrong way but as we ran down a sea I could turn just enough to steal a bit.

And the more we stole the better it got.

Grey pre-dawn arrived and the beach was much further than we'd thought, like when we had arrived off Sicily. Judging distance at night is impossible. With the dawn came a slight reduction in the windspeed.

Just slight.

Just a little.

But it helped.

We began to creep towards Crotone, covering ground we had covered before and still getting thrown around and still getting drenched but heartened a little.

The further we crept east the better it became.

After another half an hour the sun bathed everything in bright light and the sky was blue. The sea was blue too where it wasn't white and seething as each wave crest shredded itself.

But more and more we were able to turn towards Crotone until finally we could head for the waypoint once more without getting thrown around too much.

Crotone, Italy, 150 miles to Gouvia. Day 107

The sea was calm around Capo Rizzuto and we started to put everything straight. The offshore oilrigs spoilt the view but showed us the way and we motored into the harbour behind a small fisherman in a small fishing boat. We had talked about it in the four hours it had taken to round the cape and get this far and we had decided to continue to Greece. 'While the weather is good,' Ann said but she looked tired and I felt shattered. Were we even capable of making the right decision?

First we needed the fuel. We actually had enough to get us all the way to Greece but nothing spare so we were going to fill the tank. In any case we were too early to leave for Gouvia, we had to time our arrival off the Greek island of Corfu so that we arrived in daylight.

We shouldered some fishermen off the fuel quay and arrived at eight-thirty as the owner pulled up. He was old and thin, tanned and grizzled and looked like he should be retired and enjoying a drink in a sunny bar.

He pulled the hose from inside a shed across the quay from us and I asked him for water too. Ann told me we had plenty and I wish I'd listened harder but the old guy gave me the water hose. I took the filler caps off the diesel and the water and fed the hoses into each tank. He wanted us to watch the tally on the diesel pump for some reason and since this was inside the shed and Ann couldn't get off the boat because the jetty was too high we started fussing about getting the binoculars.

Then I noticed the water running down the side decks and screamed *'Acqua, acqua!'* and everyone froze. I jammed my hands despairingly over the diesel filler but it did little good, the torrent of water was disappearing down into the diesel tank.

Ann realised what was happening and threw the water hose onto the jetty. The old man belatedly realised too and turned off the tap. But it was all too late.

And all my fault because the one thing we do not do, ever, is have both fillers open at once. It's a guarantee that one way or another something will get contaminated.

'We didn't even need water,' Ann sounded despairing, lost.

'We're still floating,' I said, 'and we have a water separator.'

We finished filling the diesel and started the engine. It ran for about ten seconds and stopped. If I had not been tired, if I could have thought it through, I would not have started the engine because now all the fuel lines, filters and the injectors were full of water, like the tank.

A young, flash guy drove up on a scooter and talked to the old man, then he came over to us and spoke English: 'Captain, My father says you have water in your diesel tank and it is his fault.'

'It was an accident,' I said, but if he wanted to claim blame I wasn't going to stop him. Then I had a flash of guilt: 'A mistake.' I added lamely.

'Mister, I know what to do.' He already had his mobile to his ear, 'a friend who owns the boatyard he has a machine that will clear the water from your tank in minutes. I have called him and he is coming.'

'We can still make it provided we leave before noon.' Ann said, but I was going off the idea. How much was this going to cost?

The son came on board and shook his head. Then he looked at the filler pipe and shook his head again. 'Problem, problem,' he said, 'the machine has a very big hose to fit in ships tanks.' Then he looked a the filter and water separator and shook his head again, 'Problem.'

Half and hour later three men arrived in a truck and unloaded a machine that looked like the twin air-tanks SCUBA divers sometimes use but in glass. There was a boss who was dressed in immaculate whites and had posh Italian shoes and expensive sunglasses, a man I took to be a mechanic who was a burly Italian and a tiny stringy black man who looked like Sammy Davis Jr. and who was obviously the technician because it was he who had to unload the lorry.

The boss shook my hand and came aboard and looked and shook his head. 'Problem,' he sighed, 'look at my pipe, it is so big for this hole.' I waited for Ann to blush but her tan covered it well.

'*Signore*, I have thought of a solution,' I said, 'there is an inspection cover and we can take it off.' So I showed him and even got a spanner and started to loosen some of the bolts. To my amazement they came free easily.

'No, no! You must stop.' He told me and said something in Italian to the wiry black man who jumped eagerly on board, wrestled the spanner from me and continued unscrewing all the other bolts while the boss and the mechanic smoked and watched.

It was cruelly hot and the work in the locker was making our new best friend drip with sweat. Ann found him a towel and gave him a bottle of drinking water. 'Don't they look after their staff?' she whispered, 'Poor guy, he's doing all the work.'

'Division of labour, hon,' I whispered back, 'delegation. How many inkwells did you fill when you were a college director?'

'What is ink?' she asked.

It took all morning to get the cover plate off and set the machine to work slurping our contaminated diesel through the filters. Later on the team decided that they didn't have enough empty containers to put the cleaned diesel in and they all had to go off in the truck to get some more.

'Does it really take three of them?' Ann asked but she knew it would, one to give orders, one to watch and one to do.

'You're lucky they don't have quality control, project managers and health and safety people or we would still be writing specs and risk assessments.'

'They couldn't get them all in the truck,' she said, 'and you forgot Human Resources.'

They came back and slurped some more diesel then started packing up their tools. The boss came over 'It is time for food then we will come back in two hours but we might have to go to another job then come later.'

Then they left.

In all it took three men six hours to clean our diesel and our tank. Of the three men the only one who actively did anything was the small black guy except that the boss was the only one who was allowed to touch the controls of the machine. We began to wonder what three man-days was going to cost.

'I will not break your bank.' the boss said when we asked him.

Then the black man put it all back together with my spanners and keys and put a new fuel filter on and emptied the water out of the separator. The boss returned the cleaned diesel to the cleaned tank and told me to start the engine.

'Don't you need to drain the fuel lines? The engine is full of water where I tried to start it,' I said but this didn't seem to interest them. With visions of broken pistons where incompressible water was forced into the cylinders I lifted the decompressor lever in the hope that it would help. Then, believing that the boss knew more than me I pressed the starter.

The starter motor turned over and nothing else happened. The engine didn't start.

There began a relay of mechanics each of whom turned up and did what they thought would solve the problem then each shook his head and phoned someone else and congregated on the quayside where they all shook their heads and looked glum. Once a guy in soiled jeans and tee-shirt arrived in a very posh BMW and shouted angrily at the boss until I thought there must be a fight. The boss spoke calmly to him and he angrily stamped onboard and did something then stood on the quayside, shook his head and made a phone call and everyone shook their heads and looked glum.

Another mechanic arrived, possibly the dirtiest – and thus perhaps the busiest - of them all, he clambered into the engine space and started taking things off and dropping them dirty onto our clean wooden decks. Then he undid the fuel lines to the injectors and told me to turn over the engine. Water sprayed everywhere but he signalled to me to keep turning over. Then diesel sprayed everywhere and I still had to keep turning over. Finally he was satisfied and reconnected the pipes. I pressed the button and the engine coughed and caught.

'I thought so,' I said quietly to Ann but she only smiled.

On the quayside the mechanics all nodded and smiled and clapped each other on the shoulders and made phone calls. Ann and I beamed and thanked the mechanic who had sprayed our boat with diesel. He told us to run the engine for half an hour and laconically wandered back to the quayside to collect the plaudits from his peers.

Suddenly everyone left. The little black guy had long since packed up the kit and the man in the BMW shouted once more at the boss and stormed away. The fuel guys went off on the scooter and left only me and the boss who took two hundred and fifty euros in cash and no receipts please and don't mention this to anyone.

Among the audience were two marina *Capos* and they led us to a berth. That is how we arrived in Crotone. And that is how we became stuck in Crotone because we'd lost our window and the screaming wind ratcheted up the scale and that was it for a week.

The Crotone marina is in the *Porto Vecchio* and the berths are on the outer breakwater. Looking across to the town the view is of tall apartment blocks of six or more floors and painted in drab greys and creams. They line the waterfront and climb the hill behind it.

Where the quayside meets the shore is not a pretty place. It has rundown yards and workshops, decaying roads and pavements slippery with fish oil and escaped ice. It has fish merchants and another quay for the fishing boats.

The *Wanted: Outlaw* posters on every lamppost and tree had a picture of a rat. 'Catch a rat, get the reward, pass the rat to the local curry house and we win twice.'

'No curry houses,' Ann shot my profitable scheme dead.

Walk right and the road continues passed the boatyard of our rescuer and the Porto Nouvo and high on the left is the citadel and the old town. Walk left and soon the run-down buildings are replaced by the restaurants and ice-cream sellers and tourist shops and so on and the pavements become clean and well paved. And after a while you arrive at a beach which is cleaned each morning and has a view of the oilrigs and jelly-fish float in the surf.

Crotone is a town of two halves. Walk up the hill from the beach and you reach the commercial centre which has a fantastic open market and modern, fashionable shops.

Den was a delivery captain, short and tough looking like Chay Blyth, and was waiting for a wind to blow him to Malta. He sat in the cockpit of the thirty foot sailing boat next to us and bemoaned the life of the delivery man: 'The GPS doesn't work, nor the chartplotter,' he'd brought his own, 'the engine is underpowered and I have to keep fixing the rigging. The toilet is a joke, the bunks are too small and the sternland leaks. We didn't want to be here at all but there wasn't any wind and I've used all the fuel.' He was happier now that the wind was northerly and twenty knots.

'How can you do it?' I asked him, 'We go running for shelter in the conditions you're *hoping* for.'

'It's not a reflection on you,' he said, 'if you had this boat you'd be alright.' I hoped *Aderyn Glas* wasn't insulted, it wasn't her fault she had bilge keels and rolled a bit. Well, rather a lot really.

He left next day, Crotone to Malta in a few days.

We climbed up onto the seawall to look at the waves and climbed down again, shocked. To us it was a storm.

A forty-nine foot Italian sailing yacht with a young couple on board took his space but left a gap of three feet or so between us and him.

On the port side a motor cruiser left us with half a berth too so we were straddling two berths.

Some time later a passing *Capo* asked us to move across to create a full space. He asked if we wanted to move upwind or downwind which was an unusual question so we took the easy option and let the wind blow us across to the Italian next door. The *Capo* started waving his arms and whistling loudly and it was then I noticed a huge Austrian yacht, twice our length, travelling up and down taking in sails and putting out fenders.

The *Capo* shouted to him and indicated the slot next to us. The captain shook his head in disbelief and waved to a berth at the end of the marina which was directly into wind and therefore easy to enter.

'They can't be going to put that ship in here.' Ann looked worried.

Next door the Italian guy said: 'That yacht is too big to put alongside your small boat.' He and his wife came to watch so did the man on the boat next door to him. All along the quayside people caught a sense of impending doom and stopped what they were doing to watch.

The captain of the huge yacht said again that our boat was too small for him to rest against and that he was going to go into the upwind berth. The *Capo* whistled and shook his head and refused. Our Italian neighbour went and spoke to the *Capo* but nothing would change his mind.

I thought it was time to do something and the something was to move *Aderyn Glas* to the other side of the double berth so that this sixty foot monster could rest against the Italian fifty-foot pocket monster.

Ann was on the side-deck and ready to fend him off so I started to move her way to tell her what I wanted and to talk to the *Capo* and at that moment the monster started motoring rapidly backward into the space.

He almost made it. But as his shrouds ran passed our davits the crosswind took him sideways and he hooked the port one. There were noises of expensive things breaking. Suddenly people and hands came from everywhere, people I'd never seen before rushing onto our stern and pushing so hard to try to shove the monster away. Ann was shouting and crying. The yacht's bow-thruster was screaming. I was swearing and calling the captain the worst names. Ropes were snapping. Metal was bending and wire stays ripped or broke: all mine.

Three men were helping me push to try to hold him off. Two more on the monster. Another was wrapping the bow-line around his winch to pull him tight and away from us. And the *Capo* wandered away as if it was nothing to do with him.

When it was all over, when the yacht was secure, we could look at the broken davit and the broken antenna and marvel that the damage was not worse. I was so grateful to everyone who piled onboard to help. I was so angry with a stupid *Capo* who should have known better and should have listened to those who did. So sad that *Aderyn Glas* had been damaged when she was so nearly at the end of the odyssey. So sad for Ann who had cried.

Some of my anger was reserved for the captain of the monster. At the end of the day we all know that whatever the *Capo* says it is the captain who makes the final decision. I'd called him some pretty foul names and now I wanted him to cough up the insurance.

'Accidents happen captain,' I said to him, 'it's my view that accidents should be forgotten but it's what happens next which determines whether or not you are an honourable man.'

He was. The crew were exhausted from travelling in the conditions for two days and they mostly wanted to go below and sleep but the captain climbed over into our cockpit in the time it took him to gather his papers. Within minutes we had his details and a few minutes later he had called his insurers and told them it was his fault. As much as I was able I warmed to him.

'It's a beautiful boat.' I said, looking at the shiny maroon hull with not a scratch on it.

'There are only three like this,' he replied, 'I commissioned her last year and this is the first time we have been able to sail her in such good conditions.'

'Will it ever end?' Ann was uncharacteristically down, 'We've had an alternator failure, a storm and now a collision all in the last week or so. Not to mention the leaking sterngland and nearly dying in Elba. The weather out there is terrifying and we've still got another night to do.'

'We could stay here,' I said, 'the boatyard is okay and cheaper than Preveza.' but I wasn't really serious. To get this close and stop would be a failure. *Aderyn Glas* wasn't badly damaged. The dinghy was intact and I'd already strapped it into a new position and tied its buckled davit to the rail. The solar panels that sit on top of the davits were still working and the antenna that had been ripped off was for the *Navtex* weather text service and we could live without it for a while.

To cheer ourselves up we wandered into the old town behind the citadel on top of the hill. From there we looked out over the marina and tried to find *Aderyn Glas*. After a while we realised that she was completely hidden by the yachts either side of her. 'Poor little thing,' I thought aloud, 'battered, damaged, dirty, listing like a drunk, and now invisible too.'

And so it continued, a marina full of crews waiting for a gap in the weather. A town empty of happy holidayers who couldn't take the wind either. The beach deserted, the pavements clear, the shops busy, the kids moaning, clouds in the sky. There was a sense of the season running down. In Britain the season would end in a week when the kids went back to school and maybe it was true here. The Austrian monster yacht was hurrying home up the Adriatic to Croatia and Venice because the holiday was over and work beckoned. Luca, the Italian who had helped us had to head home after a six month sabbatical around the Med in his new boat. For us, the odyssey was nearly over and we were beginning to feel like going home and it was starting to fill our conversations. There was a coolness in the air too, not much of a drop in temperature but enough to have us wearing more clothes in the evenings. And it grew dark so early.

Next day we woke to the sound of the monster starting his engines. Ann and I looked at each other in disbelief. Even without moving from our bunk we knew the wind was high.

The captain sat behind the wheel and his crew had taken up stations. The only one whose judgement I had learned to trust was a Croatian and he came over to me as I climbed into the cockpit.

'Are you joking?' I asked. He looked grim.

'We have to get home,' he said with a sad shake of his head, 'can you lower your sternline I don't want the keel to catch it.'

'I think you won't have to worry, your shrouds will finish tearing my dinghy off before you get that far.'

I let the line go and I lowered the dinghy into the water and pulled it out of the way.

The Croatian went back to watching the wind patterns and the captain called the windspeed, continuously 'twenty-five… twenty… twenty-five…' – this was knots of crosswind. Ann and I waited. Luca, the Italian, dropped his line too and waited to push the monster away when it swung into him.

The captain continued calling the windspeed. The Croatian watched the patterns and the other two stood by their ropes. I noticed the captain had the wheel hard over the wrong way. I called to the Croatian who shrugged 'I have told him what to do,' he said but I doubted whether the captain had enough experience to know how to do it. Our eyes met, the Croatian and me, and we both knew – we both saw the whole thing played out before us. As things stood the monster would slew her stern into us. I just laughed; there was nothing I could do to prevent what was going to happen.

'Twenty-five… twenty…'

One of his crew had a telephone to his ear and called out to the captain. Suddenly it was all over, the ropes were re-tightened, the engine slowed to a tick-over, the Croatian came over and told me there was no space in the next marina so they would have to stay here. So it all ended, the tension seeped away. Luca went below, the monster's crew disappeared into the huge cockpit, the quayside cleared and Ann and I went below for breakfast. Only the cheated wind stayed and screamed in frustration.

Next day was a repeat but now the wind was lower. The Croatian was behind the wheel and he and I exchanged looks and grins which meant: no problem, it's going to be okay. The captain seemed happier and we chatted briefly about his boat and how well she was going to sail today. He'd called his insurers again to make sure there would be no problem 'Send them the bill,' he said. I wished all insurance claims could be so easy.

And then they left, a little touch of bow thruster, a turn of the wheel to steer the stern around and a *'bon voyage'* from Ann and me and they popped out and into the harbour. There they pulled up the sails and tied down everything that could move because it was rough outside.

Luca, Ann, and I climbed to the top of the breakwater where there was already a small audience. Five people, four nationalities, one language: a Maltese, two Welsh, an Italian and a German all speaking English. We were quizzed about the accident and I learned about Maltese politics, we were quizzed about the monster boat and Ann learned about the Gulf of Squalls. It's wonderful this camaraderie: sailors stuck in a port together.

The monster left and we watched the progress out to sea. She displaced twenty-eight tonnes and she was being hurled around like a toy. The five of us watched as she crept into the waves and finally, when we knew she was safe and we knew she was definitely leaving, we all drifted apart and back to our own boats.

For us another day stuck in a port with little to do but check the boat again and make a few phone calls and check the weather and eat. Ann uploaded photos to her blog and her dad had his gall bladder removed, these two things are not related.

Ann became friends with Luca and swapped cards. In the evening his wife, Chiara, went ashore dressed like a princess and next day she dressed like a deckhand and hauled at the ropes as they made for the sea. We watched them go from the top of the breakwater and took some photographs as their mast and sails swept the sky and were silhouetted against the sun.

We turned around and photographed poor little *Aderyn Glas*. She looked every inch the hard working boat from her torn Red Ensign to the bent pulpit and back to her battered davit. She was festooned with ropes, new and old, that hung and coiled and writhed so much that it was impossible to see how you could walk along her decks. Fenders hung at crazy angles, all shapes and sizes, no two the same but all showing the marks of fighting with quaysides. Her windscreen was covered with a white shield that stretched across like a blindfold as if she hid in shame and her deck was littered with the bikes I had put in a bag in the Porquerolles almost one hundred days before. Two bikes, a plank, a sail in a bag that hadn't seen daylight since about the time the bikes were put away, and a ladder we thought would come in handy but was so well tied on that to use it was too much pain. Her list was worse than ever the boot-top on her port side dipped so low that grass grew above it. She was our home. Tough, sturdy, reliable, beautiful *Blue Bird. Diolch yn fawr, Aderyn Glas.*

A little later a German in a small motor cruiser left and later still he came back. We went and spoke to him, it was too rough he told us. We checked the weather forecast again for the tenth time. We thought we had a slot if we started in the early afternoon we could miss the weather coming south in the night. So we hung around. Waiting. The worst thing of all is waiting for a window to open.

And then it was time. Time to go. The *Capo* came and wished us well and I would have killed him in another life. His mate climbed up on the wall with the German and it was our turn to provide the entertainment. In the harbour we hauled out a sail for stability then turned and headed for the oil rigs. The seas were rough from the start but we had expected nothing less, and we were prepared for the rocking and the soaking. *Aderyn Glas* buried her bows and threw water around. The tang of salt filled the air and the noise of the wind and surf was intimidating but Ann had a plan and we were happy to be moving. In the heads the little bin hurled itself into the toilet again.

Chapter 20

Crotone, Italy, 150 miles to Gouvia. Day 112

Ann's plan was simple: wait. Have some tenacity, hang on in there. Become stoic. Wait, and motor towards the oilrigs and Greece and all will become calm.

She was right. After two hours the seabed dropped from fifty to two hundred metres and the seas dropped from white capped two metre high horrors to a rolling swell that was far kinder on the nerves. We left Crotone and the gas rigs behind. We left Italy behind and Sicily and Sardinia and Corsica and Elba and France. We left behind all those great people we'd met and all the great places we'd been and all the things we'd seen. We left behind adventure and terror and the discovery of the new: and we headed towards peace and the familiar and a flight home; wherever that was.

And the wind dropped then sprang up again in the evening. It was quiet. We pulled out full sail hoping to sail to Greece as a concluding statement, but gave up after an hour and a half at two knots. So instead we motored into the night. Certain of our safety.

Our last sunset at sea. Again. It was a beacon for us and we motored towards it watching it turn the horizon pink and outlining the little grey clouds. Then it sank and the clouds changed through grey to disappear against the black sky. The stars lit up. First the brightest then down the scale until the arch of the Milky Way was dusted above us again. A short time later the blood red moon crawled into the sky turning white as it climbed and dimming the fainter stars. The moon cast a bright, glittering road for us to follow.

But Aeolus and Poseidon hadn't finished with us yet. The wind and the seas were from the north and grew stronger as the night wore on and *Aderyn Glas* started rolling again. All our worst weather has been in the middle of the night, while I was trying to sleep, and so it was that at about three o'clock I couldn't stand the motion any more and Ann and I had a shouting match about how she was unable to stop the boat rolling by aiming a little off course. 'Zigzag!' I shouted in anger.

So I took over the helm, tired and frustrated and turned the boat until the rolling stopped. Ann had gone below to prevent herself throwing me over the side but now she stuck her head out of the saloon 'It's certainly calmer like this,' she said, 'but do you actually know where you're heading?'

Telling her I didn't care was childish and she waited until I looked at the compass and the GPS.

'Africa?' I said. We were heading due south. The bubble burst and we laughed hysterically for a moment.

So I changed course again and put up with some of the rolling and Ann went to sleep. Rachel had an alternative destination to the south of Corfu, the little harbour of Lakka on Paxos island, so I dialled up that route and that helped a little. But it was still a slow uncomfortable grind.

Behind us we had a shadow, another yacht had caught us and slowed down to keep pace with us. It is amazing how reassuring it is to have someone else around. We never knew who he was.

Eventually the sky turned grey and the stars died away. The sea turned from ink-black to cerulean blue. As the final pinpoints of the brightest stars died and the sky changed to blue our shadow turned left and headed north into the Adriatic.

'Ships that pass in the night,' Ann watched him go. He must have wanted the company too because he could so easily have turned north at any time during the night.

The wind eased and shifted as dawn came and we turned a little northwards and once more headed to the top of Corfu.

I've said I don't like passages that take their time to get started and this one must be the ultimate: it's about a hundred and twenty nautical miles from Crotone to the north west tip of Corfu, so you might think that after sixty miles you would be closer to Corfu than Italy. Not a bit of it. Halfway through the route you are only about twenty miles from Italy and are still getting closer to it: at the closest the heel of Italy is just seventeen miles from the course. The distance from the heel to Corfu is only fifty-five miles so it's not until you are within twenty-seven miles of Corfu that you are actually closer to Greece. This is why so many people cross the Gulf of Taranto to Santa Maria di Leuca at the southernmost tip of the heel then hop to Greece.

The first sign of Greece were the cumulus clouds that hung in the sky where the outlying islands would be. An hour later a pale line on the horizon hinted at land. An hour after that we could see the white cliffs of Othonoi and Mathraki. This was Greece. We grinned like fools and hugged and kissed and did a little dance and thought it was all over.

Six hours later it was. Some kind of triumphal entry into Gouvia marina would have been lovely but we slipped in and had to hang around while a man in the uniform of the marina with sunglasses and fag found us a berth. He spoke English and told us if we wanted drinking water it would cost extra and welcome to Gouvia. We told him we'd sailed from France but if it impressed him he hid it well. We felt robbed of a climax somehow.

'Did you notice,' said Ann, 'we've stopped worrying?'

'After what we've been through what's left to worry us?' It was true. At some point we must have accrued enough experience to believe we could deal with everything that was thrown at us. But then the thought started to worry me so I poured more wine.

Gouvia is great, it's surrounded by trees and greenery and has picturesque corners with local fishing boats and I wish all marinas had a choice of restaurant and chandlery and even a swimming pool. It's not even too expensive and the bus to Corfu town is a doddle. And for us this wasn't quite the end because we still had further to go: we were booked into Preveza for the winter and had a date to meet. But it was the end of the odyssey. These Ionian islands were familiar to us from all those holidays all that time ago, as familiar as our home town, and so the adventure was over. There would be more problems, more excitement, before we reached Preveza but we wouldn't see the Milky Way and the shooting stars again, nor the vast empty intimidating seas. We wouldn't see the breathtaking beauty of Sardinian shores nor the ruggedness of Corsica. Dolphins would not fly horizontally out of the face of breaking waves nor flying-fish scamper over the surface.

It was over.

'Time to go,' said Ann, and smiled sadly.

Some sailor's terms

If you're not a sailor then some of the terms will have perplexed you. I didn't want to slow up the narrative by explaining each term as I wrote it so here is a list of the important ones.

Sailing has it's own lexicon and, like the Inuit who have many words for 'snow', sailors have many words to distinguish between what are for land dwellers very similar things. Thus *halliards*, *warps*, *sheets*, *lines*, *rodes*, *in-hauls* and *out-hauls*, *reefing lines* and *snubbers* are all some form of rope each of which has it's own special use.

The *boot top* is the part of the body or *hull* at the *waterline* while *keels*, on *Aderyn Glas* anyway, are weighted plates pointing downward from the hull. The *log* is an instrument that tells us how fast the boat is moving through the water (which is not the same as over the seabed due to currents). The *sounder* tells us how deep the water is.

A *genoa* is a big sail at the front of a boat and on *Aderyn Glas* provides most of the power when we are sailing. The *mainsail* is the triangular sail that kids draw when they draw a sailing boat and is strung between the *mast* and the horizontal *boom*. *Shrouds* and *stays* hold the mast up side to side and front to back.

Starboard is the right hand side looking forward and *port* is the left. The *bow* is the front and the bit that cuts through the water is called the *stem*. The *stern* is the back and a *transom* is that type of stern that looks like it has been sawn off, rather than a pointed one.

Heads is either the bathroom or the toilet itself. The living room is called the *saloon* and the bedroom is the *cabin*. The *galley* is the kitchen and the *cockpit* is the outside area where the boat is controlled from, it has the wheel, the throttle controls and the ropes needed to manage the sails (at least on our boat).

Sailing boats can't sail directly into the wind so they aim off by maybe 45° or so on a *tack* either port or starboard. To *tack* (i.e. a verb) means to change from a starboard tack to a port one or vice versa which is done by swinging the boat's bow through the wind and moving the sails to the other side. *Gybing* is similar but with the wind behind.

End Note

I hope you enjoyed the book. Ann wrote the diary on which the book was founded: she logged all the information and much more than appears here including how much wine we'd drunk (to the nearest litre) and how much fuel we'd used (approximately). I took the diaries and turned them into this book. Some of our experiences after arriving in Preveza are described in Ann's blog here: **www.aniberry.co.uk** which you may also enjoy and if you fancy the part-time liveaboard life have a look at our website: **www.seasolutions.co.uk**.

If you are going to follow our route in your own yacht then please be aware that the information in this book may be out of date now. As sailors I'm sure you will be wise enough to check the latest local charts, guides and almanacs.

And when you make it to Preveza we'd love to meet you; *Aderyn Glas* isn't hard to find.

But right now, It's Time to Go…

David Berry
South Wales
2016